KU-587-580

11

2

?

6

6

WITHDRAWN

N 0081109 2

Leadership, Organizations
and Culture

Leadership, Organizations and Culture

An Event Management Model

Peter B. Smith and Mark F. Peterson

NEWMAN COLLEGE
BARTLEY GREEN
BIRMINGHAM, 32

CLASS	658.4
BARCODE	00811092
AUTHOR	SMI

SAGE Publications
London · Newbury Park · Beverly Hills · New Delhi

© Peter B. Smith and Mark F. Peterson 1988

First published 1988
Reprinted 1989 (twice)
Reprinted 1990

All rights reserved. No part of this publication may be
reproduced, stored in a retrieval system, transmitted or utilized
in any form or by any means, electronic, mechanical,
photocopying, recording or otherwise, without permission in
writing from the Publishers.

SAGE Publications Ltd
28 Banner Street
London EC1Y 8QE

SAGE Publications Inc
2111 West Hillcrest Drive
Newbury Park, California 91320

SAGE Publications Inc
275 South Beverly Drive
Beverly Hills, California 90212

SAGE Publications India Pvt Ltd
32, M-Block Market
Greater Kailash - I
New Delhi 110 048

British Library Cataloguing in Publication Data

Smith, Peter B.
  Leadership, organizations and culture: an
  event management model.
  1. Organisations. Leadership. Theories
  I. Title   II. Peterson, Mark F.

  ISBN 0-8039-8083-3
  ISBN 0-8039-8084-1 Pbk

Library of Congress catalog card number 88–061487

Typeset by AKM Associates (UK) Ltd
Ajmal House, Hayes Road, Southall, London
Printed in Great Britain by J.W. Arrowsmith Ltd, Bristol

This hardback has been supplied at paperback price

Contents

Acknowledgements

We are grateful to Frank Heller, Ian Morley, Gun Semin and Ritch Sorenson for their comments on earlier drafts of parts of this book. Thanks are due to the McGraw–Hill Book Company for permission to reprint excerpts from pp. 73–4 and 116–17 of L.R. Sayles, *Leadership: What Effective Managers Really Do . . . And How They Do It* (1979).

We also owe a particular debt of gratitude to Jyuji Misumi, Michael Bond and Monir Tayeb for their help and encouragement in our attempts to develop an adequately cross-cultural view of the process of leadership. As Western individualists we must nonetheless acknowledge, in accordance with our cultural norms, that the failings and shortcomings of this book are ours and ours alone.

To our respective role sets

Anne, Toby and Jonathan
Susan, Janice and Daniel

PART ONE

AN OVERVIEW OF THE EVOLVING CONCEPT OF LEADERSHIP

1
The Search for the Philosophers' Stone

The notion that by studying leaders we shall come to understand the behaviour of groups, organizations and even societies has a long history. In this book we hope to provide an overview of the way in which the study of leadership has evolved, particularly over the past few decades. We shall propose that the models of leadership that have found most favour have been ones which embody the implicit value-systems of Western advanced industrial cultures. While we can lay no more claim than others to stand outside such value-systems, we shall nonetheless proceed to outline a model of leadership processes which incorporates a substantially greater attention to the cultures and contexts within which leadership acts occur. Since our analysis will stress the way in which the study of leadership has entailed differing assumptions at different times, it follows that we cannot begin by defining our subject matter on an agreed basis. It is precisely the question of what issues and factors are crucial to an understanding of leadership which will preoccupy us throughout the book.

The present chapter will look at and evaluate conceptualizations of the leadership process which were already in existence by the 1940s. Chapters 2, 3 and 4 follow through this sequence of historical analysis up to the present day, laying most stress on research studies done recently, even where the theories of leadership which they address were first formulated some time ago. Cumulatively, these chapters delineate the impasse which many researchers of leadership have diagnosed in recent years, and which has led quite a few practitioners to conclude that research into leadership has little to offer them. Readers already familiar with the development of the field may wish to skip at least the first two chapters, although they are written from a viewpoint which seeks to draw out points which are emphasized later. Chapter 4 provides a contemporary model of the processes whereby a leader decides to act in a particular manner.

In Chapters 5, 6 and 7 we present a more broadly based model of the leadership process, which while not entirely new, places the concept of leadership in a context which we believe illuminates it, and which makes it easier to distinguish elements likely to be fixed and immutable from elements which are infinitely variable. Chapters 8, 9 and 10 develop this model by examining leader behaviour from the perspective of the leader's superior, the leader's colleagues, and the leader's subordinates. Finally, in Chapter 11 we summarize the model and contrast it with those outlined in Part One of the book. We then explore the relevance of the type of model we have presented to certain practical issues which are of continuing interest, such as the training of leaders and the management of culturally diverse organizations.

The origins of the leadership concept

The lay conception of leadership has long been focused on the actions of major historical figures such as Churchill, Gandhi or Hitler. Analysing the actions of such figures may provide a poor basis for theorizing about less glamorous and more everyday types of leadership, but if such figures have indeed shaped everyday conceptions of the nature of leadership, that is where we should begin our analysis. Perhaps the earliest sophisticated discussion of the processes of leadership is that provided by Machiavelli (1977) in the sixteenth century. Machiavelli analyses the balance between principle and opportunism which in his view provided the best guide for the actions of a prince in the medieval Italian city states. His prescriptions extend not only to relations with other city states, but also to the most effective styles with which to relate to advisers and to one's subjects. On the subject of flattery, for instance, he offers the following view:

> Courts are always full of flatterers; men take such pleasure in their own concerns, and are so easily deceived about them, that this plague of flattery is hard to escape. Besides, in defending against flattery, one runs the further risk of incurring contempt. For there is no way to protect yourself from flattery except by letting men know that you will not be offended by hearing the truth. But when anyone can tell you the truth, you will not have much respect. Hence a prudent prince should adopt a third course, bringing wise men into his council and giving them alone free licence to speak the truth – and only on points where the prince asks for it, not on others. But he should ask them about everything, hear his advisers out, and make his decision after thinking things over, according to his own style . . . But apart from these counselors, he should not listen to anyone . . . (1977: 67)

Effective leadership in Machiavelli's view was therefore a matter of maintaining an adequate flow of accurate information on the issues to be decided, while at the same time maintaining sufficient respect to enable decisive actions to be taken. His analysis thus has a good deal in common with those of much more recent theorists who have identified two dimensions of the leadership process, that concerning task organization and that concerning the maintenance of good working relationships with others. There are perhaps two differences between Machiavelli's approach and the more recent ones. These are firstly, the more systematic manner in which modern theorists have sought to analyse the various elements in the process of leadership, and secondly, the wide variety of methods which have been devised which seek to test the validity of such analyses empirically.

Some first steps toward more systematic analysis are found during the nineteenth century. Carlyle's (1841) discussion of heroic leadership and Galton's (1870) emphasis on the inheritance of leadership qualities were influential at this time. At the beginning of this century, Weber (1947) distinguished three bases upon which a leader's authority might rest. These he identified as:

1 Rational grounds – resting on a belief in the legality of patterns of normative rules and the right of those elevated to authority under such rules to issue commands (legal authority).
2 Traditional grounds – resting on an established belief in the sanctity of immemorial traditions and the legitimacy of the status of those exercising authority under them (traditional authority).
3 Charismatic grounds – resting on devotion to specific and exceptional sanctity, heroism or exemplary character of an individual person, and of the normative patterns or order revealed or ordained by him (charismatic authority). (1947: 328)

Weber's conception of leadership, like Machiavelli's, clearly envisages the leader as a source of influence over others, but it introduces a distinction between bases of influence which reside primarily within the leader as a person, and those which derive from the social and organizational context within which the leader operates. The personal qualities identified by Weber are defined as charisma, while qualities of the leader's environment are seen as deriving either from tradition or from rational–legal structures. Weber stresses that his analysis has sought to identify a series of 'ideal types' and that in practice, authority may often be found to rest on a variety of bases. Even in the case of the personal 'gift' of charisma he makes clear that the gift is dependent upon the ability of followers to recognize it as such:

It is recognition on the part of those subject to authority which is decisive for the validity of charisma. This is freely given and guaranteed by what is held to be a 'sign' or 'proof', originally always a miracle, and consists in devotion to the corresponding revelation, hero worship, or absolute trust in the leader. But where charisma is genuine, it is not this which is the basis for the claim to legitimacy. This base lies rather in the conception that it is the duty of those who have been called to a charismatic mission to recognize its quality and to act accordingly. Psychologically this 'recognition' is a matter of complete personal devotion to the possessor of the quality, arising out of enthusiasm, or of despair and hope. (1947: 359)

Weber goes on to discuss various ways in which charisma may frequently become 'routinized', of which the most relevant to modern organizations occurs where office-holding is on an elective basis. We shall return a little later to the work of those who have recently sought to study charisma empirically.

Leadership as a personal trait

The early part of this century saw a rapid growth in the development of psychometric assessment procedures. While such a development was only one among several contributing to the growth of an empirically based psychology, it was the one which lent itself most readily to the further study of leadership. Since both leadership and abilities such as intelligence were widely believed to be qualities which were inherited, it made sense to study the degree to which they were empirically associated. By so doing it should become possible to understand in a more precise manner the nature of what Weber had termed 'personal charisma'. Typical of such early studies was that by Terman (1904) who asked teachers to describe playground leaders. They were reported to be active, quick, skilful in devising and playing games, and good-looking. In addition boy leaders were said to be larger, stronger and brighter, whereas girl leaders were said to be of good disposition and temper. The numerous later studies which used not only the reputations of leaders, but also self-reports and ability tests as these were developed, have been frequently reviewed. Stogdill (1948) located 104 studies while Mann (1959) located about 75. Later commentators, such as Stogdill (1974), Yukl (1981) and Bryman (1986) have all noted the substantial effect of the earlier reviews upon later conceptualization of the leadership process. Both the Mann and the Stogdill reviews concluded that personality variables account for only a minor proportion of variance in leadership behaviour. In so doing, they paved the way for the growth in popularity of the view that different settings require different types of leadership. As Stogdill (1948) put it: 'A person does not become a leader by virtue of the possession of some combination of traits, but the pattern of personal characteristics of the leader must bear some relevant relationship to the characteristics, activities, and goals of the followers' (reprinted in Stogdill, 1974: 63–4). Mann conducted his review by computing median correlations between leadership and each of the variables studied. Since most studies included more than one set of correlations, he was able to include more than 1400 correlations in his computations. The highest relationship found was a median correlation of 0.25 between leadership and intelligence.

There are a number of reasons why a cautious reinterpretation of the

Stogdill–Mann reviews is required. Firstly, the studies which they reviewed were predominantly concerned with the behaviour of children and of students in unstructured settings. While such a research area is of as much interest as any other, the findings have often been discussed with reference to the behaviour of adult leaders in formally structured organizations, where different variables are likely to be important. Secondly, very few of these studies looked at the 'effectiveness' of the leaders studied. The focus was more upon which persons emerged as leaders, an emphasis which reflects the unstructured settings studied. Finally, by treating each of the correlations between a trait and leadership as a separate observation Mann makes unwarranted statistical assumptions, since predictor ratings deriving from the same source may be spuriously intercorrelated. Lord, de Vader and Alliger (1986) have attempted to update the validity of Mann's conclusions, both by re-examining the studies he reviewed and adding other more recent ones. They found within Mann's sample only 19 studies which gave sufficient statistical detail for further analysis, and to these were added another 12 more recent studies. They used a statistical technique known as validity generalization procedure to estimate the true relation of variables in the sample. This led to an estimate of the correlation between intelligence and leadership of 0.52, compared to Mann's estimate of 0.25. The changed figure is not simply a product of the additional studies, since the correlations were in fact weaker in the more modern studies. In a similar manner, Kenny and Zaccaro (1983) reanalysed data from a previous study in which Barnlund (1962) had concluded that task situation not traits determined leader emergence in laboratory experimental groups. The reanalysis indicated that 49 to 82 per cent of the variance in leader emergence was due to some stable characteristic of the person. Kenny and Zaccaro suggest that this characteristic may be not so much a traditional trait, but rather an ability to size up the type of leadership required in a range of varying situations. Such an ability would fall within most definitions of intelligence. Thus the most recent view is that intelligence and possibly other personal qualities do play a quite substantial role in the emergence of leaders in unstructured settings.

Stogdill (1974) examines a further series of 163 studies linking personality and leadership, which had been published since his earlier review. However, in this review Stogdill includes indiscriminately studies which assessed the leader's effectiveness, and those which assessed leader emergence. Many more of the studies included concerned leadership behaviour by adults within formal organizations. He concludes that the earlier reviews had underestimated the role of personality in effective leadership, and that personality must be considered as one among many factors which contributes to leadership.

Yukl (1981) points out that many of the attributes included in Stogdill's second survey are better thought of as skills or abilities rather than traits. The qualities which Stogdill reports as most frequently linked to leadership are activity, intelligence, dominance, self-confidence, achievement drive and interpersonal skills. Unlike Mann, however, he makes no estimate of the size of the relationship with these variables.

The majority of recent studies in this area have been focused upon the identification of managerial talent. In some studies this is done through assessment centres, which set up simulations of settings managers are likely to encounter in their work. In other studies, evaluations are made of actual managers' performance in relation to self-report measures of personality. In evaluating such studies it is important to note how substantially different is their implicit conception of leadership compared to that of earlier studies. In the earlier studies leadership was seen as a function or process which would emerge within an unstructured setting. In the more recent ones leadership is seen as synonymous with occupancy of a managerial role, and the effectiveness of leaders is judged in terms of criteria which reflect the concerns of top management, such as promotability or ratings of competence by more senior managers. For these reasons it is not surprising that the findings of these studies are somewhat different. An assessment centre survey by Bray, Campbell and Grant (1974) found that managers most frequently promoted within the American Telephone and Telegraph company were those who had been assessed early in their careers as high on oral communication skill, human relations skill, need for advancement, resistance to stress and tolerance for uncertainty.

A further line of study has been to examine the motives of managers and follow the pattern of their subsequent promotions. A series of studies initiated by McClelland (1975) used the TAT projective test procedure. This requires the respondent to make up stories explaining what might be happening in a series of ambiguous pictures. The stories are then coded for their degree of emphasis on motives such as power, achievement and affiliation. McClelland sees a high need for power as a prerequisite for the filling of a managerial position, but he concedes that an overall measure of power needs may be too crude to identify precisely what is required. He distinguishes a personalized or self-seeking power concern from a socialized power concern, which is more likely to be used in the service of the organization's needs. The most recent studies in this tradition examine the utility of particular patterns of motives. Four studies of Leadership Motive Pattern (LMP) consider the relative importance of needs for power, affiliation, and achievement for success at various levels and in various settings. Follow-ups of

237 AT&T managers indicated that high need for achievement predicts success for lower-level managers (McClelland and Boyatzis, 1982). A combination of moderate to high need for power, low need for affiliation, and high activity inhibitions – the Leadership Motive Pattern – predicts success for most other managers, except in technical and engineering areas. In a service organization doing technical and professional work, high need for affiliation by first-line supervisors predicted positive evaluations by their own superordinates and positive attitudes by their subordinates (Cornelius and Lane, 1984). LMP predicted a manager's assignment to prestigious work centres, but not other criteria.

The preceding two studies used the traditional projective tests to measure needs. Two other studies have used a job choice exercise. Respondents are asked to indicate their relative preference for jobs having characteristics that appeal to different needs. One of these studies found that scientists, engineers and Air Force officer/students preferred jobs providing opportunities to satisfy achievement needs. Executives had the highest power needs (Harrell and Stahl, 1981). Need for achievement was reflected in performance as measured by officer/student grade point average and publications by scientists and engineers. Based on studies of 172 managers in various settings, Stahl (1983) argued that high managerial motivation consisted in high need for achievement and high need for power.

A similar series of studies by Miner (1978) examined the motives of those who were most frequently promoted, using a form of projective test which required the manager to finish off a series of incomplete sentences. The motives most strongly linked to promotion were desire to exercise power, desire to compete with peers and positive attitudes toward authority. Recent research using versions of this instrument indicates that power motivation is particularly important in predicting career plans to work as a manager (Miner and Crane, 1981). The professional success (a composite of publications, rank and other indicators) of professors on the other hand is predicted by preference for professional rather than hierarchical inducements. Miner (1982) develops a set of predictions as to which types of motives will be favoured within organizations which offer different types of inducements. In so doing, he moves his theory from a personality-based model to the type of contingency model to be considered in Chapter 2.

The methods used by researchers in this area have mostly involved measuring a set of psychological orientations using paper and pencil indicators that do not include any kind of psychological scaling. Correlations are then identified with independently measured success criteria. Researchers then speculate about intervening processes providing the links between predispositions and success. Such speculations rest on assumptions about the intervening processes which cause people of certain personality types to be evaluated as effective leaders. However, the particular studies reported tell us little about what these people actually do as they perform their day-to-day leadership tasks. Assessment centre research studies bring us somewhat nearer to such an understanding, but they provide us with only a fragmentary list of traits and skills found to be predictive, rather than a theory which could tell us why those particular traits are important and whether they would always be so. The first attempts to produce such theories were made by the theorists of leadership style and it is to these that we now turn.

Leadership as a behavioural style

Those whose work we have so far examined have chosen to define leadership as a quality which is inherent in particular persons. This quality has been seen as enabling such persons to achieve roles in society which legitimize the exercise of influence over others, and as ensuring that they use such powers effectively. A modification of this view became popular from the 1930s onwards, stimulated in particular by the energies of Kurt Lewin. In this view there are a specifiable set of behaviours which we may delineate as the skills of leadership, but they are not inherent in the person. Indeed, once identified, the skills may be taught to others, who may thereby become effective leaders. The classic study in this tradition was that by Lewin, Lippitt and White (1939), who examined the impact of three different leadership styles upon boys' clubs. By using three club leaders, each of whom role-played each leader style in turn, the effect of personality upon the results was essentially eliminated. The researchers' decision to compare autocratic and democratic styles of leadership was an expression of their preoccupation with the political events of the late thirties. The impact of the study shows how widely shared were those preoccupations.

Like many classic research studies the experiment has frequently been cited in a manner which distorts the researchers' original conclusions. The study did not show that the 'democratic' leader style was most effective. It showed that which style of leadership was most effective depended upon which criterion of effectiveness was used. The morale of the clubs was best under democratic leadership. But under autocratic leader style a greater number of aeroplane models were constructed, at least while the leader remained present. It is not, of course, a usual function of youth clubs to seek to maximize productivity at the expense of morale, but the fact remains that in this study different criteria were in conflict as to the most effective leader style.

The Lewin, Lippitt and White study had a substantial effect upon the developing field of leadership research in North America after World War II. What is less well known is that the study was subsequently replicated in other parts of the world, yielding entirely different results. In the late 1940s Misumi and his co-workers conducted a modified version of the study in Japan (Misumi, 1985). They found that on school tasks, the democratic style was more effective where the task was easy, and the autocratic style where the task was more difficult. Meade (1967) also repeated the study, this time in India, and found the autocratic style superior on all criteria. We may therefore note in passing that even were a certain style to be found effective in North America, we would need to hesitate before assuming that such a finding would prove replicable in other cultural settings.

The studies of Lewin and his co-workers were based on experimental manipulations of leader style. Most of the research which followed opted instead for examination of the styles of leadership of those already in posts within established organizations. In this way one could be more confident that the leader styles studied were truly representative of those occurring within everyday settings. Researchers within this tradition assumed that the most effective method by which to identify such styles was the development of a range of questionnaires upon which subordinates as well as leaders themselves would record their perceptions of the leader's behaviour. Reflecting the behaviouristic and pragmatic influences of the time, their purpose was to obtain valid and objective measures of leader behaviour. A great deal of research effort was invested in attempts of this kind to define effective leader styles during the fifties and sixties. The project which stimulated the greatest number of publications was that based at Ohio State University (Stogdill and Coons, 1957). The series of Ohio State studies was one among several programmes of research that reached the conclusion that leadership style could best be described as varying along two dimensions. These were defined as 'Consideration' and 'Initiating Structure'. In other words an effective leader would be one who behaved towards others in a considerate manner, but who nonetheless provided appropriate structures to enable the tasks to be done. Such conclusions are based upon factor analysis of large samples of responses to inductively designed questionnaire items. The goal of the researchers was to develop a standardized set of validated questionnaires which could then be used in identical versions in a wide variety of settings. A series of studies at the International Harvester Company were reported (Fleishman, 1953; Fleishman and Harris, 1962) which showed a clear pattern of relationships between Consideration and Initiating Structure by the supervisor on the one hand and various performance measures on the other. At around the same time, Parsons, Bales and Shils (1953) were proposing that there were two fundamental dimensions of behaviour in both small groups and larger social systems. These were identified as 'task' and 'social' aspects of social systems. Cartwright and Zander (1953) popularized a similar distinction between task and group maintenance functions in small groups. Likert (1961) summarized extensive research at the University of Michigan into the behaviour of supervisors within a wide range of organizations. Effective supervisors were found to be those whose role as supervisor was differentiated from that of their subordinates, who were seen as 'employee-oriented' rather than 'production-oriented', and whose style of task supervision was less detailed and close than others. Blake and Mouton (1964) formulated an extensive programme of management training and organizational development based around their concept of the 'Managerial Grid'. This proposes in essence that effective managers are those who show extremely high concern both for the maximizing of task performance and for those with whom they work, rather than trading off one dimension against the other.

Hopes that these various developing research initiatives would lead to a unified understanding of effective leader style did not last long. As further results were published it became clear that the relation between leader style, as it was being measured, and performance was highly variable. Korman (1966) and Kerr and Schriesheim (1974) provide the most detailed summaries of results from studies using the Ohio State measures. It is clear that while in some settings the results are as expected, in others they are not. Numerous possible reasons for this have been put forward. Perhaps the least radical is the proposition that excessive zeal in the preparation of standardized psychometric instruments has led researchers to focus on too few dimensions of leader style. Stogdill (1974) reports the development of a further ten scales. Bowers and Seashore (1966) also attempted to respond to this view by developing a four-factor leader style theory. They proposed that effective leadership entailed support for others, facilitation of interaction among others, emphasizing group work goals and facilitating the work of the group. Some support for this model was obtained within an insurance agency, but Bowers (1975) acknowledges that this model also gives varying results in different settings. Some more recent researchers have taken this line of reasoning much further. For instance, Yukl and Nemeroff (1979) advance a list of nineteen managerial behaviour categories. However, Yukl and Nemeroff's goal is no longer the detection of simple linkages between leader style and effectiveness, but rather the development of a more adequate taxonomy of managerial behaviours.

A second line of critique of the inconsistent results from the Ohio

State studies is that advanced by Blake and Mouton (1982). Blake and Mouton propose that the conceptualization which underlies the Ohio State model is flawed. The Ohio State model treats the two dimensions as independent of one another and quite separate measures of each were developed. But, argue Blake and Mouton, these scales cannot be treated as independent elements which when added together are expected to achieve a certain effect. A subordinate's response to the supervisor's action in initiating a certain structure will be coloured by the consideration with which that act and earlier acts are expressed. The two dimensions are integrally interrelated rather than separate and they must be tapped by questionnaire items which incorporate such interactions. The early Ohio State researchers do themselves discuss the possibility of such interactions between the two dimensions. Unfortunately, neither they nor Blake and Mouton have ever published studies using such measures, so the potency of this line of reasoning remains to be tested. This critique of the Ohio State measures is, however, supported by studies such as that by Lowin, Hrapchak and Kavanagh (1969). In this laboratory experimental study, students were asked to role-play supervisors who were high or low on Consideration and also high or low on Initiating Structure. The results did show the type of interaction which Blake and Mouton would expect. In other words, response to a considerate leader depended not only on the manipulation of Consideration but also on the manipulation of Initiating Structure.

Blake and Mouton are thus able to sustain their position that it is possible to specify an effective type of leader style with some plausibility. However, the absence of supporting empirical studies has led most researchers to view other avenues of exploration as more promising. Many of them felt that a third criticism of the early leader styles research was the most compelling: the research failed to reach generalizable conclusions because it failed to take account of the circumstances within which leadership acts occur. In the next chapter we turn to the reconceptualizations which followed.

The early models: a critique

The present chapter has been predominantly a story of failure, or at least of results which have fallen some way short of the aspirations of researchers. Leaving aside for the moment our initial examination of Machiavelli and Weber, there has been a period of around 70 or so years during which researchers into leadership acted as though they were medieval alchemists in search of the philosophers' stone. Repeated attempts to distil the 'essence' of leadership yielded no great insight, but researchers nonetheless persisted with research strategies which were not substantially different. It is tempting to presume that they did so for similar reasons to those of the medieval alchemists: they knew that what they were seeking was really there, even though it was not visible. Furthermore, the researchers' patrons in government and industry were making it clear that what they were wanted extracted from organizational life was gold, rather than the all-too-evident lead. Neither were the patrons responsive to the idea that the production of gold first required thorough study of the equivalent to subatomic particles within organizational life.

What we have from all this is certainly not nothing. We can make various statements about traits, skills, styles or motives which frequently contribute to effective leadership. But equally, that knowledge is no great advance on lay conceptions of effective leadership. More importantly, this type of approach has been exhaustively studied and shown to yield little. Such a negative finding opens the way for other types of theorizing which hold more promise.

Some elements in the classic sociology of organizations find even less expression in this phase of leadership research than do individualistic qualities such as Machiavellianism, charisma and leadership traits more generally. As we noted earlier, Weber saw charisma as but one of three bases for authority. Writers about organizations early in this century paid a good deal of attention to his other bases of authority, particularly such structural issues as hierarchy and the manager's span of control. In general, this literature assumed that what was important about formal leaders was not their personality or behaviour but their occupancy of an organizational role. The scientific management conception of formal leadership saw supervisors and managers as logical extensions of the technocrats who actually specify the routinization of production processes (Taylor, 1947). Supervisors were necessary because the majority of employees, like Schmidt, the classic pig-iron handler whom Taylor studied in the early years of this century, were not seen as having adequate ability to understand the procedures laid down by the technocrats. The supervisor's role was thus to reiterate these procedures, in part as general principles guiding action and in part as guidance for particular acts at particular times. Role prescriptions from managers were viewed as coming not so much from other managers making decisions based on staff recommendations or subordinates' views, but from technically trained 'experts' in work procedures.

Not all sociological theorists have seen leadership in a positive light. Michels (1962) saw the emergency of an established leadership elite as an inevitable outgrowth of the social structures which arise from people's desire for self-determination. However, he saw this outgrowth as incompatible with the basic principles of democracy. A mass of individuals seeking self-determination inevitably find it necessary to appoint 'delegates' to carry out administrative tasks on their behalf. A progression toward the emergence of leaders quickly follows:

> At the outset, the attempt is made to depart as little as possible from pure democracy, by subordinating the delegates to the will of the masses, by tying them hand and foot . . . Gradually, however, the delegates' duties become more complicated; some individual ability becomes essential, a certain oratorical gift, and a considerable amount of objective knowledge. It thus becomes impossible to trust to blind chance, to the alphabetical order of succession, or to the order of priority, in the choice of a delegation whose members must possess certain peculiar personal aptitudes if they are to discharge their mission to the general advantage. (1962: 65, 73)

This process tends to concentrate leadership opportunities in the hands of an elite of established leaders. The creation of an elite in turn reduces democratic participation by the masses and creates a continuing power struggle between the leaders and the led. Michels argues that leadership needs to be understood because it is there, not because it is good or bad. Although he espouses a value-free approach, his own writings give strong hints of how he feels about leadership processes. Most recent writers have tended to focus upon leadership within established organizations, rather than its emergency from within an initially unstructured mass movement. Nonetheless, modern writers, particularly those with interests in participation and democracy have had to struggle with the same dilemma: whether to aim for an objective science of leadership, or whether to be advocates of a certain style.

During most of the long period under review, the majority of researchers treated leadership as something whose essence was definable without reference to its context, whether that essence be a personality, a leader style or an organizationally structured role. To be sure, there were numerous suggestions of other approaches, but these were not picked up to any substantial degree. In understanding why this occurred, we have to consider where and when the research took place. Of the authors writing within the present century referred to in this chapter all but four are American. Since many of the authors to be referred to in later chapters and who take up different theoretical positions are also American, this fact by itself establishes little. It does, however, specify the context within which these particular research strategies developed. As Gergen (1973) has argued, psychological research cannot be thought of as the discovery of absolute truths. What is investigated and what is found is itself a part of social history, and there can be no certainty that results will prove replicable at some later date. In this sense, the search by researchers for the 'essence' of leadership must be seen as part and parcel of the culture of the individualistic societies which until recently have comprised the advanced industrial nations of the world. The literature of those nations has contained frequent discussions of the essence of leadership, from Fayol's (1949) treatise on management, published during World War I, to Blanchard and Johnson's (1982) *One Minute Manager*.

Our cultural heritage makes it easiest to think of leadership as something which a leader does to a follower. Our attention is focused upon the leader as actor, not upon the subordinate or follower, who is seen much more dimly. In his 1948 review Stogdill discusses some findings by Ackerson (1942), who found that correlations between personality traits and 'followership' were not opposite to correlations between those traits and leadership, as had been expected. Such findings have been replicated in a few studies. For instance, Nelson (1964) found substantial personality similarities between liked leaders and liked followers among men overwintering in the Antarctic. Such findings suggest entirely different ways in which the research field might have developed, though there is no guarantee that they would have proved any more fruitful.

To return once more to Weber, he did not simply differentiate three bases for authority. His more important insight was that all three bases of authority did not reside simply in the leader but in the social structure of which both leader and follower are part. Some recent writers have merely debased Weber's conception, as for instance in the definition by Broussine and Guerrier (1985: 35), 'Charisma is the ability to make someone else behave in a particular way because of personality.' Others, particularly House (1977) and Bass (1985) have stayed closer to Weber's intention, by defining charisma as the basis for a particular type of leadership, and developing ways of studying the contexts in which such a type is effective. In doing so, they encounter the problem of how to conceptualize context, as we shall also in later chapters. Their approach, like the others mentioned above, involves the abandonment of the search for a simple essence of leadership, and the commencement of more sophisticated analyses.

2
Contingency Models

In this chapter we consider a series of attempts by researchers to repair what they saw as the deficiencies of the approaches to leadership outlined in the preceding chapter. These researchers were heavily influenced by the earlier work and mostly continued to analyse leadership in terms of certain leader behaviour patterns or styles acting upon a group of subordinates. However, they proposed that the emergence or effectiveness of any one style was contingent upon the environment within which the leader is operating. The earliest model of this kind continued the emphasis of early researchers upon the processes whereby leaders emerged in initially unstructured settings.

Leader role emergence and group process

The insights which Michels achieved as to the manner in which leadership evolved within political organizations could have found a use in a wide range of fields. Particularly useful is his emphasis upon the manner in which the passage of time unleashes group processes which inexorably alter the role of the leader. So potent are these forces that the ultimate role of the leader may be wholly in conflict with that originally intended, even in the most participative types of organization. Researchers within this tradition do not, however, refer back to Michels's work. In a series of early studies, Bales and Slater (1955) showed that within small groups of students, two types of leadership role quickly differentiated. They dubbed these task leaders and socio-emotional leaders, a distinction which clearly parallels that made by the survey-oriented leader style researchers considered in Chapter 1. Bales and Slater found that differentiation of the two roles occurred more in some groups than others, and attempted to discover why. Both they and subsequent researchers have proposed that such variables as the level of consensus in the group, members' attraction to the group, and how legitimate is the group's task activity may all be important.

The difficulty with such studies is to find a common way of measuring these and other aspects of group process. Hollander (1964, 1979) attempted to solve this problem through the use of a theory of exchange. Initiated by Thibaut and Kelley (1959) and Homans (1961), exchange theory portrays social behaviour as a quasi-economic exchange of rewards and punishments. It can be thought of as an attempt to apply behaviourism to the field of social psychology. Hollander suggested that whether or not an individual takes on a leadership role depends upon the balance of rewards exchanged within a group. Leader emergence thus depends not simply on the possession of certain traits, but equally on the group's tasks and norms, which will determine those skills and values which will be most rewarding for members. A leader achieves acceptance by providing adequate evidence of task competence and of conformity to group norms. Task competence is the more crucial of these attributes, and Hollander proposes that where task competence and early conformity have built up sufficient 'idiosyncrasy credits', the group may be willing to tolerate a certain amount of later non-conformity, so long as their overall reward levels are preserved. Hollander reported laboratory experiments which supported these hypotheses but later researchers proved unable to replicate them successfully (Wahrman and Pugh, 1972). However, it is by no means certain that such hypotheses could be validly tested within short-term laboratory settings.

In following a similar line of thought, Michels noted the need for technical skills, but leaves acceptance of group norms by the leader implicit. In Hollander's model the leader remains in place so long as subordinates' goal achievement is facilitated. Michels's analysis explores in detail the process whereby the initially benign leader may remain in power despite becoming a powerful oligarch. Though such a leader may initially have achieved power through taking on the charismatic role which the group required, later tenure is related to other factors. The leader acquires an increasingly broad and firm control of the resources wished for by the relatively powerless members of the group or emergent organization. This is accomplished through exchanges with those external to the organization and with the more powerful internally differentiated factions. Paradoxically, this process can occur as a direct result of the leader's seeking to accomplish goals which are valuable to the organization members' cause.

Although Michels's writing predates the formulation of exchange theory by many years, it requires only slight amendment here to show up its parallels with the Hollander model. Both theorists see leaders as being given certain powers, statuses and perquisites in exchange for doing something on behalf of their constituency. Both give the passage of time a central place in their model. However, the Michels model has the broader vision, no doubt because it was based upon analysis of ongoing social movements, rather than short-term laboratory experiments. Neither model has had substantial influence upon subsequent contingency theories, all of which focus upon leader effectiveness rather than leader emergence. This change of emphasis no doubt accords with the pressures exerted by research sponsors toward studies which had clearly applicable findings. Something was lost in this change of emphasis, particularly Michels's exposition of the manner in which leadership comes to entail contacts with a wide network of constituencies, and we shall return to this later in the book. Hollander's reliance upon exchange theory finds echoes in later theories of leader effectiveness, several of which also use reward as their focal concept. The earliest contingency theory of effectiveness and the one which has commanded the most continuing attention as well as a good deal of criticism has been that put forward by Fiedler (1967).

Fiedler's contingency theory and LPC research

The Contingency Theory of Leadership is built around the Least Preferred Coworker (LPC) measure of leader personality. Its basic premise is that a leader's description of the person with whom he or she has had the greatest difficulty working reflects a basic leadership style. Fiedler's model distinguishes high LPC leaders, whom he initially considered to be task-oriented, from low LPC leaders whom he described as relationship-oriented. This distinction appears to have a good deal in common with that proposed, for instance, by the Ohio State researchers. However, Fiedler's measure is based upon a series of semantic differential ratings of someone whom one has worked with in the past, and it is completed by the leader and not by the subordinate. In contrast, most leadership style researchers have used ratings by subordinates of their formal leader's behaviour patterns, based on the view that leaders distort their self-perceptions too much for those perceptions to be of much meaning (Korman, 1966; Misumi, 1985). Studies directed toward identifying exactly what Fiedler's measure of orientation involves – an interpersonal versus task motivation predisposition, cognitive complexity, or something else – have been a major theme in the continuing controversy surrounding his contingency theory. Researchers initially attempted to correlate LPC with other personality measures. When this yielded few significant correlations, they manipulated situational variables and used subordinates or observers to indicate how leaders with different LPC scores responded.

Fiedler's second basic premise is that the leader personality orientation (and implicitly the behavioural style) that contributes most to group performance varies according to 'situation favourability'. Situations are conceived of as allowing more or less leader influence depending primarily on three factors. These are the quality of the leader's relationship with subordinates, the leader's formal 'position' power, and the degree of task structure. Fiedler envisages a curvilinear relation between situation favourability and the most effective style, such that task-oriented leaders will do best in settings that are highly favourable, and also in those which are very unfavourable. In settings which are intermediate the relationship-oriented leader is expected to do better. Fuller details of the predictions derived from Fiedler's model are presented in many places (e.g. Bryman, 1986) and will not be repeated here. Fiedler and his colleagues have conducted numerous field and experimental tests of these predictions (Rice, 1978; 1981) and their findings have been extensively debated (Graen et al., 1972, Ashour, 1973). Numerous aspects of Fiedler's model have been criticized, including both the arbitrary basis upon which its predictions were formulated and the strength of the findings which were said to support the model (Schriesheim and Kerr, 1977). The nature of this debate has evolved over time and we shall give detailed attention only to more recent aspects. Several factors have contributed to the length of time over which Fiedler's model has continued to be actively debated. One factor is certainly that contingency models of leadership are seen as plausible. In our culture at this time it 'makes sense' that leaders do affect subordinates' behaviour and that different styles of leadership fit different settings. A second factor has been Fiedler's continuing willingness to modify and develop his original formulation. For instance, he has identified additional dimensions of environmental variance which would affect situation favourability, such as level of stress and linguistic heterogeneity. He has also discussed the effects of training and of intelligence on the relationships between the variables in his model (Fiedler and Chemers, 1984).

In recent years few studies using the LPC measure have been published, although reviews drawing conflicting conclusions continue to appear. Rice (1978) has reviewed studies bearing on the question of just what it is that Fiedler's LPC measure does in fact measure. Fiedler's original belief that it tapped an underlying and invariant personality dimension is clearly untenable. Repeated measurement of LPC from the same subjects has shown test–retest reliabilities varying from 0.01 to 0.92. Furthermore, observation of high and low LPC leaders has shown that their actual behaviour, not just its effects, varies depending upon the situation. Fiedler (1978) therefore now proposes that the LPC score reflects a leader's position in a hierarchy of motives. Those with high LPC are said to value most highly the creation of good interpersonal relations with their subordinates. However, when good relationships are already accomplished, their behaviour can become more task-oriented, reflecting their secondary motives. Conversely, low LPC leaders are seen as valuing task accomplishment most highly, so that their behaviour is predominantly task-oriented. But when task accomplishment is assured their behaviour will become more relationship-oriented. Rice (1978) proposes a somewhat similar conceptualization, whereby LPC scores are seen as measures of the leader's values. As with other measures of attitude or value, Rice would expect that the relation with actual behaviour would vary from one situation to another. These conceptions of the nature of the LPC measure help to make it clear why researchers have found few strong correlations between the LPC measure and other measures of personality traits or of leader styles.

Despite the earlier criticisms, Fiedler (1978) continues to assert that empirical support for his model is strong. As in many other fields, the most recent examinations of the literature takes the form of meta-analyses (Strube and Garcia, 1981; Vecchio, 1983; Peters, Hartke and Pohlmann, 1985), in which the sizes of the effects obtained in different studies are statistically combined. These reviews also conclude that the balance of evidence favours Fiedler's predictions. Thus the issue to be debated is not so much whether the evidence favours Fiedler's model but why it does so. Critics point to the arbitrary manner in which the model is constructed and to the consequent risk that results may spuriously support predictions. A particular weakness of the Fiedler model is the possibility of overlap between the LPC measure completed by the leader, and one of the three supposedly independent dimensions of the situation, namely leader–follower relations. Leader–follower relations in studies of Fiedler's model are ordinarily assessed on the basis of ratings made by the leader. In Fiedler's (1978) review, he asserts that the study by Chemers and Skrzypek (1972) of military groups provides some of the strongest support for his model. The data from this study were reanalysed by Shiflett (1973) in an attempt to see how far it was possible to predict the same pattern of findings which Chemers and Skrzypek had obtained using LPC as a predictor, but using the measure of leader–follower relations as a predictor instead. A large proportion of the variance did indeed prove explicable in this way. This indicates that the supposedly independent measures of leader style and situation are not at all independent, so that the pattern of findings supporting Fiedler's predictions could well be explained in ways quite different from those proposed by him and which would require the abandonment of his theory.

Rice (1981) reviews studies dealing with a secondary issue in the research programme – the relation between leader LPC and follower satisfaction. The review indicates that followers are more satisfied when there are low LPC leaders in favourable situations and high LPC leaders in unfavourable situations. It also reveals that follower satisfaction is highest in leader–follower dyads with dissimilar LPC scores.

Three other recent articles report experimental studies involving slight modifications of Fiedler's usual research method. Instead of comparing very high and very low LPC leaders as has typically been done, the studies all include intermediate LPC levels. Kennedy (1982) reanalysed data from 697 participants in 13 studies not previously used to test the basic contingency model. Situation favourability was represented by the usual three variables noted above. Supervisor and observer performance evaluations were used as criteria. As the theory postulates, leaders in the low LPC range did best in very favourable and very unfavourable situations. High LPC leaders did best in the intermediate range of situation favourability. Middle LPC leaders were generally more effective than the average of the Low and High LPC leaders. Their effectiveness was relatively unaffected by situation favourability. This is the one study among the three that deals with the pragmatically significant performance implications of the LPC.

The other two studies extend the debate about the behavioural meaning of the LPC measure. In one study, time pressure was manipulated to determine its implications for the communication frequency of leaders with one of four LPC levels (Isenberg, 1981). The results did not support the hypothesis that LPC interacts with time pressure to predict frequency of communication by the leader. In the other study, a series of laboratory experiments were conducted in India to determine the implications of LPC scores for reward allocation (Singh, 1983). The proposition guiding the study was that if high LPC leaders really are relationship-oriented, perceived subordinate attitudes should substantially affect rewards. Similarly, if low LPC leaders really are task-oriented, actual subordinate performance should affect rewards. This proposition was not supported. However, high LPC leaders tended to maintain a technically equity-oriented approach to reward distribution.

A good deal of confusion thus still surrounds Fiedler's Contingency Theory. His most recent work involves the addition to the model of measures of the leader's intelligence. The new version is referred to as Cognitive Resources Theory (Fiedler and Garcia, 1987), and it too finds some empirical support. However, it does not address the question of the confounding of the measures in the old model. Neither is the meaning of LPC and thus the psychological and social reasons for the relationships found any clearer. The attempt to construct a model which clearly differentiates elements of leader and situation must therefore be judged not to have succeeded. Schriesheim and Kerr's (1977) 'obituary' for LPC research appears to have been warranted.

The path-goal theory of leadership and its derivatives

If the undoing of Fiedler's attempt to formulate a contingency model was his reliance upon a personality measure of doubtful validity, it is interesting to note that all the other theories to be examined within the remainder of this chapter have avoided the use of personality-based measures. Instead they delineate a variety of measures which define leadership style separately from personality. Perhaps this change of emphasis reflects the fact that Fiedler first started to develop his LPC measure in the fifties, when conceptions of personality were still closely integrated with conceptions of leadership, whereas the remaining models are all of more recent parentage.

Path-goal theory derives rather clearly from the motivationally-based expectancy theories which became popular in the field of organizational behaviour in the sixties (e.g. Vroom, 1964). In essence, it asserts that subordinates will do what leaders want if leaders do two things. Firstly, they must ensure that subordinates understand how to accomplish the leader's goals. Secondly, they must see that subordinates achieve their personal goals in the process (House, 1971). The leader's task is thus to diagnose the task environment and select those behaviours which will ensure that subordinates are maximally motivated toward organizational goals. In a later version of the theory four leader styles are delineated (House and Dessler, 1974; House and Mitchell, 1974). These are termed 'instrumental', 'supportive', 'participative' and 'achievement-oriented'. In selecting one of these styles leaders need to consider the personal characteristics of their subordinates and the environment within which they work. Personal characteristics are seen as including both personal qualities and task-relevant skills. The environment includes the nature of the work group, the authority system within the organization and the nature of each particular subordinate's tasks.

The published literature of tests of path-goal theory is quite extensive (House and Baetz, 1979), but the scope of many of the studies is much more restricted than would be expected from the statement of the theory outlined above. Many researchers have used the Ohio State measures of leader style, and have in consequence only addressed themselves to the instrumental and supportive leader style dimensions. Furthermore, most typically only one dimension of environmental variance has been included, namely the degree of task structure. The results of these studies have been very mixed (Bryman, 1986). Instrumental leadership is predicted to be more appropriate where task structure is low and role clarity would therefore also be low. This prediction has sometimes been upheld in terms of satisfaction measures, but rarely in terms of performance measures. Supportive leadership is seen as appropriate where the task is stressful, frustrating or dissatisfying. A number of studies have supported this aspect of path–goal theory (Schriesheim and De Nisi, 1981) but others have not. Schriesheim and Schriesheim (1980) for instance found supportive leadership was strongly linked to satisfaction measures regardless of the level of task structure.

Several other studies making reference to path–goal theory have dealt with contingencies other than task structure. Some of these concern supervisory participativeness. Participative decision making has been linked to job satisfaction, supervisor performance ratings, and lower level employees' experience of small power differences between themselves and top management (Abdel-Halim, 1983a, b). For subordinates who have a high need for independence and are working on non-repetitive tasks, high perceived participation predicted high job satisfaction and positive performance evaluations (Abdel-Halim, 1983b). A measure combining leader participativeness and support was found to be more predictive of positive attitudes than was formal organizational participativeness in a study of 1000 members of ten organizations. Dobbins and Zaccaro (1986) examined path–goal theory predictions for satisfaction within military organizations. It was found that contrary to prediction, high group cohesiveness enhanced the relationship between Ohio State leadership measures and satisfaction. In one of very few tests of path–goal theory undertaken outside the USA, Al-Gattan (1985) studied employees of an oil company in Saudi Arabia. A complex series of hypotheses based upon measures of task structure, growth need strength and a locus of control measure were partially supported with regard to satisfaction measures, but not for ratings of performance.

Tests of path–goal theory have thus yielded findings which are highly variable. Predictions of performance measures have been particularly unsuccessful, while relations between leader styles and satisfaction measures have sometimes been as predicted. Some critics have suggested that the erratic quality of these findings may derive from use of the Ohio State leadership style measures, which are open to a variety of criticisms (Schriesheim and Kerr, 1977). Others point to the *ad hoc* manner in which different moderators of the relation between leader style and performance are included or excluded from one or another study. Presumably if path–goal theory were to be valid, one would only expect the data to support predictions to any substantial degree if all of the most substantial moderators of leader style were to be simultaneously represented in the model.

A further difficulty lies in the way of those who would advance the case for path–goal theory. Greene (1979) has argued that surveys collected at a particular point in time cannot tell us whether any relationships found are actually due to the leader's actions. It is equally possible that the qualities of the leader's task environment might cause him or her to behave in particular ways. Greene reports a study of leader–subordinate dyads over time. He found that where task structure was high, instrumental leadership increased over time. Only where task structure was low was there much indication that leadership exerted a causal effect. We shall return to this problem in Chapter 3.

A contingency theory which has some similarity with path–goal theory and which has achieved considerable popularity with practitioners is that of Hersey and Blanchard (1982). Their formulation is referred to as 'Situational' leadership theory. It relies once again upon two dimensions of leader style, which are called task behaviour and relationship behaviour. Only one dimension of the environment enters the model and this is the 'maturity' of the subordinate. Hersey and Blanchard identify four combinations of task and relationship behaviour and propose that each of these is appropriate to a particular level of subordinate maturity. Although it has been developed with reference to research findings, the measures of leadership and concepts of maturity used in it have not been subjected to the extensive empirical testing that a model of its significance would warrant. As with other contingency theories, one can only speculate that its widespread popularity rests on the fact that it 'makes sense' to a broad range of practitioners. Even by this criterion the theory has some way to go. Blake and Mouton (1982) asked samples of managers to evaluate various possible courses of action to be followed in circumstances where situational leadership theory makes predictions as to what would be effective. The large majority of managers chose alternative actions designed by Blake and Mouton rather than the ones offered by Hersey and Blanchard. An empirical study by Hambleton and Gumpert (1982) found that managers whose self-rated style matched their own estimate of subordinate maturity were evaluated as more effective by personnel managers who knew them well. This provides some support for Hersey and Blanchard. However, the results are hard to interpret as the managers' ratings of their own style were not related to the personnel managers' ratings. We therefore do not know how valid were the managers' self-assessments of leader style.

The Vroom–Yetton decision-making model

Vroom and Yetton (1973) presented a model of leadership which focuses on leadership acts in settings which require an explicit decision. They explore the criteria which can be used to determine whether and how the leader should involve subordinates in certain kinds of decision situations. Five main types of leader styles are distinguished, each with several variants and seven types of environmental contingency. In the original model, these are arrived at through a series of binary choices. Leadership is classified as either autocratic, consultative or based on group decision-making. Both the autocratic and consultative styles are subdivided into further categories. The decision environment is subdivided in terms of whether it is important to obtain the highest possible quality decision and whether it is important that others accept the decision once it is made. Where quality is important, three further choices are to be made, depending on availability of information, subordinates' acceptance of organizational goals and how structured the problem is. Where acceptance is important four further choices are required.

The elegance of this model is that it makes rather precise predictions as to the most effective decision style in a given setting. Vroom and Jago (1978) asked 96 managers to recall successful and unsuccessful decisions made by them earlier. It was found that where the managers had done as the model prescribes, 68 per cent of decisions had been successful. Where they had not, only 22 per cent were successful. Since the managers were unfamiliar with the Vroom–Yetton model this is impressive. Jago and Vroom (1980) responded to a challenge by Field (1979) that a simpler model would be equally valid. Respondents were presented with scenarios that varied according to the seven contingencies or 'problem attributes' postulated by Vroom and Yetton (1973). The results indicated that supervisors' choice of various autocratic, consultative, or participative decision-making strategies was better predicted by the original model than by Field's simplified model. Another study involved the presentation of similar stimulus scenarios, while also manipulating subjects' perspective (Heilmann et al., 1984). That is, one group of subjects was instructed to take the vantage point of a supervisor, while a second group was asked to view the scenarios from a subordinate's perspective. The results generally support Vroom and Yetton's model when subjects were instructed to respond as a supervisor. However, subjects in the role of subordinates were shown usually to prefer participative behaviour, without regard to the predictions of the model. Jago (1981) attempted to determine whether hierarchical level needed to be added to the model as an additional contingency. The results indicated that middle managers considered participation to be more important at lower levels than at upper levels when there was no quality requirement that makes one decision better than another.

The most adequate test to date of whether leaders should behave according to Vroom and Yetton's recommendations is reported by Field (1982). The study involved placing 276 students into four-person groups and asking each group to address five cases involving decision situations. A total of 115 cases were involved across all groups. The cases were designed to reflect various combinations of Vroom and Yetton's key contingencies. Leaders were instructed to use a specific one of the five decision-making approaches from the model. The results indicated that the decisions made when Vroom and Yetton's decision rules are followed were more effective than decisions made when they are not. Four of the seven contingencies had statistically significant effects on decision quality.

Vroom has continued to revise the model in an effort to increase the realism of the situations in which decisions are made (Vroom, 1984). He has done this by increasing the number of questions used to diagnose situations from seven to eleven, and by increasing the possible degree of presence of each characteristic of the situation from two to five levels. The eleven diagnostic categories are now as shown in Figure 2.1.

Questions about problem attributes

A   Does the problem possess a quality requirement? (Q)
B   Do I have sufficient information to make a high quality decision? (LI)
C   Is the problem structured? (ST)
D   Is acceptance of the decision by subordinates important for effective implementation? (A)
E   If I were to make the decision by myself, is it reasonably certain that it would be accepted by my subordinates? (PP)
F   Do subordinates share the organizational goals to be attained in solving this problem? (GC)
G   Is conflict among subordinates over preferred solutions likely? (CO)
H   How much prior information and ability do subordinates have? (SI)
I   Is there a time constraint upon problem solution? (TC)
J   How important is subordinate development? (MD)
K   How valuable is time in this situation? (MT)

Figure 2.1 *Vroom's revised decision model (adapted from Vroom, 1984: 108–9)*

The answers to these questions are used to compute the relative utility of the five decision styles for any particular situation, using a series of complex formulae. Decision effectiveness, for instance, is defined as Decision Quality + Decision Acceptance – Decision Time Costs. Each of the elements in this equation is precisely defined. For example, Decision Quality is given as:

$$\text{D Qual} = Q - Q/2 \,[(f2)\,(LI) + (f4)\,(ST) + (f3)\,(GC) + (f3)\,(SI)]$$

In this equation the values of the functions f2, f3 and f4 vary depending upon which decision method is used. The meanings of the other terms are as defined in Figure 2.1.

The prospects for the future of this model are somewhat brighter than for those reviewed earlier in this chapter, but the quantity of research generated so far is relatively small and all studies refer to the earlier version of the model rather than to the revision presented above. The studies based on reports of actual decision-making are vulnerable to the possibility that the success of a decision may bias the manager's memory of what was decided and how it was put into effect. The more recent studies based upon the use of case scenarios overcome this problem, but yield some findings which are crucial to the view which will be spelled out in later chapters of this book. In particular, Heilmann et al.'s (1984) finding that the model was supported when students took the perspective of the manager, but not when they took the perspective of the subordinate, is of considerable interest. The Vroom–Yetton model goes further than those so far reviewed in acknowledging the possibility of conflict, in so far as it differentiates between the quality of a decision and its acceptability to subordinates. Heilman et al. go further, by indicating that within their sample subordinates preferred to participate in decisions regardless of the nature of those decisions. in this way the pro-management bias of the Vroom–Yetton model is made explicit: a manager working within the guidelines of the model would presumably need to explain to subordinates that it was not within the interests of the organization that they should participate in all decisions.

Broader conceptualizations of environmental contingencies

All the contingency theorists whose work has so far been examined have focused their attention upon the immediate work environment within which the leader is operating. The image one gains of the leader within these models is of someone who has one or two subordinate workers, or at most a small group. If we were to tax the authors of these models with this point, they would most likely respond that such simplification was necessary at this stage of research if our conceptions are not to become unmanageably complex. However, what is more striking about the restricted range of variables selected by these researchers is its arbitrariness when viewed from a broader perspective. It may not be surprising that contingency theories have failed to find stronger support when so little care has been expended on selecting which aspects of environment are asked to carry the burden of reviving leadership theory.

Most of the more macroscopic models of organization deal with formal leadership as an aspect of hierarchy. Their assumption is that through the customary control processes of selection, training, goal-setting, and economic records, managers will behave reasonably predictably. March and Simon (1958) embed formal leadership within formal control systems as a part of 'programmed' decision-making. Hierarchy is a part of programming to the extent that it reinforces or supports other influences on work pacing, work activities, or product specifications. However, formal leadership is also embedded within 'discretionary' decision-making. Formal leaders can become actively and creatively involved in making decisions *within* their programmed constraints. The key contingency variable seen as distinguishing the preponderance of programmed versus non-programmed leadership actions is the degree of repetitiveness of activities by individuals (and, presumably, the degree to which situations permit repetitiveness).

The Katz and Kahn (1966/1978) formulation of leadership as 'the influential increment over and above mechanical compliance with the routine directives of the organization' (1966: 302) equates leadership with the *non-programmed* aspect of hierarchy. The contingencies posited to produce a need for leadership are (1) the incompleteness of organization design to provide sufficiently detailed and appropriate activity specifications, (2) the changing external organization environment reducing internal repetitiveness, and (3) internal dynamics and the complex processes that are characteristic of human role occupants. Katz and Kahn also recognize the function of leadership outside of hierarchy.

Many other organization design contingency models touch on leadership, Lawrence and Lorsch (1967) used Fiedler's LPC measures to try to assess leaders' behaviour style as an element in their contingency model of organizations' response to their environments. Their work did not show LPC to be an important factor in understanding the effects of an organization's environment.

Another well-known contingency model of organizations deals primarily with the role of hierarchy, but also includes a rudimentary scheme for describing supervisor role behaviour. Perrow (1970) postulates four organization types which are described as being adapted to four types of technological environments, as shown in Figure 2.2. Perrow (1970) describes the structural characteristics of the types of organizations which are found in each of the four environments. He distinguishes four characteristics as they apply at each of two levels, the middle management or technical level, and the foreman or supervision level. These four structural characteristics – discretion, power, coordination within groups, and interdependence of groups – are discussed largely according to the role demands placed on formal leaders at these two levels. For example, middle managers in craft and routine technologies are expected to be involved in work coordination through programmed, advance planning. Middle managers in non-routine and engineering technologies are expected to coordinate work

Variability of events

Search procedures	Few exceptions	Many exceptions
Unanalysable	e.g. craft industries	Non-routine
Analysable	Routine	Engineering

Figure 2.2 *Perrow's types of organizational environment (adapted from Perrow, 1970: 78)*

through mutual adjustment involving feedback in interaction with others.

A significant aspect of Perrow's perspective on formal leadership is that he considers which particular patterns of managerial behaviour are required within a broad range of organizational contexts. A second strong point is that he looks at the likelihood of evolution in the function of hierarchy as organizations change over time. In keeping with Weber's model of bureaucracy, Perrow argues that many forces drive organizations to reduce uncertainty. As a consequence of uncertainty reduction, technologies tend to move from many exceptions to few exceptions, and from unanalysable search processes to analysable search processes. The relationship between leadership and the way that organizations change over time is explored further in Chapter 8.

Heller and Wilpert (1981) take a rather different approach to that of the theoretical models just outlined. While they propose that environmental contingencies are likely to be very important in determining effective leadership styles, they prefer to search for key variables by examining a broad range of possibilities empirically. They report the findings of a project initiated a decade earlier by Heller, which examines the use of different leader styles in a variety of countries and organizations. They distinguish five leader styles, spread along an 'Influence–Power Continuum'. These styles are somewhat similar to those in the Vroom–Yetton model in so far as they focus on decision-making. They range from the leader who decides without offering an explanation, to the leader who delegates a particular decision. Managers in Heller's various studies are asked which of the five styles they use in each of 12 decision situations. The types of decision surveyed include increases in the subordinate's salary, the hiring, promotion or firing of those who work for the leader, and changes in the subordinate's work procedures. The environmental contingencies considered range from the country where the data are collected, through industry type, to the manager's perception of the particular qualities of their subordinate.

Heller and Wilpert report highly significant differences in the degree of participative decision-making used by managers in different countries. Within their sample of eight countries, Sweden and France were consistently more participative than Britain, the USA, West Germany and Israel. In a similar way, participative styles were more characteristic of the oil and electronics industries than they were of banking and public transport. When the analysis turns to the more microscopic level of analysis, it is found that decision style is heavily influenced by the nature of the specific decision. Multiple regressions showed that the variable which accounted for the largest amount of variance was the supervisor's perception of the difference in skill level between their own job and their subordinate's job. Where the perceived difference was low, participative styles were more frequently used.

The Heller and Wilpert research differs from that by Vroom and Yetton in that it asks managers how they usually decide certain matters, rather than how they did so on a specific occasion. For this reason, it would not have made sense to ask the managers whether their decisions were successful. Instead Heller and Wilpert devised a 'Management Advancement Quotient' (MAQ), which measured the relation between the manager's age and the average age found at that level and in that sector. Both those who scored high and those who scored low on MAQ related the degree of delegation to perceived skill differences with the subordinate. However, with high scorers a second factor had to do with the degree of turbulence in the broader environment within which the organization operated. For low scorers, the second factor was focused upon constraints within the workplace. In other words, those who are promoted fastest relate their leadership style to a more cosmopolitan view of the broader environment, while those who are promoted slower relate their style more to the specific situation. Heller and Wilpert caution against interpreting these findings as indicating that managers who take a more cosmopolitan view are the more effective ones. They suggest that an equally plausible view would be that managers who relate their actions to the broader context are favoured (and promoted!) by senior managers, since senior managers are also likely to be preoccupied by the broader context. Conversely, managers who take care to tailor their actions to the specific needs of their subordinates may find favour with their subordinates, but are less likely to be promoted. As was the case when we discussed the Vroom–Yetton model, it is therefore not possible to identify an uncontentious criterion of leader effectiveness. Any measure of effectiveness must be effectiveness as defined by a particular party and others may not agree with the priorities implicit within that criterion.

A further attempt to broaden the scope of contingency theories has recently been made by House (1984). Coming as it does from one of the principal protagonists of path–goal theory, one may think of the new theory as an attempt to break out of the narrowly focused research tradition which overtook path–goal theory. House (1984) once more differentiates four different leader styles, but these differ from the earlier path–goal styles. Following Mintzberg (1983), House sees a leader's power as resting upon authority, political influence, expert influence or charismatic influence. In defining the context which permits or encourages the exercise of each of these four types of power, House draws upon contingency theories developed by researchers into organizational behaviour. Hickson et al. (1971) advanced a strategic version of contingency theory. This proposed that the power of an organizational unit rests upon four variables: (1) the unit's ability to reduce uncertainty faced by other units; (2) the unit's irreplaceability by other units; (3) the linkage of the unit to the system as a whole; and (4) the degree to which the unit's activities are essential to the system as a whole. More recently, Pfeffer (1981a) has advanced a related model termed resource dependency theory. In this version, organizational power goes to those who have unambiguous control over some critical organizational resource.

On the basis of these models and a detailed literature review, House advances 60 propositions as to the personal and organizational circumstances which would predispose a particular leader to employ a specific style. Some of these specify, for example, that the use of particular styles will be limited to those styles which a leader is able to employ, both by virtue of their personal skills and their position within the organization. They will also be a function of the willingness of the target of influence to comply. House proposes that the leader will use coercive means, i.e. authority or political influence, where resistance is expected, and non-coercive means, i.e. expertise or charisma, where compliance is expected. His predictions about the use of coercive power are more fully developed in House (1988). The new House model is clearly a contingency model, and for that reason finds a place within this chapter. Its very complexity ensures that it cannot be tested as a whole, but in future years it is likely that particular aspects of it can be examined empirically. However, it also differs from all preceding contingency theories in important respects. Perhaps the most important of these is the manner in which it finally lays to rest the model of leadership which has dominated the first two chapters of this book, that of the leader who acts upon others in a unidirectional manner. Several of the more recent contingency theories acknowledge that the leader scans the environment in deciding whether to act this way or that. The House model, however, goes much further in this direction by proposing that a key element in the leader's choice of style is their expectations about how others will respond to them. While it might seem self-evident that leaders, like the rest of us, would do this, such conceptions have been at best implicit in earlier contingency theories. House's reformulation is no doubt part of the broader tide of opinion within psychology as a whole away from crudely behaviourist conceptions and towards a more detailed examination of the cognitions which guide actors' actions. We shall look in more detail at a variety of other cognitive and more radical approaches to the study of leadership in the next chapter.

3
Leader Style under the Surgeon's Knife

The rather mixed pattern of research findings reviewed in the first two chapters has encouraged various researchers to seek a variety of remedies, some more radical than others. In a notable review paper, Miner (1975) proposed that the concept of leadership had an uncertain future, and himself proposed the formulation of a model of influence processes which made no direct reference to leadership as such. Some of the approaches discussed in the next two chapters constitute relatively minor amendments to those already examined, while others come much closer to what Miner envisaged. What they all have in common is a recognition that radical rethinking of our conceptions of leadership has become urgent, and the fact that they have only become popular in the decade since Miner's paper appeared.

If leadership theory be considered as a sick person, the remedies advanced in this chapter are primarily surgical. That is, they seek to preserve the central element in leadership research by cutting away facets which are seen as confusing or based on misunderstanding. They continue to look at the leader's effect on others, but do so from a series of increasingly novel viewpoints which are opened up by the surgery they undertake. In contrast, the research reviewed in Chapter 4 has moved away from the original goal of predicting leader effects upon subordinates' behaviour, focusing instead upon the cognitive processes whereby the leader decides how to act. To continue the medical analogy, we may think of such an emphasis as dissection rather than surgery.

Returning to the present chapter, we shall place the various remedies proposed to revive leadership theory in a crude ascending ordering of their degree of radicalism.

Remedy 1: replace leader style measures by measures of reward and punishment

Researchers within this developing tradition attribute the failings of earlier questionnaire-based studies of leader style to the weaknesses of the measures which were used. They see the possibility of a more valid and reliable set of generalizations about the effects of leadership through a return to the use of those concepts which psychology has most thoroughly explored. This leads to analyses of the effects of reward and punishments given by the leader. Some researchers have drawn on the Skinnerian 'operant conditioning' tradition that emphasizes observable behaviour and the effects that one person's behaviour has on what someone else does (Ashour and Johns, 1983). Others draw upon the more recently developing cognitive–behavioural models (Larson, 1984; Podsakoff, 1982).

Although reward and punishment had been studied by earlier leadership researchers such as Hollander (Mawhinney, 1980), these concepts have been pursued more actively and more precisely since the mid-1970s than before. This is especially true of research concerning punishment. Sims (1980) summarizes several previous laboratory studies (e.g., Sims, 1977; Sims and Szilagyi, 1975) by indicating that rewarding instances of good performance tends to improve performance more than does punishing poor performance. His review indicates that although poor performance tends to elicit punishment, punishment tends not to result in improved performance. In a survey study of a non-profit organization, Podsakoff, Todor and Skov (1982) found that supervisors who were described as rewarding good performance had subordinates who performed better and were more satisfied than other subordinates. These results were not found for supervisors whom subordinates viewed as providing rewards regardless of performance, or supervisors who were viewed as punishing subordinates.

However, some recent reviews disagree with Sims (1980) by indicating that there are some conditions under which subordinates' performance has been found to be improved by punishment or informal feedback as well as by rewards (Arvey and Ivancevich, 1980; Ashour and Johns, 1983, Larson, 1984). A study of retail store managers also indicates that supervisors who have used more formal warnings and dismissals during their careers tended to be evaluated more highly than others by their own superiors (O'Reilly and Weitz, 1980).

A number of variables have been found to affect a supervisor's use of punishment (Larson, 1984; Podsakoff, 1982). Among these are the attitudes that a supervisor holds about punishment. Supervisors who had fired more employees in the past expressed a general attitude that firing people does not trouble them. In the same study, supervisors who expressed a willingness to confront problems indicated having used more formal warnings than had others (O'Reilly and Weitz, 1980). The characteristics of a supervisor's work situation and subordinates have also been found to affect disciplinary actions. Supervisors whose own rewards depended on their subordinates' performance were found in a laboratory study to give more economic rewards to poor performers than did other supervisors (Ilgen, Mitchell and Fredrickson, 1981). Engineering supervisors evaluated and rewarded one subordinate who performed poorly better when other subordinates also performed poorly than when others performed well (Ivancevich, 1983). However, similar results were not found in the same study for a separate sample of supervisors of scientists. A field experiment was conducted in which a supervisor's ability to reward good performance was removed (Greene and Podsakoff, 1981). Not only did subordinates subsequently report that rewards were used less, but they reported that punishment increased. Influence based on liking for the supervisor and on organizationally supported power were also viewed as being used less. Subordinates themselves appear able to affect the way instances of poor performance are reacted to by a supervisor. An experimental study of nursing supervisors presented leaders with an excuse that failure was due to events beyond the subordinate's control, or with apologies for failure from the subordinates. Supervisors who heard the excuses or apologies were less punitive than were other supervisors (Wood and Mitchell, 1981).

In summary, rewarding good performance appears to be more constructive than either providing rewards indiscriminately, or punishing failure. However, due to factors that bias performance evaluations, leaders are likely to make many mistakes in this area. The difficulties are increased if, as is likely, subordinates also misjudge their own performance and that of their peers. Punishment research indicates how a downward spiral in performance, or 'learned helplessness' can occur (Martinko and Gardner, 1982). A particular area of poor performance is dealt with harshly or punished if a person is generally viewed as a poor performer (James and White, 1983). Overall performance may therefore deteriorate further. Particular areas of poor performance continue to be dealt with harshly, while areas of relative strength are not rewarded.

On the face of it the replacement of leader style measures by the neo-behaviourist concepts of reward and punishment has been a positive step. A much more coherent pattern of findings has been obtained. Unfortunately, such a positive reading of the literature requires substantial qualification. The weakness of behaviourist models has long been their inability to specify, on anything other than a *post hoc* basis, just what it is that a particular individual will find rewarding. As Homans (1961) put it, 'some men find some of the damnedest things valuable'. Chomsky (1959) provides the classic critique of difficulties in applying the concepts of reward and punishment to human behaviour predictively. In order to operationalize their variables some neo-behaviorist leadership researchers have found it necessary to do much of their research within short-term laboratory settings, within which the rewards and punishments administered are not likely to have much in common with those used in everyday organizational settings. Other researchers, such as Greene and Podsakoff (1981), have indeed undertaken field surveys, but their design tells us little about how supervisors who reward or punish ordinarily do so.

The concepts of reward and punishment are in one sense broad and general, since they tell us little about the motivations of a specific individual. But they are certainly more specific in their emphasis upon individualism. It is difficult though by no means impossible to envisage how leaders and followers might influence one another through the use of rewards and punishments in parts of the world where social structures are collectivist rather than individualist. Researchers within this field also invariably treat reward and punishment as exclusive alternatives. As we discussed earlier, studies such as that by Lowin, Hrapchak and Kavanagh (1969) make clear that subordinates who find their supervisor considerate are more willing to accept initiation of structure from them. In a similar way, response to punishment is likely to be mediated by prior history of reward. Finally, even within neo-behaviourist studies, we find some acknowledgement that leaders' use of rewards and punishments is affected by their perceptions of subordinates and their circumstances (e.g. Wood and Mitchell, 1981). Later in the chapter we will return to models which give such cognitive processes a more central role.

Remedy 2: differentiate between subordinates

A second reason why many traditionally structured studies of leader style have yielded unreliable results might be that they treated all of a leader's subordinates as interchangeable. Theories have been tested either by averaging performance scores for the different members of a supervisor's work group or by looking at overall correlations between supervisor style and individual subordinate performance. Both approaches assume that there are no differences worth studying between the different subordinates of a leader, and that the leader's behaviour toward different subordinates does not vary. Practising leaders, on the other hand, from the time of Machiavelli onwards have acknowledged the value to the leader of differentiated responses to different subordinates.

Graen and his colleagues (Dansereau, Graen and Haga, 1975; Graen and Cashman, 1975; Graen and Scandura, 1987) have developed an integrated series of studies emphasizing distinctions between the exchange that leaders can develop with different individual subordinates. Within the Graen model, some dyadic relationships can be characterized as formal or legalistic. In these 'supervisory exchanges', relatively minimal, clearly specified services by a subordinate are exchanged for compensation and a minimal degree of necessary supervisory guidance and support. Other 'leadership exchanges' involve a more enthusiastic, complete, and less carefully circumscribed exchange of commitment and personal dedication by a subordinate for careful attention, personal investment and 'mentoring' by a supervisor. This model is known as the Vertical Dyad Linkage model. Its authors' use of the concept of exchange indicates that they too fall within the neo-behaviourist camp. However, the exchange of rewards which they envisage between superior and subordinate is a two-way one, thus indicating that they have moved away from the classical view that leadership is something which a leader does to a subordinate.

Research involving the Vertical Dyad Linkage model during the 1980s has not been extensive. The studies reported have mostly used cross-sectional surveys based on a questionnaire measure of leader–member exchange or LMX. Part of this research involves linking the LMX measure to various aspects of supervisory style (e.g., attention, support and performance ratings, Liden and Graen, 1980). Other studies indicate that analysing perceptions of exchange at the individual level predict labour turnover (Graen, Liden, and Hoel, 1982; Ferris, 1985), and work attitudes (Katerberg and Hom, 1981), better than does analysing group aggregate scores. An organizational change programme is also being developed based on the model. Graen, Novak and Sommerkamp (1982) found that managers trained to be aware of their vertical dyad linkages created increased productivity and subordinate satisfaction in a clerical organization. Vecchio and Gobdel (1984) found that subordinates in a bank who had a leadership exchange relationship were more productive and satisfied than were those who had only a supervisory exchange relationship with their boss. In a series of studies testing Graen's model in Japan, it has been shown that those who established a high LMX relationship with their superior were promoted more rapidly, independently of their prior qualifications (Wakabayashi and Graen, 1984). Similar results have been obtained in the USA (Scandura, Graen and Novak, 1986), although the other factors associated with high subordinate influence were different in the two countries.

The central point of Graen's proposition must be regarded as well established. A series of studies have shown that leaders do differentiate between subordinates, and that group averages of subordinate perceptions do not show the same relations with measures of leader style as do individual subordinate perceptions. The degree to which subordinates have a consensual view is likely to vary substantially in different cultures and organizations, and it is particularly impressive that Graen's results have proved replicable not only in the individualist culture of the USA but also in the collectivist culture of Japan. The most recent formulation of the model (Graen and Scandura, 1987) gives some attention to exchange relationships with superiors and peers as well as subordinates, and we shall return to this in later chapters. At a more general level, Graen's work raises more questions than it settles. If superiors differentiate between their subordinates, we need to know more about the basis upon which they decide to do so, and the effects of such differentiation on all concerned. The neo-behaviourist basis of the model and its reliance on cross-sectional surveys make it difficult for it to address such questions in much detail. However, there are more cognitively oriented researchers whose methods are relevant to these issues, and we shall now explore their work.

Remedy 3: examine leaders' perceptions of subordinates

This group of researchers has questioned the assumption implicit in traditional approaches that the leader's behaviour is in some mechanistic way imposed upon the subordinate. The leader is seen as a processor of information about the subordinate who selects leadership actions upon the basis of the information which has been processed. In line with the development of attribution theory in social psychology (Nisbett and Ross, 1980), the leader is seen as particularly interested in the question of the causes of subordinate performance, especially poor performance. The main issue this research addresses is why leaders blame instances of poor performance on subordinates' ability, their motivation, or conditions external to the subordinates (Feldman, 1981; Green and Mitchell, 1979).

Supervisors are found to be prone to blame failures on a subordinate and to accept personal responsibility for successes (Martinko and Gardner, 1982). A laboratory experiment indicated that supervisors who had not previously engaged in their subordinates' task were especially prone to blame their subordinates for failure (Mitchell and Kalb, 1982). Another experiment involving nursing supervisors indicated that the consequences of poor performance affects a supervisor's causal beliefs. When failure by a nurse resulted in harm to a patient, it was viewed as more the fault of the nurse than if there were no negative consequences (Mitchell and Kalb, 1981). Research concerning explanations that supervisors give for the causes of poor performance is consistent with general models of causal attribution (e.g., Kelley, 1972). Poor performance is seen as due to a subordinate's personal characteristics rather than the situation they are facing when (1) only that subordinate and not others perform poorly, (2) that subordinate has performed poorly before on that task, and (3) that subordinate performs poorly on similar tasks (Green and Mitchell, 1979). The consequences of an action also appear to encourage attributions to a subordinate rather than to their situation.

Besides research concerning the supervisor's interpretations of the causes for poor performance, leadership research is addressing the issue of the circumstances under which a particular level of performance is viewed most negatively or positively. A leader's prior behaviour toward subordinates may affect how the leader perceives their performance. Student supervisors in one study were instructed to lead a group of experimental subjects in either a participative way or an authoritarian way. The participative supervisors came to believe that their subordinates had more personal interest in doing their work well than did the authoritarian supervisors (Kipnis et al., 1981). Poorly performing subordinates were rated more highly in another experimental study if the leaders were led to believe that the subordinates were well liked by others (Mitchell and Liden, 1982). Poor performers may also be evaluated more positively if their performance is viewed as being affected by the actions of good performers than if it is not (Liden and Mitchell, 1983). A field study of Israeli managers indicated that when a subordinate consistently performed well, supervisors expected the good performance to continue to a greater extent than they expected repeated poor performance to continue (Bizman and Fox, 1984). Other results from the same study indicate that if subjects were led to believe that their subordinates' poor performance was due to low effort, they were more likely to evaluate performance very negatively than if it were due to a lack of ability. As a group, these studies are beginning to reveal biases that affect the way in which supervisors evaluate the acceptability of their subordinates' performance. Among the biasing factors are the way the supervisor has behaved, the performance of other subordinates, and factors that affect whether observed performance is attributed to effort or ability.

Another group of studies which follows the theme of supervisors' reactions to performance deals with how supervisors say they would respond or how they actually do respond to failure under various circumstances. For example, subordinates in one study whose poor performance was reported as being due to an extended lunch were more likely to have their pay reduced by their supervisor than were subordinates whose failure was due to a delay in receipt of material (Green and Liden, 1980). Subjects in another study indicated that supervisors should use coercion if failure was due to lack of effort more than if it were due to lack of ability, a difficult task, or misfortune (Pence et al., 1982). If a nurse's failure had substantial negative consequences for a patient, supervisors reported that they would respond more punitively than if it did not (Mitchell and Wood, 1980). Supervisors in an experimental study who were required to give negative feedback directly to a subordinate tended to distort the feedback in a favourable direction, especially for subordinates who were said to have low ability (Ilgen and Knowlton, 1980). These studies indicate how supervisors' attributions about causes of failure are linked to the supervisor's choice of subsequent behaviours. In general, a coercive or punitive response is likely if an instance of failure is viewed in a particularly negative light and if the failure is attributed to lack of effort.

Most of the studies concerning a supervisor's response to failure have been short-term laboratory studies. The use of laboratory experiments as an attempt to establish clear causal relationships has increased in the last few years. However, one field study in this area develops the perspective that although overall appraisals of 'performance' are important, there are specific performance aspects or task domains that a supervisor may view somewhat differently from others. James and White (1983) asked 377 Navy officers and senior enlisted men to identify their best subordinate and their worst subordinate. Seven kinds of task-related problems or stresses were then described to the respondents – time overload, task difficulty, underload, problems with personnel, evaluation stress, physical stress, and emergencies. The supervisors were next asked how they behave towards their best and worst subordinate in those situations where the subordinate performs most and least adequately. They were also asked to indicate why each subordinate was especially effective or ineffective in the kind of task situation that each handles most and least adequately. In general, in the areas where the *best performers* were least effective, supervisors indicate that they would allow more influence, use less persuasion and coercion to improve performance, and provide fuller explanations for orders than in areas where *poor performers* were least effective. Thus, the way these supervisors see themselves as responding to particular aspects of subordinate success or failure is related to overall subordinate performance.

The value of this and other studies concerning supervisor perceptions of and response to subordinates' performance lies in the careful analysis given to one narrow segment of leadership. The research indicates that many biases enter a leader's appraisal of a subordinate's performance and the reasons for it. Being inappropriately severe due to a misperception of the causes of a mistake might even bring about future non-cooperation (Eden, 1984; Eden and Ravid, 1982). Conversely, mistakenly attributing high ability to a subordinate might result in providing favours viewed by other subordinates as inequitable, or in assigning excessively demanding tasks at which the subordinate is likely to fail.

The research paradigm used by these studies does, however, have substantial limitations. Researchers have restricted their focus to attributions concerning subordinate performance levels and the leadership behaviours these attributions are hypothesized to produce. This restriction has certain advantages, such as limiting attention to the number of variables which can be reasonably manipulated in a laboratory experiment and described in a US-style journal paper. Researchers have also taken advantage of the distinctions made by Kelley in his theory of attribution – attribution of cause to a person or to a situation.

However, the value of their research is limited by this restriction. Leaders in work organizations spend a considerable amount of time carrying out activities which do not directly involve the evaluation of subordinate performance. Yukl and Nemeroff (1979) have identified twelve other frequent activities in addition to the use of positive reinforcement. Even at times when the leader's perceptual processes are focused upon goals for subordinate development or by markedly good or poor instances of subordinate performance, information is also being processed concerning aspects of organizational success which are not determined by subordinate performance. A complete view of the leader's selection of actions therefore needs to incorporate responses to problems of adjustment to external events, resource distribution, coordination, personal and interpersonal strain management, and aspects of subordinate socialization and group stability in addition to subordinate motivation and task ability. Although attribution theory has not been developed to address complex causal inferences about the sources of events indicating such problems which appear in an organizational context, it is relevant in principle to an understanding of such causal inferences.

The findings of attributionally oriented researchers do nonetheless provide firm empirical evidence for the view that influence-processes between superiors and subordinates are two-way rather than one-way. It might still prove to be the case that leaders influence their subordinates more than subordinates influence their leaders. But the studies make clear the manner in which subordinate actions can cause leaders to perceive subordinates in certain ways and consequently to employ certain behaviours towards them rather than others. Every act of influence down the organizational hierarchy rests upon a related flow of influence up the hierarchy. Such a reconceptualization of leader–subordinate relations takes us directly to a further and more radical 'remedy'.

Remedy 4: re-examine the basis of subordinates' perceptions of leaders

The original finding that stimulated leadership research in this area was that different people tended to view the same leadership style profile to be typical of an effective leader (Eden and Leviatan, 1975; Weiss and Adler, 1981). This body of research is basically a specific application to leadership of theories about information-processing which have been found to simplify or distort people's perceptions and memories of what they see and experience. It is referred to as implicit leadership theory research.

In a study that illustrates the perspective taken, Phillips (1984) asked 20 students to identify the extent to which 53 leadership questionnaire items were characteristic or 'prototypical' of effective leaders. Another 20 students indicated the extent to which these same items were characteristic of ineffective leaders. A fifteen-minute videotape showing a leader working with a group was then shown to two separate groups involving a total of 60 subjects. Of these subjects, 20 were told the leader was effective, 20 were told the leader was ineffective, and 20 were not told about the effectiveness of the person they were to rate. The subjects were next asked to use the leadership questionnaire to describe the leader of the group they had just seen. Even though they had all viewed the same video, the subjects who were told the leader was effective affirmed the prototypically effective items more strongly than did the other groups. Those who were told the leader was ineffective affirmed the prototypically ineffective items more strongly than did the others. Results from other experimental manipulations in this same study indicate that aspects of behaviour that are seen as neither typically effective nor ineffective are described more accurately immediately after viewing the tape than they are following a twenty-four-hour delay in waiting. This makes it clear that subjects did actually attend to the video, but that their expectations about leadership outweighed what they saw.

Other recent studies have confirmed the finding that information about the leader or group performance affects subordinates' question-naire descriptions of leader behaviour (Phillips and Lord, 1981, 1982; Foti, Fraser and Lord, 1982; Rush and Beauvais, 1981; Rush, Phillips and Lord, 1981; Larson, 1982). However, actual behaviour does also have an important effect on descriptions (Rush, Phillips and Lord, 1981). Implicit leadership theory research has further indicated that certain characteristics are viewed as typical of particular kinds of leaders, such as political leaders, compared to leaders in general (Foti, Fraser and Lord, 1982). Respondents also tend to affirm items describing behaviours that do not actually appear in a videotape to the extent that the behaviours are viewed as consistent with behaviour the leader did actually show (Phillips and Lord, 1982; Rush, Phillips and Lord, 1981). If a group is described as effective, but subjects are led to believe that its success could be explained by other factors than the leader, group performance has less of an effect on ratings of the leader (Phillips and Lord, 1981). Explicit instructions to answer only questions that subjects are sure they can answer accurately do not seem to reduce the biasing effects of performance (Rush and Beauvais, 1981). Neither the time when subjects are told the level of group performance nor the time when leader behaviour is described relative to the time the group is observed reduces performance-related biases (Phillips, 1984; Larson, 1982; Rush, Phillips and Lord, 1981).

Basically, this line of research suggests that people do not think about their leaders in terms of a large number of very specific actions in which a leader may or may not engage. Instead, people simplify; they form consistent mental images of a few types or categories of leaders and rapidly place any particular leader into one of these categories. Furthermore, the category they place a leader into is determined by their belief about how effective the leader is as well as by what they actually see the leader do. When asked about the leader, the students used as research subjects in the United States do not seem to distinguish carefully between what they have actually seen a leader do and what they think the leader would do. As long as a characterization of a leader fits the prototype they have established, they will agree with it.

The experimental research traditions described here as remedies 3 and 4 comprise the most popular innovations in US leadership research of the 1980s. In a review of implicit leadership theory and related approaches, McElroy (1982) accurately points out that this research is primarily descriptive. It provides information about how leaders are perceived without spelling out what a leader may do with this information. At this stage in the reconstruction of leadership theory, this may be no bad thing. It has been left to field researchers to spell out more fully some of the radical implications of the processes uncovered by the laboratory researchers.

Meindl, Ehrlich and Dukerich (1985) have provided the most substantial field study of this type to date. Attacking what they term 'the romance of leadership', they argue that qualities attributed to leaders by their subordinates may not be due to the actions of the leaders at all, but to publicly available information that the firm or department has experienced success on some relevant criterion. In their view, leaders are rarely influential, but many of us impute heroic qualities to them on the basis of our implicit theories as to what leaders of successful organizations must be like. They report a series of studies showing for instance that in the *Wall Street Journal* more frequent

references to the qualities of corporate leadership occurred for corporations experiencing relatively successful years than for unsuccessful
years. Laboratory experimental studies were also conducted in which
subjects were asked to explain why particular hypothetical companies
had experienced success or failure. In a further set of studies, Meindl
and Ehrlich (1987) showed that where MBA students were told that a
firm's success was attributable to leadership factors, the firm was rated
as more successful than it was where the success was attributed to other
factors.

It is clear that we do all have implicit theories as to the qualities
inherent in an effective leader. Close comparison might well show that
such implicit theories bear a marked resemblance to the traits which
researchers in Chapter 1 sought so assiduously to relate to measures of
leadership. The radicalism of the Meindl studies and of the theoretical
formulations which preceded it (Calder, 1977; Pfeffer, 1977) lies in
their proposing that it is knowledge of outcome which structures our
imputing of qualities to the leader, rather than the conventional view
that it is our experience of leadership which determines outcome. The
evidence for the radical view to date is relatively meagre. It may well
prove in due course that the proposition that it is outcome which
determines attribution of leader qualities is no more sustainable than
the reverse. If this were so, it would most probably be because in
everyday settings perceptions of outcome and perceptions of leader
style will interact with one another in a spiral fashion. Only within a
controlled laboratory experiment could one intervene within a social
process sufficiently strongly to establish that one event can cause
another. For the present, the attributional critique of leadership theory
must remain as a challenge to us to create models which do not make
unwarranted presumptions about the flow of causal inference.

Remedy 5: review the circumstances which call for leadership

Most managers and organizational scientists would recognize that a
leader's behaviour towards subordinates is only one of a number of
things that affect subordinates' performance (Katz and Kahn, 1965/
1978). However, a sufficiently large volume of research reports
focusing exclusively on the contribution of leadership appeared
through the 1950s and 1960s that leadership theories seemed to have
lost this recognition. The attention of the field has been drawn back to
the place of leadership in conjunction with other organizational
controlling and directing processes by articles concerning 'substitutes
for leadership' (House and Baetz, 1979; Kerr and Jermier, 1978).
Substitutes for leadership are variables that contribute directly to
subordinates' performance apart from what a leader does. Articles

concerning leadership substitutes have presented evidence that the low relationships often found in the United States between leadership and performance or attitude variables are due to other organizational processes. For example, there are circumstances under which self-management, self-regulation or self-supervision can fulfil some of the functions of leadership to encourage and facilitate performance (Manz and Sims, 1980; Mills, 1983; Mills and Posner, 1982). Schriesheim and Kerr (1977) show a beginning awareness of substituting processes in their examination of path–goal theory. There is indeed some link between path–goal theory's discussion of the environmental moderators of leader style effectiveness, and the emphasis of Kerr and Jermier on how environmental variables may reduce or totally eliminate the need for leadership in certain settings.

Several characteristics of subordinates have been identified that contribute to self-supervision. Subordinates' ability, training, education, experience and professional identification have been found to predict performance or work attitudes apart from what a leader does (Howell and Dorfman, 1981; Kerr and Jermier, 1978; Sheridan, Vredenburgh and Abelson, 1984). These personal skills and motivational orientations have been postulated to facilitate effective subordinate performance (Slocum and Sims, 1980; Cummings, 1978). These characteristics may also permit subordinates to establish their own goals, evaluate their own performance, and reward themselves (through self-recognition, for example). In this way, self-management can reduce the need for or substitute for achievement-oriented or pressuring behaviour by a leader (Manz and Sims, 1980). Leadership and organizational practices can also contribute to self-supervision. Lack of centralization and of support from leaders, in particular, can operate in this way (Mills, 1983; Mills and Posner, 1982).

Organizational characteristics and characteristics of the tasks people are carrying out also appear to affect the importance of leadership. Group cohesiveness, routine tasks, interesting work, tasks for which it is easy to judge one's own performance, and, especially, an established, detailed system of rules governing work activities have all been found to reduce the contribution of leadership to employee performance (Howell and Dorfman, 1981; Sheridan, Vredenburgh and Abelson, 1984; Slocum and Sims, 1980).

Attempts to identify substituting or neutralizing effects of other variables besides task structure with respect to satisfaction criteria have also had some success (Abdel-Halim, 1981; Schriesheim and De Nisi, 1981). However, the specific nature of these effects are only beginning to be identified. For instance, in explaining the non-support of their path–goal hypotheses in a large public utility, Schriesheim and

Schriesheim (1980) argue for the development of more comprehensive models of leadership substitutes.

Summary

The intentions of those who have advanced the five remedies can perhaps be classified under three headings. Firstly, these researchers have sought to relate the study of leadership more directly to theoretical advances within other areas of social and organizational psychology. Secondly, they have developed the viewpoint that understanding of leadership can only be accomplished where substantial attention is paid to the perceptions and cognitions of those being studied, both leaders and led. Finally, they have sought greater control over the phenomena to be studied, through the use of laboratory experiments, quasi-experimental field studies and increasingly sophisticated statistical techniques. Each of these emphases has yielded some benefit. Taken together they make it clear that a coherent account of leadership requires analysis of the manner in which two parties perceive and interpret one another's actions and of the manner in which this leads to processes of influence. In the next chapter we shall present a model which emphasizes the central role of cognitions in the leader's choice as to how to act in any particular setting. In so doing we seek to draw together the current emphases of American cognitive social psychology as applied to leadership.

4
An Alternative Model of Leadership Action

In this chapter we shall present a model of leadership behaviour which draws together the implications of recent research by North American social psychologists. The most striking thing about this model is the manner in which it represents a departure from the ambitions of earlier generations of leadership researchers. The implicit behaviourism of the earlier generation led them to seek to predict the effects of leader personality or behavioural style upon outcomes of value to managers. Personality was interpreted as an indicator of particular invariant styles. The further assumption was made that once the linkages between styles and outcome had been determined, we could in a similarly mechanistic manner select or train leaders to use appropriate styles. Recent research leaves to one side this earlier preoccupation with personality and style and focuses instead upon the conscious and implicit choice processes of leaders. Furthermore, 'choice' and 'cognition' are increasingly seen as containing substantial elements of irrationality, which may also be open to conceptual modelling and research. Terms like 'choice' and 'decision' are used as an explanatory convenience. As the model indicates, elements which are conscious or unconscious, rational or irrational, and chosen or unconsciously enacted must all be incorporated in revised versions of the classical notion of choice.

The focus of this chapter is thus only upon the processes whereby a leader decides whether or not to act in a given situation and if so, what type of action is likely to be enacted. Researchers who have followed this strategy have felt it wiser to narrow the focus of research in this way. It is important to note that in doing so, they leave out of account the conclusions reached at the end of Chapter 3. The decision to act is conceptualized in a wholly individualistic manner, which excludes from explicit consideration the effects that outside parties may have on chosen behaviour. As we shall argue more fully in later chapters, how each act is interpreted, what reactions follow from others, and whether it is judged to be effective may well depend upon which of various parties does the judging. Furthermore acts do not, as the models brought together in this chapter assume, occur in an initial vacuum, but are preceded by other acts by oneself and others. In this chapter we shall seek to test whether or not the simplifying assumptions made in modern cognitive research are ones which distort our views of the leadership process, and whether or not the distortions prevent us from drawing on the insights afforded by such models in later chapters. Only when the lack of conceptual integration between those who wish to construct cognitive models of leadership and those who wish to study the contexts within which leadership occurs naturally has been addressed, shall we be in a position to return to those practical issues such as training which motivated the early researchers. We shall arrive at this point in the final chapter.

A basic model outlining what occurs immediately before the decision to attempt leadership and the choice of specific leadership behaviours is presented in Figure 4.1. The model indicates that behavioural intentions are determined most immediately either by a judgemental motivated choice or by a behavioural choice which is 'programmed' (March and Simon, 1958), 'habitual' (Bettman, 1979), or policy-based (Green and Mitchell, 1979). Such choices are preceded in turn by perceptual, attributional and salience-affecting processes which determine how events are to be identified and interpreted. These processes also may be 'controlled' or at a cognitively 'high level' (Feldman, 1981; Lord and Smith, 1983; Schneider and Shiffrin, 1977; Shiffrin and Schneider, 1977), on the one hand, or else 'automatic' or 'low-level' on the other. Each element in this sequence will be affected by the actual events, context, and personal characteristics of the leader. Let us consider each of these stages in turn.

Experienced situation

Perceived events

The notion of 'event' appears occasionally in recent analyses of organizational behaviour (Lord and Kernan, 1987), but the idea has not been fully exploited or conceptually rooted. 'Events' as used by Russell (1961) and Whitehead (1929) are viewed as theoretical constructs which correspond to segments of experience and segments of reality. The examples provided by these philosophers are physical but the concepts have equal value in the analysis of social processes. Our definitions of events have a certain amount of elasticity in both space and time. That is, tentative boundaries defining an event could be placed around an exchange between a supervisor and a subordinate in an office one afternoon. The context, which would be an implicit but integral part of this event, would include things like the previous relationship between the two people, other occurrences in their respective work and personal lives, and the physical characteristics of the setting. Alternatively, an event could be defined as the entire history of the relationship between these two parties. If we choose the second perspective, the organization's history as well as occurrences within the industry or the nation must be considered as the implicit context of this event. Thus, an 'event' comprised of various 'occasions' is constructed out of the information available to an observer, whether that observer is an actor or an 'objective' outsider.

However, the imposition of boundaries around an event is not arbitrary, and it derives from what is actually done by the parties involved. The involved parties are seen as actively constructing 'Gestalts', or unified sets of perceptions, which may parallel the events constructed by observers. For example, the supervisor whose subordinate comes to the office is likely to be able to describe what occurred as an integrated event, or perhaps as a series of events, and to relate such descriptions to their context in a coherent manner. Furthermore, while the way in which one supervisor constructs events out of experience may differ somewhat from how it is done by another supervisor, or by an observer, the differences are unlikely to be so random or so gross that each person's account is incomprehensible to the other.

Whether or not such a convergence in the description of events is best thought of as 'reality' or as the result of parallel socialization processes is an issue best left on one side. A great deal of modern social psychology does continue to rest upon an assumption of an external reality. Researchers in this tradition have constructed classes of theoretical events, such as schemes, scripts and percepts which are presumed to determine how experienced events are structured. Research with these concepts has involved manipulating what are assumed to be elements of external reality, in order to understand their relation to the conscious and unconscious ways in which schemes, scripts and percepts arise from them.

In the present model, behaviour occurs in response to perceived events. Although 'actual' events do affect social perception, perception involves filtering and interpreting even at the initial point of awareness (Kiesler and Sproull, 1982). Perceptual filters have been hypothesized to act differently under two conditions of information processing (Bettman, 1979). During the uninterrupted pursuit of pre-established goals, whether these be tacit or conscious, attention is directed toward the search for goal-relevant information from both external sources and from memory. Thus, goal-relevant information is readily noticed while other information tends to be screened out.

However, a general 'scanner' is also operative during goal-directed information processing. This subconscious scanner has three functions. First, it obtains information forming the context or 'ground' against which information being consciously processed is interpreted. One set

EXPERIENCED SITUATION → CHOICE PROCESSES → BEHAVIOUR CHOICE

Perceived events
goal-directed attention-focusing processes
externally disrupted attention-interrupt processes

Schemas
initial encoding functions
storage structuring functions

Attributions
source (person, entity, context)
principle of covariation
distinctiveness, consistency, consensus
leader's processing style, available information

Salient values
situation-induced information-processing preferences
situation-induced outcome preferences

Motivated choice (E x IV)
effort-to-behaviour (E)
(estimated ability to show behaviour)
behaviour-to-outcome (I)
(estimated utility of behaviour)
outcome valence (V)
(value placed on behaviour outcome)

Cognitively programmed choice

No attempted leadership

Chosen leadership attempt

Figure 4.1 *Motivated and programmed antecedents of leadership behaviour choice*

of models of what causes biased or mistaken attributions emphasizes the role of such unconscious information processing on conscious sense-making mechanisms (e.g., Green and Liden, 1980; Nisbett and Wilson, 1977). Second, some information which passes the scanner can be processed sufficiently to proceed into long-term memory without diverting attention from goal-directed processes for more than a brief period (Kiesler and Sproull, 1982). Thus a supervisor may store repeated short-term impressions of a subordinate's conscientiousness without actively seeking the relevant information, or even consciously recalling how it has been obtained. Third, the scanner can obtain information precipitating a substantial 'attention interrupt' signal which intrudes upon and displaces prior goal-directed activities (Bettman, 1979; Carver and Scheier, 1981). Subliminal information which is highly inconsistent with significant expectations or aspirations, or else information which is highly distinctive, may precipitate such a redirection of attention (Kiesler and Sproull, 1982). Thus a subordinate's noteworthy success or failure in carrying out an assignment may redirect a supervisor's attention from other work to address that event.

Mintzberg (1973) observed that managerial behaviour tends to be characterized by a considerable number of disruptions requiring immediate, short-term attention. For example, a production manager may be consciously attending to productivity figures for various groups headed by foremen, in an effort to plan ways of guiding the foremen to synchronize better the work of different shift groups. The manager's information search may be directed toward memories of previous coordination schemes used and the current records and personal characteristics of the different foremen and their groups. While engaged in this goal-directed search, an interruption by a foreman with an immediate problem involving a machine breakdown may be sufficient to redirect attention and bring to the fore a new set of previously dormant perceptual screens. Research into the goals which a formal leader pursues under different circumstances and into attention-getting variables related to leadership behaviour are thus important in understanding the leader's choice of how to act.

Schemas
The idea of 'schema' has emerged from social psychologists' interest in the encoding and representation of experience (Markus and Zajonc, 1985). In general, greater attention has been given to inferring the origin and structure of schemas than to their implications for behaviour, especially the types of complex behaviour in which leaders engage. Individuals are seen as varying in the kinds of information for which they have established schemas. In this respect, the idea of

schema is similar to the earlier idea of attitude. The concepts of attitude and schema differ partly in their historical origins, and partly in the kinds of activity they represent. Definitions of attitude usually include reference to either oral or non-oral behaviour toward some object, as well as associated sets of cognitions. The more narrowly defined concept of schema refers to internal processes which in complex and often quite subtle ways affect the processing of information from which behaviour emerges. An integrated model referred to as 'control theory' postulates a hierarchical structuring of goal-directed and attention-interrupt processes using ideas similar to the concept of schema (Carver and Scheier, 1981, 1982). As envisaged in this model, schemas can affect goal-directed processes by structuring the information sought and used in goal-directed activity. They can also influence attention-interrupt processes by structuring the scanning and abstracting of environmental information.

Attributions

Closely involved in social perceptions are sense-making processes by which perceived objects and events are linked to a meaningful framework of person perceptions, causal inferences, and assignments of responsibility (Lord and Smith, 1983; Ross and Fletcher, 1985). Much of this recent research in the leadership area has addressed causal attributions and their consequences for leadership behaviour, as discussed in Chapter 3. Attributional models ordinarily take perception in the sense discussed in the last few pages as given. However, attribution theory has also been employed as an alternative to the concept of schema, in order to describe the manner in which inferences may be drawn from perceived experience.

Figure 4.1 indicates that attributional processes come into play in information processing once events and circumstances are perceived. Green and Mitchell (1979) provide a useful application of Kelley's (1973) attributional model to leadership by describing the attributional processes guiding a formal leader's response to subordinate performance. Various personal, relational and situational variables are identified which affect a leader's choice of the source – person (subordinate), entity (task), or context (extraneous events) – to which good or poor performance is attributed. The 'principle of covariation' provides the basis upon which attributions are made. This involves the relationship between other events and the subordinate's current performance. The key aspects of covariation are the 'distinctiveness' of the performance level for a particular task compared to typical performance (that is, is it distinctly better or worse than usual); the 'consistency' with behaviour under other circumstances; and, secondarily, the 'consensus' relative to performance by others.

Without developing an explicit model of the next steps prior to behaviour in the information-processing sequence, Green and Mitchell review several social psychological studies which indicate that performance attributions have implications for supervisory behaviour involving rewards and punishments, the closeness of supervision, expectations about future performance, and aspirations held for a member. Subsequent research (Wood and Mitchell, 1981) indicates that some behavioural reactions to attributions may be largely programmed (internal attribution of poor performance leads directly to punishment); while others may require further information processing (external attribution of poor performance leads to further situation diagnosis). Martinko and Gardner (1987a) develop this line of work further by combining the attributions of leaders and of followers into a two-way process model of leader–follower interaction.

Salient values

The last variables in the processing of information which precedes behavioural choice are the personal values which are associated with whatever outcomes a leader considers. Expectancy motivation theorists have emphasized the importance of various personal motivations for predicting the valence of outcomes (e.g., McClelland, 1961; Alderfer, 1972; Maslow, 1954). These theorists emphasize individual differences in various needs, but tend not to identify those situational characteristics which affect the salience of particular needs at particular times. In effect, an individual's outcome valences are treated as relatively stable across situations and over time. Consistent with his critique of predictions of behaviour based upon personality traits, Mischel (1968) has proposed that particular situational characteristics may alter the values that a person considers when placed in different settings. That is, short-term events do not easily change a person's values, but they can change the subset of values that guide action at a particular time. Salancik and Pfeffer's (1978) social information-processing perspective implies that long-term organizational norms as well as the values and beliefs of peers and subordinates also have the potential to affect the outcomes evaluated, as well as the needs which are made salient in assigning values to them. Thus a variety of personal characteristics (for example, typical need satisfaction levels), general or long-term situational characteristics (for example, past associations with a particular context and social forces), as well as immediate events may affect leadership behaviour choice by affecting the attractiveness of different outcomes.

Choice processes

The cognitive model shown in Figure 4.1 suggests that the decision to attempt leadership and the choice of specific leadership behaviours depend most directly upon either a judgemental process of motivated choice or a relatively inflexible, programmed response to the situation as experienced. Conscious, judgemental processes and programmed responses are actually the extreme points on a continuum. Other semi-programmed, semi-rational processes could be shown between these extremes (Lord and Kernan, 1987). The judgemental decision processes noted are those which are typically included in expectancy models of motivated choice. They include a leader's effort-to-performance expectancy (E), namely, the judgement that the various leadership and non-leadership behavioural alternatives being considered could be successfully enacted; the performance-to-outcome instrumentalities (I), namely, judgements that the various leadership behaviours would lead to desired outcomes (notably those involving successful organizational problem management); and judgements as to the immediate and long-term values attached to these outcomes (V). Although the customary expectancy formulation, specifying that behavioural choice is a multiplicative function of these three variables ($E \times IV$), originally provided a useful point of departure, various personal and situational attributes are now agreed to introduce variability into the quantitative model which best describes even relatively rational, conscious leadership behaviour choice (Mitchell, 1974). Furthermore, research would suggest that conscious behaviour choice even approximating the expectancy model occurs rather rarely (Lord and Kernan, 1987). As we shall see below, it is likely to occur only when the leadership choice is unprecedented or has obvious, very significant consequences for the person making the choice.

Programmed choices
The cognitive processing sequence at the extreme of non-rationality can be described simply, although the unconscious processes that structure it are complex in their origin and operation (Markus and Zajonc, 1985). In relation to the emphasis upon the leader's context which this book seeks to develop, once a programmed decision process is in place, there are only two points of contact between the leader's programmed choice and its context. These are the perceived event which initiates the sequence and the action which terminates it. The remaining cognitive processes are buffered from environmental input, in a manner analogous to that which Thompson (1961) attributed to the core processes of manufacturing organizations. However, it is likely that programmed choice processes are themselves one of the

most powerful expressions of the way in which culture affects the typical response of individuals to events. Semi-programmed processes, which are those sometimes regarded as script-driven, involve a movement between conscious and unconscious processes, either in the choice of a particular action or of a more complex, integrated event. Like organizational information processes, they buffer as much uncertainty as the environment will permit, within the strategic limits set by the individual.

Lord and Smith (1983) summarize various characteristics of perceived events that determine whether or not conscious, rational cognitive mechanisms are engaged. Although their discussion is restricted to attributional processes, the factors they identify are relevant to more general information processing. Perceptual processes are likely to trigger non-programmed action only when (1) observations are inconsistent with expectations or do not fit readily into existing cognitive categories (Feldman, 1981); (2) situational norms or cues, such as being asked to make a publicly visible decision, call for conscious processing; (3) information is presented in a manner conducive to conscious processing, for example in a complex, written form; (4) sufficient information-processing capacity is (or can be made) available given basic capacity and other demands; (5) the decisions made are likely to have future relevance (for example, they have personal reward significance); (6) there is a need and opportunity to exert control; (7) a personal need for cognitive consistency is operative and threatened; or (8) individual differences predispose to systematic behavioural choice. In other circumstances, judgemental processes may be simplified by pre-existing scripts or, at the extreme, replaced by a habitual, programmed response (March and Simon, 1958). Judgemental processes which occurred in the past before a now habitual response became habitual may be reconstructed from memory or rationalized, for example when requested by an evaluator or researcher. However, rapid behavioural choices may indicate that habit is being followed more than judgement.

Motivated choice
Consciously taken choices lie at the other end of the continuum to programmed choices. Early researchers paid rather more attention to motivated choice than they did to programmed choices, perhaps because motivated choices were thought until recently to be the more widespread and more important. We therefore return to expectancy motivational theories in more detail. The original theory, including a few of its implications for the antecedents and consequences of leadership, is described in the work of Vroom (1964) and Lawler (1973). Although applied most often to predicting differences in work

effort among different people, the expectancy model can also be used to predict which of several alternative behaviours will be chosen by an individual ('within-person' choice).

The results of research predicting leadership behaviour from expectancy motivation constructs has been encouraging. In one study, Nebeker and Mitchell (1974) successfully used an expectancy model to predict 11 kinds of leadership behaviour that were measured by behavioural intentions, self-reports, and subordinate reports. Using Japanese samples, Matsui, Osawa and Terai (1975) found effort-to-performance expectancies and outcome valence measures to be related to self-reports and subordinate reports of leader consideration and initiating structure behaviour. Matsui and Ohtsuka (1978) also showed that a multiplicative combination of effort-to-behaviour expectancy, behaviour-to-outcome instrumentality, and outcome valence for Consideration and Initiating Structure behaviours predicted subordinates' descriptions of their supervisors' leadership style.

Hybrids of programmed and motivated choice
The preceding treatment of choice processes not only emphasizes the extremes of programmed and motivated choice, but also implicitly assumes that choices are always of single, discrete behaviours. Such a simplification is no longer necessary. Current formulations make it possible to model leadership behaviour as a series of complex events rather than discrete behaviours (Lord and Kernan, 1987; Martinko and Gardner, 1987a). The control theory developed by Carver and Scheier (1981) actually integrates an ongoing flow of overt behaviour with both conscious and non-conscious information processing. In a similar way, script theory (Markus and Zajonc, 1985) describes how a series of programmed and motivated choices can be integrated into a pattern of behaviour, information processing and information search. Such models indicate that the separation between gathering and structuring information ('experienced situation') and using that information to select behaviour ('choice processes') will have less value in the future. As cognitive leadership researchers become able to incorporate less restrictive assumptions into their models, so those models will become more psychologically and contextually meaningful.

Behavioural choices

Most laboratory studies of behavioural choice artificially clarify and simplify the alternatives to be evaluated (e.g., Mitchell and Wood, 1980; Payne, Braunstein and Carroll, 1978; Ogilvie and Schmitt, 1979) due to an interest in what are presumed to be generic cognitive processes. However, the choice of behavioural alternatives is itself problematic in most real decisions (Bettman, 1979). A major element in making information processing humanly manageable is that of the number of behavioural alternatives considered. The problem of narrowing down the alternatives is not simply one of deciding whether to be 'supportive' or 'directive'. Instead, it involves deciding which of a large number of discrete behaviours (as illustrated by the various items in a typical leadership questionnaire), as they would be expressed within the specific conditions of a particular work setting, are to be enacted.

It has been proposed that the attributional process provides the primary filtering mechanism for narrowing the range of behaviour alternatives (e.g., Lord and Smith, 1983). The behaviours considered are those directed at modifying or reinforcing the attributed source of events which are considered functional or dysfunctional. Personal predispositions, memory, and social forces are all likely to come into play in determining the range of behaviours toward that source which are further evaluated.

The researchers whose work has provided the main focus of this chapter have paid little attention to systematic study of the behavioural choices open to the leader. While there is general agreement that the measures of leader style developed by earlier researchers do not adequately represent the range of options open to leaders, no theoretical advances have been made which might enable us to decide how best to classify the leader's options. Yukl's 19 leadership categories may be a useful basis for research (Yukl, 1981). They are more general and less cumbersome than a comprehensive list of behaviours. They do, however, encompass a broader range of behavioural alternatives than do those models which focus on leader reactions to poor subordinate performance. Even such an extended list as this is still vulnerable to the criticism of Stewart (1982c) that it focuses too much upon rational problem-solving types of behaviours, rather than taking more note of what managers can actually be observed to do in practice. We return to this point more fully in the next chapter.

Discussion

Although the information-processing perspective suggested here incorporates a broader range of variables than those covered in other cognitive models of the leader's choice to act, it is not without precedent. An expectancy model of leadership behaviour choice can be linked to other aspects of ongoing psychological processes using an information-processing model of cognition. Wynne and Hunsaker (1975) developed a 'human information-processing' (HIP) model to explain both the behaviour chosen by a leader and the response to that behaviour by subordinates. This model suggests that a formal leader's typical information-processing style is an important factor in determining the kind of information the leader abstracts from a particular situation, and thus the behaviour selected by the leader to respond to situational demands. In their review of supporting research and theory, Wynne and Hunsaker note that some of the theory surrounding Fiedler's (1967) contingency theory of leadership and Mintzberg's (1973) model of managerial work suggests that a formal leader's behaviour depends partly on the 'cognitive style' which guides the way in which the leader processes information.

Research concerning the determinants of leadership behaviour has not made such extensive use of expectancy theory as has research into the path–goal theory of leadership effectiveness (e.g., House, 1971). However, given the inherent difficulties in measuring expectancies in a way which allows their statistically adequate application to within-person behavioural choice (Mitchell, 1974), its success in predicting leadership behaviour tendencies is encouraging. This is especially true since the simplest application of expectancy theory and other quasi-rational behavioural choice models is to selecting discrete actions (for example, occupational choice: Vroom 1964; Wanous, 1972). However, its main application thus far in leadership research has been in predicting behavioural tendencies reflected in subordinates' implicit theories of leadership (Eden and Leviatan, 1975; Rush, Thomas and Lord, 1977; Rush, Phillips and Lord, 1981). The methodological difficulties inherent in separating conscious *post hoc* rationalizations of behaviour choice from the more strictly causal conscious determinants of behaviour are likely to impede further use of expectancy theory in research into cognitive models of leadership (Nisbett and Wilson, 1977).

Since expectancy theory is a 'process' theory, describing the ways in which pre-existing pieces of information are combined to reach a decision, it and similar quasi-rational models of decision-making take the values assigned to various subjective probabilities and outcome valences as given, and indicate how they may be combined to arrive at a chosen action. Other cognitive theories concerning social perception, attributional processes, information-search strategies and attitude–behaviour relationships are helpful for understanding the origins of subjective probabilities and outcome valences which provide the content for leadership behaviour choice processes. However, the links between variables representing the experienced situation and those representing motivational constructs remain largely speculative because the two kinds of models have typically not been studied simultaneously.

The information-processing approach, when compared with

expectancy theory, raises many questions for leadership theory that have been important in other areas of organizational theory since the work of March and Simon (1958). This controversy concerns the implications of human limitations on information-processing ability for the selection of behaviour. How many behavioural possibilities does a leader actually evaluate when deciding how to respond to a situation? How many of the possible desirable and undesirable consequences of these behaviours are considered? How precisely do leaders estimate the probability that they can enact each behaviour effectively and that the behaviour will have the anticipated consequences? To what extent do individuals rely on preset, habitual, or 'programmed' modes of responding to a situation? Further research dealing with cognitive antecedents of leadership will need to answer these questions more fully.

Research on cognitive theories has stressed those portions of cognition which can be directly operationalized using verbal reports of conscious experience. As we have seen, a variety of other conscious and unconscious psychological structures and processes do precede behaviour in different situations. Some of these form the 'ground' or base against which the situation is consciously experienced and evaluated, while others may affect behaviour more directly. Many such variables, especially the unconscious ones, are not easily operationalized.

The proposed sequence of cognitive events may give the appearance of an *ad hoc* assemblage of tenuously related processes. However, the notion that they reflect a meaningful sequence of related elements is given substantial indirect support by other analyses of somewhat different kinds of behavioural choices. The analysis is consistent with a general cybernetic perspective on human information processing and behavioural choice. The control theory advanced by Carver and Scheier (1982) explains behavioural choice by postulating a hierarchically arranged cognitive sequence of comparisons between a perceived situation and some point of reference. The links in the present model may be viewed similarly as involving a sequence of comparisons that is analogous to the hierarchical levels postulated in control theory. For example, a formal leader's observation of a subordinate group (perceived situation) may result in the perception of a discrepancy with the leader's ideal of efficient work. Behavioural choice at this level involves deciding whether or not the discrepancy is sufficient to warrant further attention or whether attention should be directed instead toward other technical or administrative facets of the leader's role which do not directly involve guiding subordinates (Kiesler and Sproull, 1982). In effect, this is a goal-setting decision. If more attention is considered warranted, information processing may come to be directed in greater detail to different facets of the work situation. Attention at this level would be directed toward situational cues relevant to reference values concerning the adequacy of subordinates' resources, their motivation, and their ability. These comparisons involve, in effect, the process of making causal attributions which provide a basis for further attending to how identified discrepancies can be reduced. If subordinate resources, for example, are perceived to be discrepant with required resources, more particular behavioural alternatives such as strategies for resource acquisition, resource redistribution, or task reassignment would be further considered. Increasingly, the comparisons between perceptions and reference values become more specific and, consequently, more difficult to describe abstractly. However, part of the behavioural choice evaluation at the next step might involve comparing perceived organizational resources with the needs of various internal parties competing for them. Such comparisons would involve providing information which allows a suitable estimate of the likely effectiveness of seeking out further internal resources. In working out such examples of how a leader might actually process information about an event, the classical preoccupations of leadership researchers with subordinates are expressed in a different manner. The realities of dealing with subordinates require attention to physical attributes of the situation and to parties having various organizational roles. Thus, consideration of specific examples of the cognitive processes reviewed in this chapter pushes one towards the same perspective as that inherent in more macroscopic analyses of organizations.

Together with the contingency theories reviewed in Chapter 2 and the remedies to traditional research explored in Chapter 3, the model presented in this chapter provides a particular synthesis of the point which theorizing about leadership has currently reached. There is of course no consensus among leadership researchers as to the best way forward, or even that there is a way forward. The model presented in the present chapter does have in common with the views of other contemporary US social psychologists a strong emphasis upon cognitive processes and upon the interplay between rational quasi-rational and non-rational ways in which people choose how to act (e.g. Markus and Zajonc, 1985; Sims and Gioia, 1986). It does not address itself to the effectiveness of leaders, and leaves in the background the theoretical treatment of organizational context.

One might think that if only more attention had been given to questions of behaviour choice, then questions of leader effectiveness might once more be addressed, but with the benefit of the more sophisticated cognitive models now developed. Models of behaviour choice certainly have potential for the study of leadership beyond that which has thus far developed. They can sustain our intuition that characteristics of individuals are important, even if personality measures have been of little use in predicting leader effectiveness. They can also help explain the difficulties experienced by trainers who are able to create changes in the attitudes and behaviour of leaders within training settings, but who find that those changes may not transfer to work settings. If dependable indicators of cognitive processes could be found, it might become possible to enhance the transferability of training effects.

However, models of behavioural choice also have built-in limitations, which flow directly from the nature of events, as we discussed at the start of this chapter. These limitations should warn us against returning to the mechanistic assumptions upon which so much earlier work has rested. The meanings which leaders give to external 'reality' and their internal reconstruction of the events which make up that reality are clearly important in understanding leadership. But do a leader's reports of intended actions bear a sufficiently close relation to subsequently enacted behaviours to warrant our attention? Although such correspondence is rarely explicitly argued, there can be little justification for the studies of performance attribution reviewed above unless it can be validly assumed that the relation is close. Also, are leadership behaviours in field settings sufficiently distinguishable from each other for us to be confident that observers' ratings of their meaning are valid? If observers' constructions of events differ from those of the parties involved, what basis do we have for asserting that the observers' views are the more valid ones? If positive answers to these difficulties are not forthcoming we may have little claim to have bettered the oversimplified view that predispositions produce invariant leader styles.

A more general problem with this type of model of leaders' cognitions is the manner in which they leave the passage of time out of account. Past history is represented in research supporting the model only in the sense that the various values to which the leader may refer are taken as determined by past experiences. Changes in cognitive processes over time are rarely considered within the literature which this model draws together. This omission occurs both within the organizational literature concerning cognitive processes, and to an almost equal extent in the basic literature of cognitive psychology. A related limitation is that patterns of social relationships are likely to have substantial effects on the various processes within the model, but these are not built into it. This is a limitation for any model which seeks to be predictive, since these relationships may have more significance for behaviour choice than will direct measures of cognitive processes themselves. For example, researchers with an interest in the effects of social processes over time have shown how our actions may frequently be guided by self-fulfilling prophecies (Darley and Fazio, 1980). In other words, our expectations about how someone will behave often cause us to act towards that person in such a manner that the person does then act towards us as we had expected. If such situations are widespread, then attempts to formulate models of leader action on bases which give no place to prior interactions are unlikely to prove very fruitful. It may be that we need to view leaders' behaviour as an infinitely variable tool whereby they continually seek to manage others' impressions of them and of the meanings which are attached to their actions. If this were so, we could only hope to classify leaders' behaviour choices in the most general ways, delineating elements which are more or less implicit in the very concept of leadership. Such a classification should remain tenable in whatever cultural or historical setting it were applied. We shall explore such possibilities shortly.

The cognitive model presented in this chapter attempts to make explicit the processes whereby leaders themselves give meaning to events. Certainly the application of the model and perhaps even the structure of the model itself is dependent upon the contexts to which it might be applied. In presenting it, we have neglected the possibility that the cognitive structures underlying behaviour choice may well vary by nation, region or technological sophistication (Adler, Doktor and Redding, 1986). One speculation, for example, is that the kinds of elements and relationships sought among elements in causal models may vary by culture (Maruyama, 1982). Other comparisons of cognition in Eastern and Western cultures respectively stress the use of continuity and connectedness versus distinctions and separations, comprehensive versus analytic reasoning and concrete versus abstract ideas (Adler, Doktor and Redding, 1986). The issue of whether a generic cognitive model of leadership behaviour choice is possible remains open. At present, the cognitive models brought together in this chapter seek universal applicability for the basic elements and relationships which they incorporate. Presumably, cultural variability, like individual variability of other kinds, would affect particular elements and relationships, such as the outcomes considered or the estimated probabilities where rational processes are engaged, or the cues that initiate programmed choice where they are not. However, the possibility remains that the key elements in the model or the way it is conceived are culturally bounded.

In the second half of this book we shall present a view of the leadership process which extends well beyond individual leaders and their specific actions. We shall propose that it is the social context of leadership actions which gives them their meaning and consequently their effect. This view attempts to make use of both the methodological lessons and conceptual advances of earlier work, but to avoid the mechanistic assumptions of behaviourism and the individualistic subjectivism of cognitive psychology. Although social context has not been totally ignored by the researchers whose work we have so far surveyed, we shall propose that it be given a far more central role than has mostly been the case. In this way, leadership may be seen as a particular aspect of organizational behaviour, rather than as an isolated and intractable aspect of social psychology.

PART TWO

LEADERSHIP IN ITS CULTURAL AND ORGANIZATIONAL CONTEXT

5
Leadership as the Management of Conflicting Demands

The remedies for the ailing field of leadership research which were explored in the preceding chapters have accomplished not so much a resuscitation of the patient, but rather an increased pressure for a more radical type of therapy. The remedies reviewed in Chapter 3 were indeed radical in so far as they called into question the assumption that all we need to consider is leaders' effects on subordinates. They certainly established that subordinates' perceptions and actions may also affect leaders, and in Chapter 4 some of the detail of these processes was explored. But all of the remedies advanced remain conventional in their assumption that the essence of leadership may be captured through study of the potency of influence or lack of it within the leader–subordinate dyad. The remedies illuminated some of the blindnesses which may be induced by such a narrow focus, but they fail to point us towards ways of gaining a broader view. In seeking such a view, we shall need to turn instead to the work of researchers who have been less captivated by the 'normal science' methodology of experimentation, causes and effects. This chapter commences by examining the work of researchers whose commitment to fieldwork and observation has led them to undertake quite different types of study.

Managerial role and activity research

Observation of managers' everyday actions by researchers has been undertaken in Europe for many years, commencing with the pioneering work of Carlson (1951) in Sweden. Later studies followed, by Horne and Lupton (1965) and Stewart (1976) in Britain, and by Sayles (1964) in the USA. However, interest in this type of work was generally muted until the 1973 publication of Mintzberg's book *The Nature of Managerial Work*. The book proposed that managers enact ten different roles that can be placed into three major categories: interpersonal roles, information-processing roles, and decision-making roles. Mintzberg's challenge to leadership theory was that it had become too ambitious and narrowly focused. He argued that the role of 'leader', involving direct interactions with subordinates, is just one of a manager's interpersonal roles.

Based as it was upon observations of just five chief executives, the importance of the book lies not in any conclusions it might provide, but in the stimulus it provided for the further development of such studies. Mintzberg's description of roles, his observational method, and his characterization of managerial work as involving a demanding pace, varied and short duration activities, lack of time to think and reflect, preference for conversation over documentation, and frequent interaction with peers and subordinates are noted in much subsequent work.

A substantial number of recent studies reflect Mintzberg's influence. Shapira and Dunbar (1980) dealt with the significance that the ten managerial roles might have in the context of testing to determine which people would be effective managers. The procedure they used was an 'in-basket' simulation, which is an exercise in which people are presented with a body of realistic management-related work to be done. The exercise is designed to determine which activities subjects give priority to and how they deal with particular issues. The results indicated that the way subjects responded to tasks involving generating and processing information were unrelated to their response to decision-making tasks. However, it was not possible to distinguish any more precisely among Mintzberg's ten specific roles.

Pavett and Lau (1983) did a series of attitude surveys of military, government, and private company managers to determine which roles they considered most important. In their study of 180 managers in private organizations, they found that upper-level managers considered the roles of being a 'liaison' with people outside their organization, a 'spokesman' for their group, and a 'figurehead' formally representing their organization, to be particularly important in their work. Lower-level managers emphasized the importance of their role as 'leader' of their subordinates. When different management specialisms were compared, sales managers were found to emphasize interpersonal roles, while finance and accounting managers saw their informational roles as particularly important. Research and development managers emphasized a type of role added to Mintzberg's set by Pavett and Lau, namely their technical role.

Other researchers have followed Mintzberg's example if not the details of his method or model of roles. Schneider and Mitchell (1980) used a questionnaire administered to 1282 life insurance agency managers from 50 companies to identify six behavioural functions specifically applicable to life insurance managers. Allan (1981) identified six task dimensions using a survey administered to 1436 New York City government managers. Bussom, Larson and Vicars (1982) mapped the activities of ten US police chiefs in terms of who they spent time with, where, and for what purpose.

In general, one purpose of research efforts in the Mintzberg tradition is to describe managers' jobs in a way that will be meaningful to the managers themselves. If manager selection, performance evaluation and training can be put in terms of the activities that managers consider important, and can see themselves carrying out, then the pragmatic purposes of performance improvement can be fulfilled. This series of studies also tries to develop theories that deal with the problems managers find particularly critical. This second purpose requires close attention to comparability in research methods, consistent rules for drawing inferences from data, and a coherent, reasonably general theory.

A substantial body of observational research in educational administration is represented in a study by Gronn (1983). This study indicates how a systematic, qualitative analysis of the transcript of one person's conversation with others can clarify the process by which influence is exerted. Presenting managers with analyses of transcripts of their conversations can have the same benefits in promoting behaviour change that survey feedback can have for leader behaviour, or that listening to tapes of one's own voice can have for public speaking.

Whitely (1984) illustrates a procedure that can be used to guide managers to record their own activities. He combined this method with attitude questions to determine the importance managers place on different activities. Whitely's results agree with Mintzberg's in that brief activities were typical of managers' work. However, managers viewed the longer episodes and decision-making activities to be the more important, challenging, and least certain aspects of their work.

Rosemary Stewart (1976, 1982b) has conducted an extensive research programme in Britain using a combination of open-ended interviews, observation, personal activity diaries, and group discussions with managers to understand what they do. While the initial aim of this research programme was simply to identify how managers spent their time, it has evolved towards the development of a scheme for classifying behaviours in terms of the amount of choice a manager has as to whether or not to do them. We shall discuss this model in more detail later in this chapter. The research direction implied by Stewart's work and by the other studies that directly measure leaders' actions is that effort needs to be expended to determine precisely what it is that leaders do. Survey measures such as those which have typically been used to characterize leader style have often reflected generalized patterns of activity that are difficult to connect with the specific things that a leader spends time doing.

A number of researchers have reached the conclusion that subordinates' descriptions and managers' self-descriptions of what managers do are too distorted by beliefs about what managers should do to be practically or theoretically useful (Kerr and Schriesheim, 1974). If managers' self-descriptions are used at all, it is argued, they should be structured so that actions are recorded as soon as possible after the action occurs. Those who have found these arguments persuasive have therefore sought to develop systems for observing managerial behaviour which combine the breadth of Mintzberg's interest with the specific precision of some of the more structured approaches to the study of leader style. For instance, Yukl and Nemeroff (1979) developed the Managerial Behaviour Survey, which delineated 14 categories of managerial behaviour. This was later extended to 19 (Yukl, 1981). These categories mostly concern behaviour towards subordinates, but a few, such as 'work facilitation' and 'representation', are defined in ways which refer to behaviour addressed toward superiors or colleagues.

Other recent observational systems have stayed closer to the focus of Mintzberg's theme. The Leadership Observation System (LOS) of Luthans and Lockwood (1984) has 12 categories, including 'socializing/politicking', 'processing paperwork' and 'exchanging routine information' as well as some more subordinate-oriented categories. Luthans and Lockwood made a study of 120 managers who were observed using the LOS system. They were also asked to complete questionnaire versions of the Ohio State leader style measures and of Yukl and Nemeroff's (1979) Managerial Behaviour Survey. It was found that the observers were able to code managers' behaviours with some reliability, but the correlations between the observational data and the questionnaire responses was very weak. Luthans and Lockwood discuss ways in which their approach might be developed in order to enhance the strength of such correlations. However, the implicit assumptions behind such an attempt require careful scrutiny. The view that questionnaire self-perceptions and observers' codings have only been validly measured if they correlate strongly with one another is open to question. The assumptions hidden within this view are, firstly that the observer provides an objective, dispassionate view of the 'real' meaning of a manager's actions; and, secondly that it is possible to achieve a perception of a particular event which is agreed between all parties as the 'real' version of what happened. Of course it is the case in everyday life that there is a fair degree of overlap in interpretations of many events, but to assume that where there is no such overlap there must be something wrong with the systems of measurement may be an error.

Another large recent observational study comes a little closer to addressing these issues (Martinko and Gardner, 1984a and b, 1987b). This study sought to distinguish differences in the behaviours of high- and moderate-performing elementary and high school principals. Performance was judged according to four criteria: (1) the school's performance on state minimal competence exams, with statistical controls for socio-economic factors; (2) the school's rank within the district on national achievement test scores; (3) superintendents' ranking of the schools; and (4) superintendents' ranking of the school principals. Data were obtained from 25 high-performing and 19 moderate-performing principals, using these criteria. Each principal was observed for three days by a trained graduate student. Behavioural 'events' were coded according to the role, ethnic group and gender of the person with whom it occurred. Further codings included how many people were present, the location, the mode of communication and who initiated the event. Various theory-based coding schemes were also used, including Mintzberg's event categories and his managerial role categories, the Luthans and Lockwood LOS, and several others. The authors acknowledge that in using these systems they frequently had to adapt or redefine them in search of the meaning of particular actions. For instance, if a manager talks to his secretary, the Mintzberg system classifies this as 'Desk Work', which Martinko and Gardner found to be at odds with their own perception that such interactions are frequently important and require a coding which gives them more significance. The various coding schemes used were found not to distinguish the high- from the moderate-performing principals despite the extraordinary amount of effort involved to generate the data. Substantial relationships were, however, found between various dimensions of the school context and principals' behaviour. Martinko and Gardner suggest that the differences between high- and low-performing managers may be extremely subtle, involving not so much what managers do as how they do it.

The study of leadership as an aspect of managerial work does thus continue to generate interest. However, it is still a promising idea in search of a paradigm. Although presented in the late 1970s as a challenge to existing approaches (McCall and Lombardo, 1978), it appears in danger of being absorbed by them. What this approach has accomplished is a broadening of the range of managerial behaviours which are regarded as relevant to the study of leadership. What it has not done is to generate an adequate rationale as to why one set of observational categories should be any better or worse than any other. In order to accomplish this, one needs some overall conceptual model of what it is that is basic to the process of leadership. The old paradigm implicitly assumed that what was basic was the flow of influence from superior to subordinate. In place of this, the managerial work researchers have proceeded as though it were the case that if only we had an objective picture of what leaders do, then we should clearly understand leadership. This aspiration may well be unattainable because leadership like the rest of social process can never be seen with complete objectivity. We shall develop this view further in the next section.

The leader as pig-in-the-middle

In the preceding section, a number of studies were examined focusing particularly upon attempts to describe objectively the full range of behaviours shown by samples of managers in field settings. Some of these studies also focus upon who it is that managers spend their time with. It is a matter of everyday observation that leaders do not spend time only with their subordinates, but also with superiors, colleagues and others. There has existed for many years a literature describing the difficulties faced by any leader working within an organizational hierarchy. The classic statement is provided by Roethlisberger (1945), who delineates the perils of being a first-line supervisor. As he puts it, the foreman must become adept at double-talk, and may also become its victim. In other words, foremen are very frequently required to act as transmitters of communications between their superiors and subordinates. Experience soon teaches them that the messages they have to transmit need to be filtered and distorted if they stand the best chance of acceptance by their recipients. By doing this skilfully, the foreman may even enhance the organization's effectiveness, but the distortion of communication flows may also lead both the foreman and the organization into severe difficulty.

Numerous models of leadership acknowledge the crucial role of leaders in bridging the gap between superiors and subordinates. For instance, Likert's (1961) exposition of the human relations theory of leadership (discussed in Chapter 1) lays major stress upon the leader as the 'linkpin' between a superior group within the organizational hierarchy and one or more subordinate groups. However, Likert's approach is a normative one, since he merely emphasizes the crucial importance of the leader being an effective linkpin, without saying how that is to be accomplished. Almost all of the empirical data from the University of Michigan studies reviewed by Likert are concerned with superior–subordinate relations. A single exception is the study by Pelz (1951) who showed that effective supervisors in an electrical company were those who themselves had high influence with their own superiors. A more recent example is provided by Graen et al. (1978) who showed that managers who had high LMX relationships (that is, very positive, supportive leader–member exchanges) with their superiors were able to obtain more resources for their subordinates.

To acknowledge that an adequate theory of leadership must take account of the leader's superiors as well as subordinates is certainly a step forward, since it requires us to locate leadership actions within a context of more than one interpersonal relationship at a time. However, there are grounds for further enlarging the range of relationships encompassed. Observational studies of managers show that they spend substantial amounts of time engaging in 'lateral' relationships with their peers or colleagues. Studies reviewed by Sayles (1964) showed that lateral relationships frequently took up more of the supervisor's time than did relations with subordinates. It is not necessarily meaningful to categorize the importance of activities on the basis of how long each of them takes, neither is it likely to be the case that the pursuit of lateral relationships by managers is unconnected to their relations with subordinates. Nonetheless, Sayles's data illustrate the view that the task of most managers is not simply relating to one's subordinates in effective ways, but rather the construction and maintenance of a whole set of interconnected relationships.

To consider the leader as a focal person in a network of relationships is to amend substantially the implicit assumptions within which leadership researchers have mostly worked. One of the more disturbing qualities of research in the social sciences is the manner in which once phenomena have been labelled by investigators, other relevant models become excluded from a particular research tradition. A prime example of this is provided by research following different traditions at the University of Michigan. As indicated above, Likert's (1961) normatively expressed linkpin theory of leadership makes little provision for the possibility of conflict within effectively functioning organizations. The subsequent studies using Likert's Survey of Organizations, which derives from his theory, also gave little emphasis to conflict (Taylor and Bowers, 1972). Concurrently with Likert's work, a major project was also under way at Michigan, the fruits of which were published by Kahn et al. (1964). This presented a detailed empirical study of the incidence of role conflict among managers, and the ways in which they cope with such conflict. Role conflict is seen as occurring when the different 'role senders' who make up a 'role set' make incompatible demands upon the focal person in the set. A second possibility of role conflict occurs where the demands of one or more role senders are incompatible with the intentions of the focal person him or herself. Role ambiguity is defined as occurring where the demands of the role senders are unclear. The Kahn et al. study showed that role conflict and ambiguity were sufficiently widespread among their representative survey sample of more than 750 US managers that it has to be thought of not as a pathology or aberration of some particular situation, but rather as the normal lot of a manager.

The classic work by Kahn et al. (1964) has generated its own contingent research literature, but such work has remained largely unconnected with studies of leadership. This is true even in the case of the text by Katz and Kahn (1965/1978), within which leadership and roles are considered in separate chapters. The leadership chapter stresses the different types of leadership which would be required at different levels in an organizational hierarchy, whereas the chapter on roles has extensive discussion of role conflict. The work of Kahn et al. is now seen as an early contribution to the field of research into organizational stress (e.g., Fisher and Gitelson, 1983; Fineman and Payne, 1981).

The divorce between the notions of leadership and of role dynamics is fortunately not a complete one. Pfeffer and Salancik (1975) report a study of 53 supervisors within the housing division of a large state university. The supervisors were asked to describe, on 15 scales, how they did their job, how their job would best be done, and how they were expected to perform by their superior, their colleagues and their subordinates. The measure of supervisor behaviour used was the Leader Behaviour Description Questionnaire, which derives from the Ohio State research into leader styles. They found that the supervisor's description of actual performance was correlated 0.44 with the superior's expectations, 0.22 with subordinates' expectations and 0.11 with peers' expectations. However, when a division is made between the task-related items and personally considerate items in the questionnaire, a much more sharply delineated pattern is apparent. Task-related behaviours were strongly related to the expectations of the boss, while considerate behaviours were most strongly linked to the expectations of subordinates, with some influence also from the boss. Within this particular sample the influence of peers was apparently not very large. Pfeffer and Salancik also found that men were more likely to respond to the expectations of their boss, while women were more likely to respond to subordinates. They summarize these and other findings by suggesting that supervisors' behaviour is most influenced by those whose personality and situation is most similar to their own.

The study by Pfeffer and Salancik provides empirical evidence for the view that leadership behaviour in field settings is substantially influenced by the leader's actual context. However, a potential weakness of the study is that all the measures were completed by the supervisors themselves, rather than by the various members of their role set. Hence we cannot be certain, for instance, how close is the match between the supervisor's perception of the boss's expectations and the boss's own view of those expectations. This is also a problem in several other studies. Furthermore, none of these yielded such precise estimates of the strength of relationships as did the Pfeffer–Salancik study. Salancik et al. (1975) reanalysed survey data collected from US servicemen during World War II. They found that non-commissioned officers faced with conflicting expectations from above and below were more likely to take the superior's view where the issue was important to them. However, where the issue was important to subordinates, they took the subordinates' view. Blau and Scott (1963) showed in a study of public assistance and social work agencies that supervisors who get on well with their subordinates were less likely to be close to their superiors. Smith et al. (1969) found that among British managers a polarized situation, whereby managers got along well with their superiors or their subordinates but not both, was more frequent under conditions of rapid change. Bowers (1963) tested a model of polarization among packaging supervisors. He found that there was a tendency over time for supervisors to become closer to their superiors, and proposes that this is the only way in which supervisors can defend against threats to their self-esteem. In a similar way, Bass (1965) reviews studies showing that the longer it is since one was appointed as a supervisor, the stronger is one's identification with superiors.

Kerr, Hill and Broedling (1986) undertook an analysis of the modern context in which first-line supervisory roles in the United States are enacted. They identify six contextual factors aside from subordinates which have changed the role of the supervisor away from the traditional independence of earlier years. Planning or carrying out of activities such as selection and training have been taken over by more senior management. Unionization has given increased control of wages and working conditions to union representatives and the management with whom they negotiate, and has decreased the status difference between supervisor and subordinates. Personnel and systems engineering staff have separated supervisors from higher management by increasingly handling issues for which supervisors used to be responsible. Technological change has reduced supervisors' capacity to overcome equipment problems of their work teams, while computerization requires some supervision to be handled by technical staff. Governments in the USA and in Europe have enacted legislation which restricts supervisor actions and also requires specific safety and labour practices. Increased levels of technological education have raised the aspirations of many workers and reduced the distance between them and their supervisors. These various social changes are likely to reduce the numbers of first-line supervisors required but also to exacerbate the role conflicts which they face.

While these studies all delineate the ubiquitous presence of conflicting demands from the leader's role set, they do not provide a clear model of how the leader responds to those demands. A wide variety of theorists have sought to remedy this. The most general way of categorizing models which seek to portray the position of leaders within their organizational context is to say that they are all variants of open systems theory. Such approaches have been advocated by Katz and Kahn (1965/1978) within the USA and by theorists working within the Tavistock model of socio-technical systems analysis (e.g. Miller and Rice, 1967) in Britain. Katz and Kahn portray organizations as systems seeking to maintain some kind of equitable relationship with their external environment. Leaders are seen as managers of subsystems within the organization, whose essential task is one of reconciling the different demands upon them. These demands will arise both from within the subsystem and from outside it. Katz and Kahn lay most stress upon the different demands which will affect a manager from above and below. They see these demands as likely to vary in kind at different levels within the organization, and therefore anticipate that leaders at these levels will provide predictably different styles of leadership. At junior levels a more routine administrative orientation will be required. At middle levels the piecing out of specific policies to meet problems will be needed. At senior levels, a more charismatic style will be required in order to initiate new policies or organizational changes which are responsive to changes in the external environment.

Miller and Rice are less specific in their characterization of leadership types. They see leaders as managing the boundary between their subsystem and other subsystems within the larger system. The skill of doing this resides in identifying the 'primary task' which this particular subsystem must perform in order to optimize the performance of the system as a whole. The leader must then act in such a way as to ensure the effective performance of the primary task.

The difficulty of utilizing such models of organizational behaviour is that in order to identify whether or not a leader's behaviour is optimizing the performance of an organizational subsystem, one needs a clear criterion of success against which to evaluate that success. A variety of measures of success are sometimes available, but it is rare indeed that all such measures are closely correlated with one another. Most organizations pursue a variety of goals concurrently and the single-minded pursuit of any one goal may well undermine the achievement of other goals. The assumption that there is, or at least could be, a simple and uncontentious way of measuring success is one that researchers have been slow to relinquish, no doubt because it makes their task that much harder. A parallel might be drawn with

researchers' reluctance to abandon conceptions of leader
see it as a one-way process of influence. In both cases, the
stems from a view of organizations as free of conflict, ⌐
normally free of conflict. The belief of early researchers that produ⌐
organizations would also prove to be high on job satisfaction has long
since been shown to be untenable (Brayfield and Crockett, 1955). More
recent studies have shown that even success measures for which a more
plausible linkage might be advanced, such as labour turnover,
absenteeism and job satisfaction show little evidence of being causally
linked (Mobley, 1977; Blau, 1985; Curry et al., 1986). Part of the reason
for the lack of such causal linkages is no doubt that each success
criterion is affected by different factors external to the organization.
Such external factors are frequently ignored by researchers who fail in
practice to conceptualize organizations as open systems. However, a
further reason, which is closer to the theme of this book, is that success
criteria are frequently defined by different members of the organization. The lack of a regular relationship between productivity and
satisfaction may be thought of as an expression of the conflicting
demands of senior management for high productivity and of the
workforce for satisfying work. Of course there is no reason why these
two particular success criteria should always be in conflict, but within
any organization there are likely to be available a variety of success
criteria each defined by separate persons or subsystems. If managers
can thus never have available to them unambiguous yardsticks against
which to judge success, it is important to examine the ways in which
researchers see them as coping with that uncertainty.

Models of role-making

The view of role taken here is that a role is a label for the set of
expectations about an individual's behaviour which are received from
various sources within a social structure. In a less visibly direct
manner, roles will also be affected by national, organizational and
other cultures within which they are embedded. The concept of role
provides the basic mechanism which links individuals and larger social
systems, without losing track of either the individual or the system
(Stryker and Statham, 1985).

Although the concept of role has been in existence since well before
the development of organization theory (Biddle and Thomas, 1966),
organizational researchers have not used it to best advantage. The
exchange theory of Hollander (1979) and Graen and Cashman's (1975)
vertical dyad theory, for instance, both focus predominantly upon
leader–subordinate role relationships. Even the more sophisticated of
the contingency models reviewed in Chapter 3 add to this only a

distinction between role determinants at different levels in an organi-zation. Little evidence is shown for the potentially enormous diversity of leadership roles, by function, organization and culture.

At the same time, researchers studying supervisory and managerial roles from a structural perspective tend to dismiss variability in individual roles as insignificant (Perrow, 1970). Pfeffer (1981a) typifies this type of strong statement, stressing the external constraints upon organizations and the determining influence of others' expectations upon role formation. He portrays role expectations as directly determining behaviour. The role occupant's response is treated not as some type of negotiation, but in terms of stress, dissatisfaction or job turnover.

Our present perspective seeks to keep in view both the individual and the organization as did some of Pfeffer's earlier work. Symbolic interactionists have discussed the manner in which the self is constructed out of the cyclical action and reaction of the individual and the social context (Mead, 1934). In just such a manner may roles also be constructed within organizations. Role expectations will certainly constrain behaviour, but they will do so in a probabilistic rather than a deterministic way. Links with particular senders of role expectations are not certain and may vary depending upon the flow of events. The creation of roles is an ongoing, indeterminate process, not a quickly reached conclusion. Differences and ambiguities in demands from role senders will lead role occupants to make social comparisons with relevant others and enact their roles in a manner which reflects what they want as well as what others want (Smith, 1973; Weick, 1976).

Graen (1976) has formulated a general model of this process, which he refers to as role-making. This derives from the earlier formulations of Katz and Kahn (1966/1978). A cyclical process of perception and of behavioural response is envisaged, as depicted in Figure 5.1. In the Graen model only the relationship between the role holder and a single role sender is portrayed. The central four boxes in the diagram indicate the manner in which the role sender's expectations are conveyed to the role holder, who responds with a particular behaviour. This behaviour is monitored by the role sender, which may or may not lead to the expression of a renewed role expectation. The model depicts four types of discrepancy, the magnitude of which will determine the activation of the different elements in the cycle. Two of these discrepancies, performance discrepancy and role discrepancy, are located within persons. The other two, expectation discrepancy and feedback discrepancy, are discrepancies between the perceptions of the two people in the model.

Graen's model provides a plausible portrayal of the role-making process between dyads, and as we have seen, the research done by

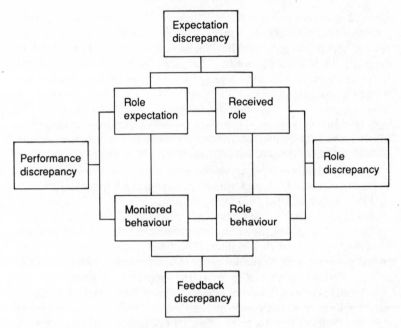

Figure 5.1 *Graen's model of role-making*

him and his colleagues is mostly focused upon leader–subordinate dyads. For the present purpose the model lacks representation of the manner in which the leader must contend with multiple role senders concurrently. It would be a relatively simple matter to redraw the diagram with multiple role senders represented, but the model thus constructed would provide no guidance as to how the role holder accommodates conflicting expectations. The four formulations of this process which remain to be presented in this chapter each make different suggestions as to how this shall be done.

A practically oriented system referred to as the 'Expectations Approach' has been developed by Machin (1980). In this system, pairs or groups of managers are asked to write down lists of all the expectations they have of one another. They also produce lists of what they believe the other party expects of them. Once these lists are complete, respondents may be asked to categorize each expectation as easy or difficult to meet, and pleasant or unpleasant to meet. Another possibility is to categorize the meeting of each expectation by the other party as 'essential', 'necessary' or 'desirable'. The parties next meet in order to compare lists, and their prioritization of the different expectations is recorded. Substantial discrepancies are almost always found (Machin, 1980; Machin and Tai, 1983), and the parties then proceed to negotiate as to what shall be done about these discrepancies. This may be done in dyads or groups. Meetings held some months later review whether negotiated changes have been adhered to. The data generated by Machin's procedures fit rather precisely the Graen model outlined above. The implicit assumptions of the Machin model are that a substantial amount of role conflict is explicable in terms of misperception and miscommunication, or as Graen would have it, expectation discrepancy. A somewhat similar procedure developed by Harrison (1972) known as 'role negotiation' is more behaviourally oriented. Under this system managers are encouraged to negotiate contracts with one another along the lines of 'If you do more of A, then I agree to do more of B'. In terms of the Graen model, role negotiation might be expected to reduce feedback discrepancy.

Another element within Machin's procedure, the prioritizing of different expectations, indicates the influence of the work of Rosemary Stewart. Stewart's work, like that of Mintzberg, has developed from an initially open-ended examination of managerial behaviour towards inductively derived ways of categorizing. Impressed by the diversity of managerial behaviour, Stewart reasoned that the unique circumstances under which each manager operated might indeed require widely differing behaviours. In attempting to classify the essence of such varying circumstances (Stewart, 1976), she distinguished those behaviours which the manager's job *demanded*, those factors internal and external to the organization which placed *constraints* upon the manager's possible range of behaviours, and the *choices* which enabled a specific manager to behave differently from someone else occupying a similar role. Her more recent writing (Stewart, 1982b, c) lays increasing stress on the importance of the manager learning to differentiate demands from choices. For the most part, the demands, constraints and choices inherent in a job are described by Stewart as objectively determinable, although she does acknowledge that some managers may exaggerate their perceptions of the demands under which they labour. For this reason, observation and interview are seen as more valid procedures than questionnaires (Marshall and Stewart, 1981a, b).

Perhaps the principal burden of Stewart's work is the argument that many of the habitual ways of classifying different types of manager, for instance by function, seniority or leader style, are simply less meaningful than a classification which differentiates demands from choices. Similar distinctions have also been advanced by some US researchers. For instance, Kotter (1982) studied 15 general managers, and distinguished what their activities had in common from what varied between them. A parallel distinction is that of Hunt and Osborn (1982) between required leadership and discretionary leadership.

Some of Stewart's earlier work also distinguished types of managers who were involved in different patterns of communication. For instance, she identified such types as 'Peer-dependent' (mostly with colleagues), 'External' (contacts outside the organization), 'Man-management' (head of a self-contained team) and 'Hub' (time with subordinates, peers, boss and colleagues). The Hub type was most frequently found. However, the research showed that these different communication patterns were frequently a matter of choice rather than demand. Despite this, it was found that some jobs had higher demands than others for 'boss-dependence', a finding which is reminiscent of Kerr and Jermier's model of substitutes for leadership, which was considered in Chapter 3.

Stewart's emphasis on choice as the key element in the manager's accommodation of conflicting expectations is reminiscent of a much earlier formulation by Kay (1963). Kay reports a questionnaire study of 153 supervisors in factories in New Hampshire and a further 278 members of the role sets of these supervisors. These included superiors, colleagues, subordinates and union stewards. Substantial differences were found between expectations and behaviour of the foremen, as perceived by each of these groups. Divergences for each group were particularly marked on questionnaire items which Kay terms 'role-centric', that is, related to the needs of the role sender. Kay reports that foremen were best able to cope with conflicting demands where they saw the demands as role-based rather than addressed to them in a personal sense. Thus, awareness of conflicting demands was actually a precondition for an effective exercise of choice.

Kay's project did not attempt to spell out any explicit criteria as to what was an effective way of handling role demands. As has been argued above, it is increasingly difficult to argue that there are any such objective criteria available. Research by Tsui (1984a, b) acknowledges this and proposes that we therefore focus upon managerial reputations, as defined by the role set. In line with the argument of the present chapter, she proposes that there will be no necessary consensus among role senders, since each will make their evaluations in accordance with their own priorities and expectations. Tsui's sample included 217 US middle managers and 863 members of their role sets. Her research method was to obtain ratings of the focal manager's behaviour on six of Mintzberg's ten behaviours as well as ratings of how far the role set members' expectations of the manager were met and how effective the managers were overall. The first finding of this study was that although there was some divergence in the behaviours which were most strongly related to reputational effectiveness as judged by different role senders, this was not significant. However, there was a substantial difference between the behaviours upon which self-evaluations were made and the behaviours upon which evaluations were made by the role set. Her findings thus suggest that managers' central dilemma is how to adhere to their own conception of what they should do while still addressing the demands from others. Tsui found that no more than 11 per cent of the focal managers were judged reputationally effective by all the constituencies of role senders, so that most were found wanting by at least one of their constituencies. She concurs with the views of Salancik et al. (1975) that the effective manager may prove to be the one who comes closest to meeting the demands of all constituencies of role senders.

This chapter has explored conceptualizations of leadership which seek to locate the leader within a more broadly defined context than have most of the studies reviewed in Part One. It has led us to see conflict and choice as crucial elements in the situation of most leaders. However, the methods of researchers whose work has been examined in this chapter have varied widely. Some have seen conflict and choice as qualities which may be objectively determined, while others give more of their attention to the processes whereby leaders construe and interpret the meaning of events around them. The task of the next two chapters will be to explore more fully this latter perspective.

6
A Model of Event Management

As Tsui's research has emphasized, the greatest role conflict may be between organizational life as experienced by the manager and the sum total of demands placed upon the manager by others. This chapter is addressed directly to the question of how managers and other organization members can cope with the various problems which their work poses for them. Organizations have been portrayed by Georgopoulos (1972) as problem-solving systems. He classifies the problems facing organizations under six headings: adaptation, resource allocation, coordination, structural maintenance, integration and strain and tension management. These problems are inherent in the properties of organizations as systems (Cooke and Rousseau, 1981). However, organizational life does not present organization members with discrete problems, but with an unending flow of 'events', as the studies of Mintzberg, Stewart, Kotter and others show.

The process of event management

The idea of event provides a linkage between the findings of research into organizational processes, which we reviewed in Chapter 5, and theories of cognitive processes, such as those contained in Chapter 4. The cognitive perspective presented in Chapter 4 treats events as something constructed from experience by an observer based both on internal knowledge structures (such as schemas) and external processes being observed. From an organizational standpoint, events may be viewed as abstracted segments of ongoing, continuous organizational processes which can only be somewhat artificially separated from these processes. From such an integrative viewpoint, events may be seen as segments of organizational processes which, while they implicitly contain the whole of some process, are given a particular meaning when they have actually been abstracted through individual cognition. The concept of event fulfils an analogous function to the concept of role. The concept of role provides a point of contact between organization structures and individual cognitive structures (reflected in personality), while the concept of event links organizational processes to individual cognitive processing. The ideas of role and event are equally amenable, if not over-rationalized, to the symbolic interactionist position that social influences affect even relatively structured, stable patterns of behaviour. The value of both concepts is that, while they link two levels of analysis, they can be used in a manner which does not imply the predominance of either one over the other. In this way, role theory can establish a place for concepts such as 'leader', which is distinct from the processes of leadership and which still has meaning both at the level of the individual and of organizational structure. Similarly, a theory of events should enable us to define leadership processes in a manner which has meaning when speaking both of individuals and organizations, and which stands apart from rational behaviouristic definitions. Both concepts reflect the practical resolution that real people ordinarily make of their paradoxical experience of being both autonomous individuals and elements in various social systems.

Any particular event is likely to be relevant to several organizational problems rather than just one, so that the skill of a manager will lie in managing each event in a manner that takes account of those problems most relevant to valued stakeholders. Certainly, an organization's problems are never solved. That is, organizations never finally and permanently achieve coordinated work activities or well-integrated membership. When work events are handled in a way which promotes continued work performance, meeting the criteria set by particular stakeholders, organization members usually consider them as being adequately managed (Cooke and Rousseau, 1981). Leadership which contributes to effective event management can be defined as *actions by a person which handle organizational problems as expressed in the events faced by others.* This formulation will serve as a definition of organizational leadership, although such a definition constitutes a major departure from the more restrictive definitions used by the traditional leadership researchers. The virtue of adopting such a definition is that it does not imply that leadership is something only done by leaders who are formally appointed. Neither does it imply that leadership influence processes flow only from more powerful members of an organization to less powerful ones. It also provides a multi-dimensional type of perspective on effectiveness which does not adopt the viewpoint of any single stakeholder (such as management), but covers the aspects of organization functioning on which various stakeholders are likely to place meaning. In so doing the problem, frequently encountered in leadership research, of attempting to interpret the effects of theoretically sophisticated leadership constructs in relation to theoretically arbitrary criteria such as global 'performance' or 'satisfaction' measures, can be avoided.

Figure 6.1 depicts categories of social processes which are simultaneously available for interpreting events to anyone who is an

Sources of event meanings for leaders

Formality of structures	Rules	Subordinates	Peers	Superiors	Self
Explicit structures	Formal rules	Formal downward influence	Formal lateral influence	Formal upward influence	Formal self-management
Implicit conventions	Established norms	Established downward influence	Established lateral influence	Established upward influence	Established self-management
Emergent aspects of culture	Emerging norms	*Ad hoc* downward influence	*Ad hoc* lateral influence	*Ad hoc* upward influence	*Ad hoc* self-management

Figure 6.1 *Types of event management processes experienced in leader roles*

actual or potential leader. The processes identified are mostly referred to as processes of influence, but this should not be taken as implying that influence occurs in only one direction. As we shall explore more fully later, all influence processes can more fruitfully be conceptualized as two-way negotiation. Since the figure includes subordinates, peers and superiors as potential sources of event meaning, it is most readily applicable to the occupant of a formal managerial role.

Three levels of structural support are envisaged. Where explicit structures are present the manager has the option of using them, and in some circumstances may be required to do so. Where implicit conventions are established, these also enhance the range of event management processes open to the manager. In the limiting case where established organizational supports are few or none, the manager will be restricted to emergent or *ad hoc* behaviours.

Five types of procedure are shown in the table, whereby managers may give meaning to an event. They may apply rules, interact with their own superiors, peers or subordinates, or be self-reliant. The essence of rules is that they are established agreements, whether they derive from legislation, company rulebooks or established conventions at the workplace. The source of rules has either an impersonal or a supra-personal quality, so that they have a 'reality' apart from any particular individual transmitting them. This quality distinguishes the application of rules from all the other sources of meaning. Downward influence as it is here understood comprises much of what is ordinarily thought of as leadership, namely attempts by superiors to structure events in terms of organizational priorities, but to do so in a way that does not neglect the needs and motivations of employees.

Lateral influence involves joint contributions to event management. A number of qualities of the contemporary Western organization combine to make this a relatively infrequent mode of event management in some settings. These may include individualistic, competitive payment systems, promotion policies and contingent rivalries between departments or functions. For this reason, the event meanings to be accomplished through lateral influence are much more obviously based upon processes of negotiation and renegotiation than are downward influence processes.

Upward influence is distinguished from lateral influence by the difference in power between the two parties. Upward influence might be thought of simply as the 'opposite' of downward influence, but the two processes differ in terms of where we focus our attention. Many researchers into downward influence have studied participation. But in doing so they focus on its effectiveness *for the leader* in achieving the leader's goals. It is assumed that it is the leader's goals rather than the subordinate's goals which will be closest to organizational goals. In distinguishing upward influence we examine instead the possibilities for a manager in a subordinate role to influence the meaning of events from below. The final source of event meaning is termed self-management. Here the leader defines the meaning of events through use of prior expertise and training. This can be particularly important in organizations in which staff have a high level of technical or professional training. Self-management may also arise from prior experience within this or related jobs.

Event management processes are frequently used in combination rather than separately, although the emphasis placed on one rather than another is likely to be stronger at a particular time. The description of sources of event meaning thus far presented implies an undifferentiated flow of problematic events. However, managers, particularly more senior ones, will be faced with the need to distinguish second-order or strategic event management processes from the more everyday flow of events. These second-order processes will be those which establish procedures, rules, structures and programmes that seek to control the manner in which first-order processes are used to give meaning to particular events.

Each of the different sources of event meaning describes a context within which the models of cognitive processes discussed in Chapter 4 can occur. As we saw, for instance in Figure 5.1 on p. 75, the models of these processes which have so far been formulated have said little about organizational context. The different categories within Figure 6.1 identify alternative contexts which are to some extent in competition as the manager attempts to construct the meaning of an event. In other words, the more a manager chooses to define an event's meaning through influencing and being influenced by subordinates, for instance, the more constrained become the manager's choices as to the event's meaning in relation to other sources.

Concepts related to event management

Concepts similar to the processes of event management have appeared under various guises in the organization theory literature. However, they are typically described for the purpose of clarifying specific ways of coordinating work, particularly that involving more than one department (Georgopoulos and Cooke, 1979), rather than for conceptualizing leadership processes. The use of rules is similar to what March and Simon (1958) call 'programmed' decision-making, while the other formally legitimized event management processes are only programmed at a secondary level of establishing the rules whereby upward, downward, lateral or self-directed processes are to be carried out. Those other event management processes which are not legitimized would generally be 'non-programmed' in the March and Simon sense. However the status of established but not formally legitimized processes could be ambiguous in so far as they are programmed for individuals but not intentionally programmed by the organization.

Galbraith (1973) proposes a sequence of the mechanisms which organizations use to process information. This sequence makes optimal information processing contingent upon departmental inter-dependence, work uncertainty and complexity. In Galbraith's frame-work, rules and hierarchy can be equated respectively with formal rules and formal downward influence within the present model. Goal-setting becomes a special way of using organizational rules within the constraints of which those processes here termed lateral and self-directed come into play. Some of Galbraith's lateral linking arrange-ments involve second-order event management processes which establish formal structures that either promote lateral judgemental decision-making (such as liaison roles, teams, task forces) or promote the use of certain kinds of downward and lateral influence (such as managerial linking roles, integrating managers, matrix hierarchies). The focus of the work by March and Simon and by Galbraith is on the information requirements of different mechanisms for coordinating work, not on linking these mechanisms to a theory of leadership.

Mintzberg (1979) distinguishes the coordinating mechanism of direct supervision – a concept related to leadership as formal downward influence – from mutual adjustment and three kinds of standardization. He suggests that these are basic management processes by which all structural arrangements promote coordination. Like Galbraith's framework, Mintzberg's model is not designed to accomplish some of the present purposes, such as clarifying the conceptual place of informal downward influence or to distinguish lateral influence from self-management. Neither is emphasis placed on any organizational problems except coordination. In fact, the mechanisms which parallel sources of event meaning are labelled 'coordinating mechanisms'. Although approaches like those of Galbraith and Mintzberg to understanding structures and mechanisms for promoting coordination have been very useful in developing integrated models of organization design, the concept of the sources of event meaning develops a similar theme in a way better suited to integrating a model of leadership with the larger issues of organization theory.

Researchers developing the 'substitutes for leadership' idea (Kerr and Jermier, 1978) have taken alternative sources of event meaning into account, but without much systematic theorizing. Instead of attempting to develop an organizational theory of leadership, current attention is being directed to statistical criteria that distinguish between variables thought to neutralize or enhance the effects of leadership (Howell, Dorfman and Kerr, 1986). The small amount of theory which is used derives from the traditional conception of leadership as a one-way process of downward influence. Many of the characteristics of subordinates and of the tasks that are described in the 'substitutes' model are conceptually related either to the ability of people in subordinate positions to use self-management to interpret events, or to their motivation to do so. A difficulty shared by the path–goal and substitutes for leadership models is that of conceptualizing categories of variables which are likely to affect the effectiveness of a leader. Of course it is useful to distinguish between 'task characteristics' and subordinate 'ability' and 'motivation' variables, in order to indicate that both work responsibilities and people can be changed. However, it may not make sense to talk about task characteristics such as structure except in relation to the ability and motivation either of people in general or of individuals. For example, subordinate training, one leadership substitute, increases the capacity for self-management of particular tasks. As training and experience in a task increase, events related to that task are likely to be experienced as more structured. Thus task structure and task ability are not logically separable. Similarly, the routineness of a task depends on the amount of prior experience a person has had with it. Other individual and task characteristics included in the leadership substitutes model, such as need for independence, professional orientation, indifference towards rewards, and the intrinsic satisfaction of a task, are likely to affect the willingness of subordinates to accept formal downward influence from leaders or to engage in self-management.

The relevance that the subordinate and task characteristics described in substitutes for leadership research have for leadership is not in their separate abstract qualities. It is in their implications for whether subordinates are willing and able to decide for themselves not only how to do their work but how to coordinate their activities with others, ensure personal goal achievement through their work, promote adaptation to unexpected changes, and handle conflicts that arise in work relationships. Rather than being epiphenomena that should be treated as error variance in leadership field research, subordinate judgements about the need for and appropriateness of leadership may provide a useful basis for developing leadership which is responsive to a multitude of important contingencies.

Some of the organizational characteristics which have been identified as leadership substitutes – notably formalization and inflexibility – are closely related to the use of formal rules as a source of event meaning. Several others – specialized staff functions, leader control of rewards, spatial distance between supervisor and subordinates – are directly related to superior–subordinate interdependence, which should strengthen downward influence relative to alternative sources of event meaning. Another organizational characteristic in the 'substitutes' model – group cohesion – has implications for group member preferences for lateral influence and self-management rather than other sources of meaning. The event management model thus provides a further clarification of why the various substitutes for leadership enumerated by Kerr and Jermier can enable some organizations to function without traditional leadership.

The relative usefulness of the different sources of event meaning is difficult to anticipate in particular organizational settings. Contingency models of leadership and organization design have indicated the variety of individual, social and organizational factors which must be considered. In some circumstances formal downward influence and self-management are likely to be equally adequate from the perspective of accomplishing necessary work. Even then, one might still be better received than another due to preferences of a work group based on prior collective experiences, established norms or other factors. Subordinate preferences will change over time through an interaction among basic personality characteristics, personal experiences, and the cultural factors characterizing the group, organization and country within which they are situated (Kerr, Hill and Broedling, 1986; Manz, 1986).

Such difficulties serve to emphasize the virtues of models such as that of Stewart (1982b), which do not seek to predict effective behaviours, but instead emphasize the degree to which managers have choices as to how they cope with their specific circumstances. Stewart's characterizations of peer-dependent, man-management and hub managers, which we discussed in the previous chapter, have clear parallels with types of manager whose circumstances lead them to utilize one or other particular pattern of event meaning sources.

The choice of event meaning sources is likely to evolve over time in two different senses. One is a progression through the history of work systems, and the second is a progression within single organizations. Historically, the sequence begins with self-management, especially in the pre-nineteenth-century craft industries. The formal/informal distinction would have been less important in this pre-organizational stage of history, since organizations are the source of formalization. Even at this point, however, licensing and craft associations provided some degree of formal legitimation to craft workers' self-management. Somewhat later, formal downward influence provided the pre-bureaucratic control of work. It was this 'charismatic' emphasis which Weber cautioned against and which Michels felt was inevitable. This dominance by relatively unconstrained supervisors was in turn replaced by internal legalism – formal rules designed not only to influence how events were interpreted but to give direct guidance to employees and to constrain managers (Edwards, 1979: 145). Modern organizations continue to invest considerable effort in establishing appropriate systems of formal rules.

This briefly sketched historical progression is primarily one of the intended or socially recognized approaches to management. There may not have been as much of a progression in the actual sources of meaning which managers utilize. Established informal rules, upward influence and self-management continue to be significant within contemporary organizations. A rudimentary recognition of their operation was made in the classic observational studies made at the Western Electric plant in Hawthorne near Chicago (Roethlisberger and Dickson, 1939). The apparent current redirection of managerial emphasis may be partly one of strengthening established lateral and upward influence processes through formal legitimation. A major recent redirection of managerial emphasis since that time has been away from using formal rules, formal participation, and formal self-management (as legitimized through individual job design) to control particular activities and work behaviour. The new emphasis has been on using these sources of event meaning as second-order processes to manage the informal processes which in practice have always had the more direct effects on actual work behaviour. This has been accomplished by using formalized sources of information as sources of meaning which make events intelligible. Thus balance sheets, productivity records and inventories become usable by leaders and by others as the definers of the meaning of organizational events.

In addition to the changes over the past few centuries, relative use of event management processes is likely to change over time within individual organizations. Within single organizations, models such as that of Mintzberg (1979) indicate that the evolution in emphasis on various event management processes is likely to follow regular patterns. Mintzberg identifies the comprehensibility of an organization's work, the predictability of the work, the diversity of the work, and the environmentally required speed of organizational response as factors which determine the most appropriate structure for the control of work processes. By incorporating these factors into the event management model, several speculations become possible about the formal emphasis likely to be placed upon each event management process. For example, if an organization's work evolves toward greater complexity or reduced comprehensibility, formalization is likely to move away from rules which specify work procedures, firstly toward expert downward influence and self-management by experts, and later toward lateral and upward influence throughout the system. If an organization's increased age and size raises the predictability of work, formalization may come to rest on rules, supplemented by self-management of individuals who have been rigorously screened to ensure that they have desired skills and attitudes. This situation of high predictability seems to be the one envisaged by the traditional leadership researchers whose work we reviewed in Chapters 2 and 3. Organizational growth, however, can also generate diverse work, producing complex departmental interdependencies which encourage managers to become involved in formalized lateral influence processes. Finally, Mintzberg's notion of speed of response implies that external threat can generate various event management processes depending upon the nature and locus of the threat.

In both of the passages of the present chapter where we use organization theory to speculate about the effects of organizational context on managerial roles, it is notable that formalized event management processes are emphasized. There appears to be a sentiment amongst some organization theorists that less explicit event management processes either fall outside the legitimate domain of organization theory, or that they are simply less significant for understanding what organizations do than are formalized processes. We now seek to link event management more directly to cognitive processes.

Leader cognition in organizational context

The leader role can be understood as one which is continually enacted in the context of alternative sources of meaning and a series of organizational events. By identifying links between these contextual processes and the cognitive processes described in Chapter 4, we can develop a leadership theory which represents an individual leader's view without being excessively individualistic or focused upon downward influence. Two tools are required. One is the structural concept of role, as interpreted within the symbolic interactionist tradition, which stresses the manner in which roles are constantly created and recreated, rather than fixed and rigid. The other tool is the process concept of event, where an event is something actively constructed and only partially constrained by physical events. In order to continue examining the linkage of events to roles, significant disciplinary boundaries will need to be crossed. Since Western research traditions have mostly segregated organization theory, social influence processes and models of cognition, linkages will need to be cautiously established. The following discussion is thus tentative and will need to await more substantial research support.

Current theorists in cognitive social psychology (Markus and Zajonc, 1985) would take it as axiomatic that externally anchored interpretive frameworks such as the sources of meaning postulated here have their effects mediated by cognitive structures and processes such as those discussed in Chapter 4. Different sources of meaning could even affect very basic aspects of event perception, such as attention-focusing and attention-interrupt processes. In one electronics manufacturing company with which the authors have been working, organizational rules about timekeeping tend to focus a manager's attention at the beginning of the day on employees' arrival times. However, under unusual circumstances, the effect of formal time-keeping rules may be reduced. During a recent production downturn, knowledge of impending cutbacks was likely to cause managers to notice other attributes of employees which would have greater value in the self-management of later events. Despite the consistency of organizational requirements to attend to latecoming in a legalistic way, managers might find it more important in these circumstances to attend to more personal cues such as workers' feelings about the layoffs.

Going back to a more normal working day, a manager could interpret late arrival at work from several perspectives. The event could be largely interpreted through a schema derived from the processes of self-management. This self-constructed schema would contain personal memories of events and interpretations associated with lateness. Among these would be the emotions, behaviours and social contexts linked with the manager's prior experience of confronting those who arrive late to work. Alternatively, the manager could be receptive to *ad hoc* upward influence, expressed through the accounts, descriptions, apologies and images provided by the late-arriving employee. A third possibility would derive from reference to the informal norms of the setting, as exemplified by widely known organizational stories about latecomers and what 'really' happens to them. In the particular manufacturing plant we were working with, stories reported by employees indicated that formal lateness rules were fully enforced.

A supervisor's options in the case of a machine stoppage due to breakdown could also be thought of in terms of schemas. Under various circumstances the supervisor might show the subordinate how to mend the machine, mend it him or herself, order spare parts or specialists, apply organizational safety rules or speak to superiors about ordering new equipment or machines. A more technically oriented supervisor will process events in terms of machine-fixing, whereas others would consider safety, social process, political and management implications. Each of these aspects is represented in the context of the event by other parties who will speak for an interpretation of events which acknowledges their particular constituency. A crucial element in the present approach is to assert that those who draw upon 'external' sources of meaning are just as much involved in the use of schemas as are those who use only internal sources. Social psychologists have described those who process information rapidly and predictably as 'schematics', in contrast to aschematics who do not (Markus and Zajonc, 1985). While this distinction has some value, it omits reference to the social context. As we have argued, the social context does provide a range of alternative, articulated sources of meaning, upon which those deemed to be aschematic are likely to be drawing.

Alternative sources of event meaning are also likely to be important in the other cognitive processes discussed in Chapter 4, such as attribution, salience and behaviour choice. While some researchers have sought to link cognitive processes and organizational behaviour within specific domains (Mitchell, 1974; Martinko and Gardner, 1987a; Lord and Kernan, 1987), much remains to be done. Further work should be possible within the experimental paradigm, provided that studies are set up in a manner which enhances their validity. Care is required in using subjects within experiments who do have experience of the types of organizational processes being studied. Information also needs to be presented in the manner in which it would actually be received within organizations, so that alternative sources of event meaning are actually accessible to the subject. These requirements have not often been followed by experimenters seeking to apply ideas derived from attribution theory to organizational life. As we saw in Chapter 3, this area currently presents a curious blend of behaviourism and a highly structured cognitive theory. This blend is understandable in so far as the most attractive processes to study within organizational life are likely to be those such as reward and punishment, which have traditionally been thought of by psychologists as clear and unambiguous concepts. The difficulty is that what appears clear and unambiguous within a laboratory experiment is likely to be open to different interpretations within ongoing organizational life. From the viewpoint of a leader, the number of occasions when it is appropriate to administer an explicit reward or punishment is rather few. Furthermore the leader's choice to use rewards or punishments will rest upon a range of possible event meanings which do not all derive from the actions of the superior–subordinate dyads upon which most of this work focuses. The implicit model of leader behaviour within experimental studies is a heroic one, which does not withstand close scrutiny. As Kotter (1982) puts it, making a related point: 'My students make more big decisions in their case discussions in one day

than most of the General Managers could be seen making in a month.'
If experimental work is to become more valid, it will need to become
rooted in the types of causal issues that managers do actually face and
the elements which they do experience as significant in their attributions. More field-based, qualitative approaches will be helpful in
accomplishing this.

A bilateral view of event management

Event management has thus far been presented as an activity carried
through by an individual within an organizational context. We need
now to broaden this view by acknowledging that all other members of
the organization will also be seeking to manage events which impinge
upon them. In order not to make the picture overcomplex let us simply
consider the processes of event management in which a leader's
subordinate may engage. These processes are shown in Figure 6.2,
which complements the formal leader's perspective shown in Figure
6.1. Only slight differences are apparent in the two tables, all of which
are based upon the assumption that the subordinate does not have any
subordinates of their own.

The point of creating a separate Figure 6.2 is to emphasize that
subordinates also have an extensive range of ways of defining event
meaning. The traditional view of leadership focuses only upon the
manner in which the leader structures the task and provides support
for subordinates. As is clear from putting Figures 6.1 and 6.2 together,
events which are managed by the leader through downward influence
are also managed by the subordinate in terms of upward influence. The
interplay of these two modes of event management is likely to be a
great deal more subtle than is conveyed simply by describing them as
the structuring of tasks and the provision of support. Leader
structuring of the task may include explaining various aspects of a
work process, attempting to force through policies despite subordinates' reasoning, or resolving conflicting advice the subordinate has
received from others. A leader may also promote task structuring
indirectly by calling a meeting of subordinates to work out mutual
problems, or providing training which would strengthen self-management. In fact, Kerr, Hill and Broedling (1986) point out the value of
supervision which strengthens the use of alternative sources of event
meaning, where supervisors are not likely to be forever available for
the exercise of primary downward influence. Such second-order event
management processes can be of considerable value.

While the leader seeks to exert these various kinds of downward
influence, the subordinate has available an equally wide range of
modes for interpreting the events which are constituted by the leader's

Sources of event meanings for subordinates

Formality of structures	Rules	Subordinates	Peers	Superiors	Self
Explicit structures	Formal rules	—	Formal lateral influence	Formal upward influence	Formal self-management
Implicit conventions	Established norms	—	Established lateral influence	Established upward influence	Established self-management
Emergent aspects of culture	Emerging norms	—	*Ad hoc* lateral influence	*Ad hoc* upward influence	*Ad hoc* self-management

Figure 6.2 *Types of event management processes experienced in subordinate roles*

actions. Therein lies the potential for continuing confusion or conflict between leader and subordinate. The event which the leader seeks to manage through the application of rules may be one which the subordinate has developed their own new ways of handling, or which subordinates are determined not to carry through. Organizational rule systems, whether they be formal or merely established convention, are often differentially applicable to various parties, and differentially known and understood according to their personal applicability.

The greatest value in differentiating the leader's and the subordinate's systems of event management is apparent when considering those aspects which are least programmed or rule-determined. As we have seen, writers such as Katz and Kahn (1965/1978) reserve the label 'leadership' for those actions which are not rule-governed. Cohen, March and Olsen's (1972) 'garbage can' model of organization focuses upon the way in which many organizational events are amenable to alternative interpretations. Their interest, however, was in defining the bounds of organizational rationality. Our present focus on leadership concerns not just the process of organizational decision-making but the broader question of how it is that superior and subordinate are able to interrelate their sometimes conflicting modes of event management.

This chapter has presented a framework for analysing how leaders seek to manage events. In order to escape from the charge that the model is no less individualistic than those it seeks to replace, we must attend more fully to the ways in which interactions occur and meanings are communicated between members of an organization. To do this we need to step back for a while from the field of leadership research and explore its cultural context.

7

Leadership as Situated Action

The past few decades have seen a substantial change of emphasis in the explanatory models favoured by psychologists. The behaviourism of rewards, punishments and incentives has gradually been yielding ground to a more cognitively oriented view of the person (Markus and Zajonc, 1985). This cognitive emphasis has even influenced the work of leadership researchers who use the language of reward and punishment to describe the subjective experience of followers (Podsakoff, Todor and Skov, 1982) and the intentions of formal leaders (Mitchell and Kalb, 1982). It has become increasingly clear that to understand human behaviour we must comprehend fully the complex ways in which human beings process information, rather than seeing them as passive recipients of externally administered sticks and carrots. Theorists of leadership have by no means been in the vanguard of such a changing emphasis. Among the approaches to leadership detailed earlier in this book, only the work of those who have sought to develop attribution theory and the other cognitive theories reviewed in Chapter 4 can be said to fit in wholeheartedly with this orientation. Leadership research which uses the language of reward and punishment is best seen as showing an uneasy ambivalence between behaviourist and cognitive orientations. If it can be established that the responses of leaders and subordinates to one another are contingent not only on how they act but also on their perceptions of *why* they think the other party is behaving in that particular manner, a substantial step forward has been achieved. That step forward may nonetheless be insufficient to break the hold of implicitly behaviourist thinking over leadership theories.

Consider the typical research design used in one line of attribution-oriented leadership research. Leaders are asked to indicate how they would respond to some predefined subordinate action, such as persistent latecoming to work. Extenuating circumstances are shown to affect the leader's attributions and therefore his subsequent choice of action. Part of the implicit behaviourism within this scenario lies in the researcher's provision of a pre-defined subordinate action which is labelled as persistent latecoming to work. It was argued in the previous chapter that there are frequently conflicting perceptions of an action as between superior and subordinate. To define one of these perceptions as the objectively correct one and use it as the basis of an attempt to predict what happens next is implicitly behaviouristic. A further problem is that this type of design assumes that once the superior has selected the appropriate response to latecoming, the meaning of this response will also be self-evident to the subordinate. We may hope to come closer to understanding what occurs if we treat the perceptions and attributions of both parties to the transaction as having equal validity.

This chapter will explore some attempts to understand leadership which emphasize the manner in which the context of actions helps to define their meaning to those concerned. It is possible to draw conclusions favouring such a view even from studies which have been done within the behaviourist tradition. For instance, the study by Podsakoff, Todor and Skov (1982) showed that subordinates reacted differently to rewards which they saw as contingent upon performance than they did to those which were not contingent. If one subtracts from this finding the traditional assumption that a specified reward is always the same thing, we can express the findings as showing that the context of behaviours intended by the supervisor to be rewarding redefines their meaning. In a study which did not make behaviourist assumptions, Peterson (1979, 1985) showed that subordinates' reactions to particular leadership styles vary sharply, depending upon whether the subordinates felt the style was required by the situation. For instance, schoolteachers reacted positively to being told what needed to be done, except when they judged that they already knew what was required. Such effects of context are likely to be widespread, if not universal.

Consider once more an extension of our hypothetical example. A supervisor meets the subordinate with the lateness problem early in the morning and greets them warmly. A conventional analysis of this transaction would lead us to expect that the subordinate will see the superior as considerate and supportive. But suppose we add the information that the supervisor already greeted the subordinate five minutes earlier. In this case the subordinate might interpret the identical actions as forgetful and absent-minded. In a similar manner, the subordinate's interpretation of the gesture will be affected by the time at which it occurs. If the subordinate is in fact on time on this day, the greeting could be interpreted as a task-centred reward. If it is late, the greeting might even be seen as a warning that a reprimand was on its way as soon as work was under way. The greeting could also be interpreted in the light of whatever successes or failures occurred during the previous day's work. One could go on for some time inventing different ways in which the same action might be interpreted. However, even this example is vulnerable to the accusation advanced earlier: it too is implicitly behaviouristic, since it assumes that there is an objectively definable action which can be labelled as greeting someone warmly. In seeking to escape from such traps we shall need to draw upon concepts first developed by anthropologists and upon studies done outside North America.

Leadership in different cultures

While studies of leadership have been published by researchers in most parts of the world, almost all such studies indicate an awareness of the research models and methods developed in the United States. In examining such studies we are not therefore sampling a universe of studies which are entirely independent of the US tradition. The best we can hope to do is to see whether studies whose methods and hypotheses are often closely derived from the work of US researchers have yielded results which are comparable to those which might have been expected within the USA. Before embarking upon such a survey we need a conceptual framework within which to fit the results.

The most appropriate definition for the concept of culture has been debated extensively (Geertz, 1973). For present purposes we shall define culture as 'agreed ways of interpreting signs, symbols, artefacts and actions'. As we argued a little earlier, the meanings of actions as perceived by superiors and subordinates may not always be agreed. This would leave the culture of a setting as embracing all those aspects of that setting which *are* consensually defined. National cultures, and the cultures of large organizations, may well prove to embody subcultures. Early researchers into the leadership attitudes and actions of managers in different countries (e.g., Haire, Ghiselli and Porter, 1966; Bass and Burger, 1979) necessarily compared the responses of managers to their questionnaires without having any particular theory as to how the results would vary from one country to the next. More recently, the work of Hofstede (1980) has provided a framework for classifying work-related values in different national cultures which makes our task a good deal easier. Hofstede analysed the questionnaire responses of over 116,000 employees of an American-owned multi-national firm. The firm has employees in 67 countries, but there were only enough data to analyse from 40 of these. The questionnaire included several questions about the type of boss which the respondent currently had and would like to have. Hofstede concluded from his study that it was possible to classify the work-related values of those in his sample along four dimensions. These were termed individualism versus collectivism, power distance, uncertainty avoidance, and masculinity versus femininity. A complex set of transformations of the data and factor analyses enabled him to plot the average of responses from each country on each dimension, thereby facilitating comparisons.

Since our present purpose is to see how non-American leadership research compares with American results, a useful starting point is to see where the USA itself is positioned upon these scales. On the individualism scale, USA ranks highest of all 40 countries. In other words, within Hofstede's sample US respondents laid greatest stress upon the autonomy of the individual, whereas in other countries comparatively greater emphasis was laid upon the way that the person's identity resides within a collective group or organization. On the power distance scale, USA rated 26th with all the countries below it being West European, with the addition of Canada, Australia and New Zealand. In these countries therefore a lesser psychological distance is reported between superior and subordinate than elsewhere. On uncertainty avoidance the USA ranked 32. Risk-taking was thus more highly valued than in many countries. On masculinity USA ranked 13. In other words, in the USA there was relatively high emphasis on striving, advancement and success.

Critics have queried some aspects of Hofstede's results. For instance, the employees of a single organization may provide a highly aberrant representation of the values current within a particular country. Furthermore, the findings are based upon responses to attitude questionnaires, which may bear little relation to the actual experience of leaders and followers in a given culture. Nonetheless, the study is much more substantial than what went before, and its findings are not implausible in terms of the results of other approaches, so that we can place some trust in them. The implications for comparisons of the findings of leadership studies are clear. The USA is atypical of most countries in its particularly strong emphasis upon individualism.

Of course every country has unique cultural elements, and US culture has not prevented the formulation of certain non-individualistic theories of organization upon which we have already focused. But the particular uniqueness of the USA should alert us to the possibility that the individualistic nature of much American-derived leadership theory is a facet of US culture, rather than a firm base upon which to build leadership theories of universal applicability.

Bearing this in mind, we can now examine separately the research findings from other individualistic countries, such as those in Western Europe, and from countries which are more collectively oriented. Studies of effective leader styles in Europe have yielded findings which are as inconsistent as those from North America. For instance, in Britain, Argyle, Gardner and Cioffi (1958) found productivity higher in electrical engineering plants where supervisors were democratic and non-punitive, whereas Cooper (1966) found supervisors rated high on task relevance to be the most effective ones in an oil-processing plant. Bryman et al. (1987) found relationship-oriented supervisors to be most effective on construction sites. Sadler (1970) found that among a sample of over 1500 British industrial managers, the leadership style which they preferred their own boss to use was a consultative one. The most extensive data concerning the effects of different leader styles in Europe are those collected by Heller and Wilpert (1981), whose contingency model was discussed in Chapter 3. Their data show that the effective leader style of senior executives depends upon a variety of environmental contingencies, which they then attempt to identify. A related project by the Industrial Democracy in Europe research group compared decision-making in 12 European countries. Environmental contingencies such as differences in legislation were found to exert a large influence upon the manner in which decisions were made, particularly major ones (IDE International Research Group, 1981). Some of the early tests of Fiedler's (1967) contingency theory were carried out in Belgium and Holland. Although the results in the Belgian study were not as Fiedler had expected, due to the potency of the linguistic conflict in that country, they nonetheless made it very plain that different leader styles were required in different settings. Results from Israel, which scores at the median of Hofstede's individualism–collectivism scale have also been mixed. Fleishman and Simmons (1970) found that Israeli foremen who were effective scored high on both Initiating Structure and Consideration. However, Mannheim, Rim and Grinberg (1967) reported that both among manual workers and clerical workers, preferred supervisors were those who were high on Consideration, without regard to the level of their Initiation of Structure.

In contrast to these results, studies conducted in collectively oriented societies have given much more consistent support to theories of leader style which specify two components of effectiveness. The research conducted by Misumi (1985) over 40 years in Japan has shown that effective supervisors in that country are those who score high both in their orientation toward task performance (which he terms P) and in their orientation toward team maintenance (M). This finding has been replicated in coal mines, shipbuilding yards, banks, local government offices, bus companies and many others. Further replications in families, schools and sports settings suggest that these findings are consistent with Japanese culture in general, not just the work culture. The P and M measures used in Misumi's experiments and surveys are not conceptualized in the same way as the Ohio State measures, but an English translation of the M scale has been found to correlate very highly with Consideration items and the P scale has components which have some similarity to Production Emphasis and

Initiating Structure measures (Peterson, Maiya and Herreid, 1987; Peterson, Smith and Tayeb, 1987).

In a similar manner Bond and Hwang (1986) review studies of leader style undertaken in Taiwan. Translations of the Ohio State leader style measure show positive relations between both Consideration and Initiating Structure and performance measures in factories, local government offices, and schools. Sinha's (1981, 1984) studies in India support the view that the effective leader can be characterized as a Nurturant Task or NT leader. The two dimensions of NT leader behaviour again appear related to the Ohio State scales. Furthermore, Ayman and Chemers (1983) found both Ohio State leadership scales related to productivity in a factory in Iran, although in this case both scales loaded on a single factor. In Brazil, bank employees reacted positively to supervisors who were considerate but provided close supervision (Farris and Butterfield, 1972). Workers in Peru were found to favour supervisors who emphasized production but were thought to understand the problems of workers (Whyte and Williams, 1963). This last study also explored cultural differences in the manner in which Consideration might be expressed. Group meetings were welcomed by workers in an American factory, but not in the Peruvian one.

There is a certain irony about this pattern of findings. The theories first formulated in the USA would appear to be most strongly supported in those parts of the world which are less like the USA, and must be rejected in the USA and in the countries in Europe and elsewhere which are more similar to it. We should nevertheless hesitate before accepting such a bold conclusion in its entirety. It is quite possible that the differences found are partially explicable through the use of more numerous and more tough-minded criterion measures in the North American studies. Furthermore, the measures used in many of these studies have been adapted for use in the countries concerned. Ayman and Chemers' questionnaire included the item 'The supervisor is like a kind father.' Sinha's nurturance scale includes the item 'Does your superior help you to grow up and assume responsibility?' While these items may well be valid components of a Consideration factor in the countries where they have been used, they are not likely to prove comprehensible to respondents or to factor together with US-based Consideration items if used in Western countries. In the study by Goldthorpe et al. (1968) of British car workers, the most frequent reason given for getting along well with one's supervisor was that he left one alone. This action also was no doubt regarded as considerate. The fact that measures have had to be adapted for use within the various Western and non-Western countries where studies have been conducted indicates that the surprising consensus of findings from non-Western countries may require closer scrutiny. What these studies do clearly show is that certain general aspects of leader behaviour are related to performance in a variety of collectively oriented cultures. The specific way in which these aspects are construed appears much more variable. As with the hypothetical example at the start of the chapter, subordinates in many organizations may value a warm greeting from a supervisor, but the precise actions which convey this are likely to be culture-specific.

It could well prove to be the case that leaders in organizations from all parts of the world do indeed need to attend both to the task in hand and also to the maintenance of good relationships within the work team. But *how* this is to be accomplished in each setting will be dependent upon the meanings given to particular leadership acts in that setting. A supervisor who frequently checks up that work is done correctly may be seen as a kind father in one setting, as task-centred in another setting, officious and mistrustful in a third. The meaning of acts is given by the cultural context within which they occur. In collective cultures, the attribution of meaning is likely to be much more consensually shared than would be the case in more individualist societies. So, one possible explanation for the more consistent findings on leadership in non-Western countries is that in collective cultures there is a much more unified view of how the actions of formal leaders are to be interpreted and of what contribution they should make. The focal person in a role set in a non-Western country may experience conflicting demands from others, but the cultural norms will indicate what should be done about those demands. In an individualistic Western culture the individual would experience much more uncertainty about which demands to accommodate and which to resist. A second possibility is that the sharpness of the distinction which US researchers made between 'task' behaviour and 'group maintenance' is itself culture-bound and will be variously blended in a different manner in different cultures. Even within European cultures, some of which are almost as individualistic as the USA, it could be that the boundaries between what is 'task structure' and what is 'consideration' are drawn differently. On this view, whether or not the two dimensions come out as linked to high performance in any particular culture depends on the meanings given to specific behaviours within that culture. A third view would be the culture-specific one that different leader styles really are required in different cultures. Existing studies certainly provide some encouragement for this view, but substantial variability in the samples and types of measurement used in different countries requires our continuing caution.

Organizational culture

The framework provided by Hofstede's work has made it possible to address a series of questions about the manner in which national cultures found in different parts of the world define the meaning of a leader's actions. Several other groups of recent researchers see some promise in the concept of culture as applied not to nations but to organizations. Differences between the cultures of different organizations are likely to be more subtle than those between the cultures of different countries. The study of organizational culture may nonetheless be equally important in creating a model of leadership which gives adequate coverage to the context of the leader's actions. In examining the literature on organizational culture, a degree of historically rooted scepticism can be useful. Many recent writers advance the value of studies of organizational culture as though they were something entirely new. Yet the concepts they employ do not appear radically different from those espoused a generation ago by those who sought an understanding of what was then called informal organization (Barnard, 1938) or its descendant, organizational climate (Payne and Pugh, 1976). It is perhaps true that researchers within the current wave of interest use concepts which are a little more sharply delineated, and that they have devised rather different ways of collecting data. While researchers into organizational climate most typically used survey questionnaires, students of organizational culture have usually relied upon methods derived from anthropology which are more qualitative and more sensitive to nuances of meaning.

A concise view of organizational culture is given by van Maanen and Barley (1985). They see it as a product of four attributes: ecological context, differential interaction, collective understandings, and reproductive and adaptive capacity. The first two of these are structural prerequisites, whereby cultures can only develop where people are in proximity to one another and interacting with one another. The third attribute, the development of collective understanding is seen as central. 'Only when members of a group assign similar meanings to facets of their situation can collectives devise, through interaction, unique responses to problems that later take on trappings of rule, ritual and value' (van Maanen and Barley, 1985: 34). One might add at this point that the processes whereby organizations recruit members and frequently assign them to work with others having similar interests and abilities will enhance the development of collective understandings. The manner in which van Maanen and Barley conceptualize organizational culture leads them to argue that it would be rare, though not impossible, that an organization would have a unified culture. The more usual situation would be that with the passage of time departments, functions or workgroups would develop distinctive subcultures. Such a view of organizational culture is compatible with the view advanced in the preceding chapter that the normal state within most organizations is some degree of conflict and difference in perceptions and priorities rather than consensus.

Van Maanen and Barley's fourth factor, the presence of a reproductive and adaptive capacity, underlines the fact that cultures are not necessarily fixed and immutable. Historically salient events may play a key role in forming the culture both of work groups and of large organizations (Pettigrew, 1979). But the potency of such events does not necessarily preclude subsequent change induced by more recent events. When new supervisors or managers are appointed, a work group with a pre-existing culture ordinarily precedes them. The appointee's entry into the role will entail both learning the nature of the existing culture and seeking to create some changes within it. Crouch and Yetton (1988) provide an illuminating illustration of how this process occurs. They hypothesize that when a manager joins a work group, relations with the group will move towards one or other of two equilibrium positions. In the first of these both manager and subordinate performance will be high, as will ratings of mutual trust. The second position is where both manager and subordinate performance is low, and there is mutual distrust. A survey of 165 management teams in Australia showed strong support for these predictions. Thus neither the prior qualities of the manager, nor the prior qualities of the team, was adequate to explain what happened. An interactive model is required.

The conception of organizational culture advanced by Schein (1985) is closely related to that of van Maanen and Barley, perhaps because they have worked in the same organizational subculture at MIT. However, Schein lays more emphasis upon the way in which collective understandings come to be taken for granted as time passes. Consequently, when a consultant or a new recruit enters an organization, established members may be unable to describe to them the basic assumptions which make up the local culture. Schein provides a summary of the types of assumptions he has in mind, which is reproduced as Figure 7.1. Each of these general headings can clearly subsume a multitude of specific assumptions which might arise within a particular organization. Schein provides detailed suggestions as to how to surface the basic assumptions of an organization's culture. He sees this as not simply a matter of asking the right questions, although asking questions may well be a useful first step. Cultural assumptions become apparent as one begins to see a way of making sense of responses which initially seem contradictory or silly.

A third and more radical group of writers about organizational

1. **Humanity's relationship to nature**
At the organizational level do the key members view the relationship of the organization to its environment as one of dominance, submission, harmonizing finding an appropriate niche or what?

2. **The nature of reality and truth**
The linguistic and behavioural rules that define what is real and what is not, what is a 'fact', how truth is ultimately to be determined, and whether truth is revealed or discovered; basic concepts of time and space.

3. **The nature of human nature**
What does it mean to be 'human' and what attributes are considered intrinsic or ultimate? Is human nature good, evil or neutral? Are human beings perfectable or not?

4. **The nature of human activity**
What is the 'right' thing for human beings to do, on the basis of the above assumptions about reality, the environment and human nature: to be active, passive, self-developmental, fatalistic or what? What is work and what is play?

5. **The nature of human relationships**
What is considered to be the 'right' way for people to relate to each other, to distribute power and love? Is life cooperative or competitive; individualistic, group collaborative or communal; based on traditional lineal authority, law, charisma or what?

Figure 7.1 *Schein's underlying assumptions of cultures (Schein, 1985: 86)*

culture criticize the notion that culture can be thought of as a separable quality which organizations possess. Smircich (1985), for instance, asserts that organizations *are* cultures. What is required in her view is cultural analysis of organizational life. This entails discovering the meanings which organization members give to events. Since not all meanings will be within the conscious awareness of organization members, some of the methods of traditional anthropology may be more valuable than questionnaires or interviews. Particular attention can be given to symbols, myths and rituals, since it is these which most closely embody the ideologies and belief systems which sustain the organization. Trice and Beyer (1984), and Pondy et al. (1983) illustrate the use of such methods in North America, and Marshall and McLean (1985) do so in a British car components firm. Some of these writers would accept van Maanen and Barley's view that subcultures frequently differentiate within large organizations, but the focus of their work is mostly upon myths or stories which are widely known within the organization. An equally rich source of data is provided by the mixture of technical jargon and slang which embodies the culture of organizations as diverse as the Navy (Evered, 1983) and participants in corporate takeovers (Hirsch and Andrews, 1983). The breadth of coverage of this type of approach is particularly well illustrated by the view of Meyer (1984) that formal organizational structures such as those depicted by organization charts can be thought of as organizational myths. Thus the classical view which distinguishes prescribed structures from emergent organizational processes is turned on its head: the organization chart is to be studied as a myth providing clues to the implicit ideology of the organization, and the role of individual managers is seen as symbolic of the organization's rationality and control.

A more cautious approach to the concept of organizational culture is made by Morey and Luthans (1985). They argue that the original utility of the concept of culture lay in its application to small geographically separated non-Western societies. In 'displacing' the concept to the study of large organizations within Western societies, we need to take care that we are not stretching it beyond the point where it can be of value. They conclude that the displacement of the concept has in any event been initiated by urban anthropologists, and it can be effectively accomplished so long as some refinement of the concept takes place in the process. In particular they propose that it will not for long be satisfactory merely to describe the diversity of organizational cultures, as viewed from the inside. A second stage will be required where we start to formulate generalizations based upon analytic categories about types of cultures. In this way it should become possible to build connections between our understanding of culture and prior theorizing in fields such as leadership. Morey and Luthans clearly expect this to be a slow and difficult task. Some steps in this direction are already apparent. For instance, Martin et al. (1983) give seven examples of supposedly unique stories which organization members tell as illustrating how things are done in their particular organization, but which in fact recur over and over again in different organizations. Three categories of their stories are particularly relevant to understanding how impressions of organizational leadership are communicated. One set concerns 'Is the big boss human?' that is, when presented with an opportunity to perform a status-equalizing act, does he or she do so? Another set involves 'rule breaking' stories in which a senior manager breaks a rule and is confronted by a very junior person. The punch line depends on whether the senior executive conforms when confronted. A third set involves 'how will the boss react to mistakes?'

Other more popular writers with an enhanced sense of urgency (e.g. Peters and Waterman, 1982; Deal and Kennedy, 1982; Peters and Austin, 1985) have long since set about the task of arguing that if we can specify effective organizational cultures, then management should be able to create and control them. We shall return to this debate in the following chapter, but first we must seek to place the current North

American interest in organizational culture into its cross-cultural context.

Universals and specifics within the leader's cultural context

With but three exceptions, all of the publications on organizational culture referred to in the preceding section were written by North Americans. Just as we did earlier with leadership research, we should now enquire whether there is any obvious way in which models of organizational culture are influenced by the type of culture within which they have been formulated. As the research of Hofstede (1980) emphasized, one of the most distinctive qualities of North American and West European cultures is their stress on the individual rather than the collective. On the face of it, culture is a concept which can only be defined collectively, so there should not be too great a difficulty. However, this is an oversimple view. The Western stress upon distinguishing the individual from the group, organization or society is but one of a whole series of binary splits, which have been central to the modes of thinking of Western societies for some centuries. Others are mind–body, thinking–feeling and leader–follower. There is no reason to believe that Western cultures have always had such an orientation, although it may have started to develop in ancient Greece. Williams (1961), for instance, discusses how the concept of the individual has gradually evolved since medieval times, at which point 'individual' was understood to mean 'member of a group', that is, someone who was indivisible from a group. The Reformation played a major part in its change of meaning. By the time of Newton and Descartes, the predominant mode of thought had become one where abstract entities were differentiated and cause–effect relationships sought between them. In contrast, Needham (1978) shows how a different system for comprehending the world evolved in ancient China. This was much more holistic and emphasized the mutual responsiveness of the specific elements of a system.

It would be a gross oversimplification to categorize East or West as entirely dominated by either of the two thought-systems. The nineteenth-century British philosopher John Stuart Mill (1973) identified several ways of inferring causation of which the two that are best known are the method of difference and the method of agreement. The method of difference leads us directly to the logic of Western scientific method. The method of agreement involves searching for instances where an event occurs, without seeking to eliminate or control the circumstances surrounding it. This second method is clearly much closer to the thought-systems which Needham identifies as prevalent through much of the Orient. A more directly relevant instance of this type of thinking within Western science is given by writers who advocate a systems theory of organization. It is interesting to note, furthermore, that systems theories of leadership have proved much more popular among researchers in Europe than in North America (Miller and Rice, 1967; Graumann and Moscovici, 1986), as the Hofstede ratings for individualism in each country might lead us to expect. Graumann (1986), a German social psychologist, analyses the manner in which Kurt Lewin's 'Galilean' advocacy of field theory was transformed into more individualistic or 'Aristotelian' concerns by his US followers. There is no evident basis upon which one could evaluate either mode of inferring causal relationships as superior to the other. Western scientific method has proved invaluable within the physical sciences, but its application to the study of leadership and other social processes has yielded a much more meagre return. It is for this reason that procedures deriving from Mill's 'method of agreement' are worthy of fuller exploration.

To return to our specific theme, it is clear that any conception of organizational culture which sees culture as opposed to the individual, or as something which acts upon the individual, is unlikely to prove helpful in non-Western cultures. On the other hand, more radical conceptions such as those of Smircich (1985) that cultures and organizations are part of one another will make for less easy reading by Westerners, but should prove more durable cross-culturally. Adler, Doktor and Redding (1986) outline the perils of undertaking cross-cultural research into management without a full understanding of these issues. They assert that the fundamental problem in cross-cultural research is the difference in the way that people *think* in different parts of the world. Careful translation of questionnaires or interview schedules will not overcome this problem unless the researcher can find a way of gaining access to the logic of the culture studied. Their cautions sound surprisingly similar to those of Schein (1985), when he discusses the difficulties he faces as a consultant trying to surface the basic assumptions of organizations within the USA.

The dilemma of all research into culture is that of how to find an appropriate vantage point from which to conduct a study. Researchers who immerse themselves in a culture for long enough will begin to comprehend the meanings of events within that culture, but will still have difficulty relating those meanings to knowledge about other cultures. Researchers who set up some kind comparative research across cultures run the risk that their comparative measures simply do not tap the right dimensions to make a comparison valid or useful. Cross-cultural psychologists have struggled with this conundrum for some time (Berry, 1980), in terms of what they call 'emic' versus 'etic' strategies. Emic studies are those done within a single culture, while etic studies are comparative ones. The emic–etic distinction originated within the field of linguistics (Pike, 1967), where the comparative study of languages started from a very strong basis in classical and Western languages. When doing research within other linguistic groups, linguists found that the study of indigenous phonemes (hence 'emic') required very specific focus upon the sounds and symbolic actions of communicators within a linguistic group. Models based upon Western phonemes were found simply to be not useful within other linguistic groupings. The cross-linguistic study of phonetics (hence 'etic') has often erred by imposing what is really a phonemic analysis from the researcher's own linguistic group on to other groups. The debate continues within cross-cultural psychology as to how one may best escape similar dilemmas within the field or psychological research. The skill of resolving such a dilemma, as any Zen master would know, must lie in not becoming ensnared by the attractions of either half of yet another Western polarization, but inventing instead a strategy which transcends the choice. For guidance on possible ways forward we turn to one of very few non-Western theorists to have presented a systematic theory of leadership.

The model of leadership behaviour advanced by Misumi (1985) arises from nearly forty years of empirical research, initially triggered by contacts between Kurt Lewin and Japanese social psychologists (Misumi and Peterson, 1985; House, 1987). Its progress has been further influenced by personal relationships and exchanges with social psychologists such as Cartwright, Festinger and Kelley. Some of Misumi's empirical findings were touched upon earlier, but the focus of interest here is upon his overall conceptualization of leadership behaviour. This is presented as Figure 7.2. It can be seen that he makes a distinction between the behavioural forms of leadership, which he represents as the morphology of leadership, and the behavioural

	Situation	
Dimension	General characteristics	Specific situational expressions
Behavioural forms (morphology dimension)	General behavioural morphology	Specific behavioural morphology
Behavioural causes (dynamics dimension)	General behavioural dynamics	Specific behavioural dynamics

Figure 7.2 *Misumi's paradigm for the science of leadership behaviour (Misumi, 1985: 8)*

causes of leadership, which he represents as the dynamics of leadership. Such a distinction is not made by Western leadership researchers. The chapters of Misumi's book which cover morphology seek to establish a taxonomy of leadership types with high situational generality. In contrast the dynamics chapters are based upon experimental studies that test models of causal relationships.

Of more interest is Misumi's distinction between the general characteristics of leadership and their specific situational expression. Again, no distinction of this type is to be found in major current Western leadership theories. Misumi's view is that there are certain general contributions to group processes which are required of any leader. These are the general morphological characteristics, and he describes them as comprising two leadership functions which he terms Performance and Maintenance. However, the manner by which the leader addresses the questions of task performance and group maintenance must of necessity vary depending upon the specific situation of any leader. This may sound a little like a Western contingency theory, but it is not. In line with customary Western thought patterns, Fiedler's (1967) contingency theory, for instance, differentiates the leader from the environment and then hypothesizes the interaction of a fixed series of environmental attributes upon a fixed measure of leader style, which was initially interpreted as reflecting actual behaviour. In contrast, Misumi argues that each time one studies a substantially new setting one needs to construct new measures of the kinds of specific behaviours which represent the general P and M functions in that setting. The specific elements which Western theorists have sought to measure in an invariant way are allowed to vary, based upon factor analyses of items derived from interviews with practitioners. The presence of the two general functions is a theoretical premise which is justified by reference to laboratory studies and the general pattern of factor analyses derived from the many settings in which Misumi has worked. His model thus transcends the individual–organization culture polarization. In studying effective leader behaviours in a given setting, one is also studying the culture of that setting.

A distinctive feature of Misumi's programmatic approach has been his use of successive approximations in making simultaneous progress in his studies of both the morphology and the dynamics of leadership. As a contrast, we may consider the four stages of an idealized leadership research advocated by the US writers Sashkin and Garland (1979). One starts with observation, including a consideration of prior research in related fields. Secondly, one identifies discrete concepts that can be operationalized with an experimental design, so that causal relationships may be confidently established. Thirdly, one conducts survey and other field research to check applicability of the findings. Only after these stages are complete does one move into the final stage of application. In many ways the prescriptions of Sashkin and Garland would afford a substantial advance on most Western leadership research. It was indeed formulated in reaction to the current situation where each researcher tends to become a specialist in one or other segment of the process, as well as in one or other conception of leadership. Current US academic policies encourage the publication of discrete articles rather than of book-length accounts of integrated research programmes.

In contrast, Misumi's work as researcher and consultant has followed what we call the logic of successive approximation (Misumi, 1985; Peterson, in press). Although some tendency to move from observation through experiment to application is evident, the prevailing sequence is much less clear-cut. Apart from retaining the concepts of Performance and Maintenance in order to preserve coherence over time, tremendous reciprocal influence is found between change programmes, development of new measures, experiments using new tasks or criteria and modifications required by applications made outside Japan. Presumably this process is made possible by the culture of Japanese academic and business life. The result has been that Misumi has been able to undertake etic analyses within and outside of Japan, while not being constrained by the 'rational' sequence advocated by Sashkin and Garland. Although the work is undoubtedly affected by the emic qualities of its original context, it need not be theoretically bound to it. If Misumi's approach is to be found more widely useful, some problems of cross-cultural communication will need to be overcome. In particular, it will be necessary to demonstrate that for Westerners to interpret the dimensions of Performance and Maintenance as being equivalent to the old behaviouristically defined leader style dimensions is to miss the main point. It will also be necessary to show that statistical interpretations of the way in which the P and M dimensions interact do not successfully capture Misumi's meaning. To state the problem more generally, successful cross-cultural transmission of leadership research requires that the receiving culture attempt as far as possible an emic analysis of the sending culture. This kind of analysis is obviously difficult, but it will be necessary if we are to escape the confines of what Berry (1980) terms 'imposed-etic' analyses, in other words the forcing of data from one culture into categories provided by another.

Misumi's studies within Japanese groups and organizations are impressive. The next step in evaluating them is to test their relevance to other cultures. A series of studies has recently been undertaken in an attempt to make a start on this (Peterson, Smith and Tayeb, 1987;

Smith, Misumi, Tayeb, Peterson and Bond, in press; Smith, Tayeb, Sinha and Bennett, 1987). In each of these studies subordinates have been asked to make ratings of the leadership style of their superiors, using one or other of the established measures of leader style. Such measures are largely composed of rather broad general characterizations of leader behaviour. For instance, one Ohio State item used was, 'Is your superior friendly and approachable?' Respondents are then asked to complete a further series of 36 specific questions, asking about the superior's behaviour much more precisely. Thus they are asked when the superior comes to work, where he eats lunch, who he has meetings with, who he talks to and how often, and so forth. Correlations are then computed separately for each country's data between the perceived style of the supervisor and each one of the 36 specific behaviours. Data have been collected from shop-floor assembly workers in Britain, the USA, Hong Kong and Japan, and from samples of middle managers in Britain, the USA, Japan and India. Results are so far available for measures of Misumi's PM leadership styles and for Blake and Mouton's (1982) 9,9 and Paternalism scales.

The overall pattern of findings is relatively clear. Eight to ten of the 36 specific behaviours prove to correlate consistently positively with one or other of the style measures in all the countries sampled. For instance, talking sympathetically with a subordinate who has personal difficulties is seen as considerate in all cultures, and frequency of talking about work progress is seen as task-centred in all cultures. But the remaining 16 behaviours show wide and frequently significant differences between countries in correlation with the style measures. For example, it was found that a supervisor who talks about a subordinate's personal difficulties to his colleagues when the person is absent was deemed inconsiderate in Britain and the USA, but considerate in Hong Kong and Japan. The supervisor who shows disapproval of latecomers to work is seen as task-centred in Britain and Hong Kong, unfriendly and inconsiderate in the USA, and neither of these things in Japan. Like these differences, many of the others found are readily explicable in terms of existing knowledge from emic studies of the cultures concerned.

This series of studies has also shown that in all the countries included in the sample, subordinates who evaluated their current work situation highly also evaluated their supervisor as high on both P and M, just as Misumi's theory predicts. Western researchers might well argue that such a concordance of the various different ratings by the subordinates points to some kind of halo effect due to the use of a set of relatively similar rating scales. However, for the present purpose this need not be a problem. At the very least the study shows that in all four countries the scales measuring P and M leader styles have high social desirability. At the same time the data show that the specific meanings of the P and M styles vary by culture. These studies therefore support the value of Misumi's distinction between general leader attributes and specific ones. They raise the possibility that there may be universal qualities required of all leaders but which Western researchers have failed to find because they have searched for them with measures which are too static and individualistic. Likewise the findings support the view that by studying the specific actions of leaders and their associates, rather than generalized measures of style, we can better understand the reciprocal interplay which is their cultural context.

Further evidence as to the wide applicability of Misumi's distinction between general and specific aspects of leader behaviour is given by the work of Gioia and Sims (1985) in the USA. These researchers reasoned that generalized measures of leader behaviour, such as the Ohio State Leader Behavior Description Questionnaire, were vulnerable to distorted perceptions based upon respondents' implicit leadership theories. Conversely, specific measures, which they call behaviourally oriented measures, should not be so vulnerable to bias. Their experiment showed that when subjects were told that the leader they were watching on videotape was a good performer or a poor performer, ratings on the LBDQ scale were strongly affected, whereas the specific measures were not.

Some interim conclusions

In Chapter 5 we presented a model of the leadership process which stressed the degree to which leaders were subjected to conflicting demands from different role senders. The emphasis upon the distinctiveness of North American culture in the present chapter suggests a need to review whether or not role conflict might be a phenomenon distinctive to individualist cultures. There is little or no empirical literature directly comparable to the type of studies done in North America to aid such a review. However, more general ethnographic studies from many parts of the world make clear that some form of role conflict is a very widespread phenomenon. A more plausible hypothesis might therefore be that in individualist cultures, role conflict might frequently take the form of what Kahn et al. (1964) termed inter-role conflict, where the focal person receives conflicting demands from different role senders. Conversely, in collectivist cultures one might expect a greater incidence of person–role conflict, where the role holder has difficulty integrating the collective expectations of others with his or her own experiences or abilities.

In the next three chapters, we shall seek to explore in more detail the implications of thinking about leadership in its cultural and organizational context. The most obvious implication of the viewpoint which has been outlined is that leadership involves attending to all members of one's role set, not merely one's subordinates. With this in mind, we give separate attention to the behaviours required when seeking to lead one's subordinates, one's colleagues and one's superiors. In terms of the event management model this involves the processes of downward, lateral and upward influence respectively. The second implication is that within each of these areas it will be fruitful to distinguish between the generalized goals of leaders and the specific means which make sense in their particular cultural setting. What leaders strive to accomplish or to symbolize may have great generality. How they accomplish it may be infinitely variable.

8
Leadership as the Management of Meaning

In a certain sense this chapter returns to the issues which were uppermost in the minds of those who studied leadership in the thirties and forties. Our concern is with the ability of leaders to shape the whole strategy and culture of an organization from the top down. However, the focus of current attention can be a little more precisely focused than it was at that time, as a result of more extensive debate about ways of defining leadership. From the perspective of someone enacting a leadership role, the sources of event meaning which concern us here are those identified as downward influence. In other words, we are here considering managers while their attention is predominantly directed toward those who are formally subordinate or informally more junior than themselves. In contrast to the other sources of event meaning to be addressed later, such as upward and lateral influence, few authors would dissent from the view that these processes are central to leadership.

Some writers have, however, proposed that leadership be considered only one among several modes of social influence. A recent debate has focused on the relationship between the concepts of leadership and of management. To Mintzberg (1982), management is what managers in the real world do, whereas leadership is an increasingly arcane concept, cultivated by academics and poorly related to any kind of practice. A more moderate view is that of Dachler (1984) who defines management as 'the design, change, development of, and giving directions to social systems embedded in their environment'. In contrast, leadership is seen as 'the design, change, development of and giving directions to social *sub*-systems embedded in their environment' (1984: 102). He specifically points out that it would be a misinterpretation of his definitions to conclude that he is saying that management is what is done by senior managers and leadership is what is done by junior managers. In his view management is an attribute not of individuals but of social systems.

A rather different set of definitions are those popularized by Katz and Kahn (1965/1978), who argue that the tasks of leaders differ systematically depending upon their seniority within the organization. In their view, the leadership required of senior managers is that they originate changes in policies and structure, using their charisma and view of the system as a whole to achieve this. Middle managers are required to interpret and make specific the structures which implement pre-existing policies. This means that they need a two-way perspective on what is required from above and below and considerable skill in integrating these demands upon them. Junior managers or supervisors are required to use their knowledge of rules and of technical matters to administer the existing structure. Katz, Kahn and Dachler would most probably all consider themselves to be systems theorists, but the divergence of their views is largely one of whether they focus primarily upon the organizational system as a whole, or upon the subsystems within it. In this chapter we shall mostly be examining the attempts of senior managers to create large and visible changes, since these have been more frequently studied empirically. Many of the researchers in this area do not emphasize the leader's relations with a particular group of subordinates. Instead, they focus more on the individual's contribution in the context of the whole organization. We shall argue, however, that change in organizations may be created at any level where leaders and followers agree to place new meanings on events.

Charisma

As we indicated in Chapter 1, Weber's interest in charismatic leadership predates almost all other approaches to the study of leadership. Recent interest in charisma has been fuelled by disillusion with other approaches, but the triggers for renewed interest were provided by House (1977) and Burns (1978). House proposes that charismatic leaders differ from other types of leaders in that they achieve:

> follower trust in the correctness of the leader's beliefs, similarity of followers' beliefs to those of the leader, unquestioning acceptance of the leader, affection for the leader, willing obedience to the leader, identification with and emulation of the leader, emotional involvement of the follower in the mission, heightened goals of the follower, and the feeling on the part of followers that they will be able to accomplish, or to contribute to the accomplishment of, the mission. (House, 1977: 191)

House proposes that leadership thus defined does occur with some frequency within modern organizations and argues for the restoration of the concept of charisma in the analysis of leadership effects. In relation to the distinctions advanced by Katz and Kahn (1965/1978), House would expect to find charismatic leadership at senior rather than middle or junior levels within large organizations. Charismatic leadership is thus seen as one among several types of leadership and contrasted with more routine types of management or administration.

Burns (1978) also provides definitions against which charismatic leadership is to be contrasted. He discusses the relationship of the concepts of power-holder and leader. Power-holders are those who for whatever reason have the capacity to influence others. Leaders are actual or potential power-holders, but not all power-holders are leaders. In order to be considered a leader, someone must be able to induce 'followers to act for certain goals that represent the values and the motivations – the wants and needs, the aspirations and expectations – *of both leaders and followers*' (Burns, 1978: 19, emphasis in original). Thus Burns accepts, more strongly than most theorists, that leadership must be defined not as the action of one person upon another, but as a two-way process between leader and follower. He goes on to distinguish two forms of leadership, transactional and transforming. In transactional leadership a mutual exchange occurs between leader and follower. The exchange could be economic, political or psychological, but there is no enduring bond between the parties. The exchange continues only as long as both parties find it to be to their benefit. Such exchange relationships are widespread in many work organizations, whereby subordinates agree to accept leadership from appointed leaders on the basis of their paid employment (Jacobs, 1970). Burns contrasts this to transforming leadership, within which 'one or more persons engage with *others* in such a way that leaders and followers raise one another to higher levels of motivation and morality' (Burns, 1978: 20). Although he sees the functions of leaders and followers in such a relationship as fused, he still makes clear that it is the leader who does most of the initiating. Such leadership must entail an acute sensitivity to the follower's wants and needs, as well as one's own. The exchange envisaged by Burns in transactional leadership is clearly a more minimal one than the leader–member exchange posited by Graen's Vertical Dyad theory. High LMX as defined by Graen sounds closer to transforming leadership, although Graen and Scandura (1987) assert that high LMX does not include affective reactions such as liking.

Burns's analysis is based largely upon the study of major political leaders, both historical and contemporary. His interest clearly lies with transforming types of leader, just as House focused upon charismatic rather than the more mundane types of leadership. They differ in respect of the amount of attention they give to the follower's role in leadership. Paradoxically, those who have sought to develop Burns's ideas have rendered them more individualistic, while House's 1984 paper pays much more attention to contextual factors than did his 1977 paper.

The main protagonist of Burns's concepts has been Bass (1985), who has developed questionnaire measures of what he terms transactional and transformational leader styles. Transactional leadership is assessed by two scales which are referred to as 'Contingent Reward' and 'Management by Exception'. Transformational leadership is assessed by four scales, known as 'Charisma', 'Individualized Consideration', 'Intellectual Stimulation' and 'Inspiration'. The case for using these particular scales is derived from Burns's more detailed exposition of the nature of his two types of leadership. Bass's scales are completed by a leader's subordinates and by leaders themselves, much as were the earlier generation of US leader style measures. Studies using the Bass questionnaire have uniformly shown that subordinates who rate their superior high on the transformational scales also rate them high on effectiveness, whereas those rated high on the transactional scales are seen as less effective. This finding has been obtained in the USA (Bass, 1985; Avolio and Bass, 1988), India (Pereira, 1986) and New Zealand (Singer, 1985; Singer and Singer, 1986). Bass et al. (1987) have also shown that where New Zealand managers are seen as transformational, their subordinates at the next level down are also seen as transformational by *their* subordinates. Furthermore, Waldman, Bass and Einstein (1987) have shown that subordinates who receive positive performance appraisals tend to be those whose superiors are rated highly by them on transformational leadership. On the face of it, such findings are interesting, not least because of their apparent replicability in widely varying cultures. However, it is debatable as to whether or not the measures do indeed capture the meaning of Burns's definitions. Although Bass (1985) does present an analysis of leader–follower relations, his questionnaire items do not focus upon the two-way aspect of leader–follower relations which is so strongly stressed by Burns. Representative transforming supervisor behaviours asked about in the questionnaire are ' . . . arouses in me the effort to work harder and better', and ' . . . places heavy emphasis upon careful problem-solving before taking action'. Furthermore, some of the transactional items are written in a manner which already implies that the leader is ineffective. For instance, some supposedly transactional supervisor behaviours are ' . . . takes corrective action if I make mistakes' and ' . . . is content to let me continue doing my job in the same way as always'. The finding of superior effectiveness for the transformational scales is thus enhanced by the manner in which the items are written. The measure will require substantial revision before it gets us much nearer to an understanding of charisma. A further problem with Bass's measures is that in most cases both the description of leader styles and the measures of leader effectiveness derive from ratings by subordinates. A fuller range of measures of leader effectiveness will be required to establish the validity of the findings obtained.

One of the assumptions of Bass's version of the Burns model is that transformational leadership is under all circumstances preferable to transactional leadership. In contrast, House (1984) has advanced what amounts to a contingency theory within which charisma is one of four possible types of power. The other three types are authority, expertise and political influence. Leaders are seen as more likely to exercise charismatic power where they possess the relevant personal qualities, where they anticipate compliance to their influence attempts and where the norms of the follower group are humanistic and supportive. House reviews studies from North America which found that inspirational leaders were rated as effective in military settings (Yukl and van Fleet, 1982) and that charismatic leaders were found to have followers who rated high on 'charismatic follower syndrome'.

The principal difficulty in evaluating the success of current attempts to revive the concept of charismatic leadership remains one of definition. It has been well established since the time of the Ohio State research studies that subordinates frequently respond positively to leaders with whom they can establish warm and friendly relations. As was detailed in earlier chapters, the relationship of supervisor Consideration to performance measures is much more varied. What is not clear is whether researchers into charisma have succeeded in identifying a style of leadership which is different from supervisor warmth. Bass (1985) uses 'Individualized Consideration' as one subscale of his transformational leadership measure, and he also reports correlations of around +0.4 between transformational leadership and the Ohio State Consideration measure. House (1984) now equates charisma with French and Raven's (1959) concept of referent power, in other words as power based upon liking and friendship. There is thus a danger that charisma will come to be interpreted empirically in a manner which makes it increasingly difficult to distinguish from the concepts it seeks to displace. If charisma is defined individualistically as a power or quality which the leader has, Burns's emphasis upon the *fusion* of leader and follower has been lost. Sashkin and Fulmer (1988) attempt to overcome this individualistic emphasis by devising separate measures of charismatic leader behaviour and organization culture and examining their interrelation. While such an approach may provide instruments for tests of further aspects of House's contingency theory, it still falls short of Burns's definition.

The transformation of organizational cultures

Modern researchers into charisma have thus had only limited success in escaping from individualistic conceptions. They have come closest to doing so when they have sought to relate charisma to a specific cultural context. The problem remains of defining how one may best relate charisma, or other types of leadership, to culture or more particularly organizational culture. In the previous chapter we explored the proposition that cultures and subcultures define the meaning placed upon the actions of leaders. Leaders who wish to change an organization's culture, or to preserve it as it is, need before all else to be aware of what those meanings are. As Schein (1985: 2) puts it, 'there is a possibility . . . that the *only thing of real importance that leaders do is to create and manage culture* and that the unique talent of leaders is their ability to work with culture' (emphasis in original). He goes on to propose that leaders embed and transmit organizational culture in five different ways: (1) by what they pay attention to, measure and control; (2) by their reactions to critical incidents and crises; (3) by deliberate role-modelling, coaching and teaching; (4) by their choice of criteria for allocation of reward and status; and (5) by their choice of criteria for recruitment, selection, promotion, retirement and 'excommunication'. The role of founding fathers in establishing an organization's initial culture is seen as crucial, but Schein sees a continuing role for managers in monitoring and influencing culture through these same mechanisms. He acknowledges that leaders are not always consistent in their actions and that the five types of mechanism outlined above may on occasion pull in differing directions and yield a culture which is confused or contradictory. He also lists a further set of five 'secondary' articulation and reinforcement mechanisms. These are mechanisms which will enhance the impact of the leader's actions if they are consistent with what the leader does. The secondary mechanisms are (1) the organization's design and structure; (2) organizational systems and procedures; (3) the design of physical space, façades and buildings; (4) stories, myths, legends and parables about important events and people; and (5) formal statements of organizational philosophy, creeds and charters. These five mechanisms can also be thought of as specific instances of the second-order event management processes discussed above. Through each of them the manager exerts some kind of influence over the way in which organization members interpret events.

Schein's analysis makes no use of the concept of charisma. His five mechanisms by which leaders embed and transmit culture are clearly a blend of the styles of leadership which Burns differentiated as transactional and transforming. However, he shares with Burns a strong commitment to the view that analysis of leader behaviour and organizational culture are inseparable from one another. Another distinction which is lost in the Schein model is the division between leadership or charisma as a source of change, and management as a source of routine administration. This may be no bad thing. It could be that the distinction between stability and change is one of those Western dichotomies which obscure rather than clarify the processes we are seeking to understand. As Schein would put it, the leader's actions and reactions imbue events with particular meaning. That meaning can be conveyed simply by the manager's attention to certain events and inattention to others. Whether the implications of this attention are for change or for continuity is not of crucial importance.

The essence of Schein's analysis lies in the view that no definitive judgements are possible about the value of a particular organizational culture. Just as leaders can only be judged effective in terms of some criterion, so cultures are only good or bad in relation to one or another value. Since organizations espouse multiple values, each of which is likely to be more strongly emphasized by some subgroups within the organization, conflicting evaluations are inevitable. This viewpoint is in sharp contrast to that advanced by Peters and Waterman in their 1982 best-seller *In Search of Excellence*. In this and other related recent books, it is argued that successful companies have cultures which are in important ways similar. The culture of excellence is said to have eight attributes: (1) a bias for action; (2) staying close to the customer; (3) fostering of leaders and innovators; (4) respect for individuals; (5) 'hands-on value driven' (that is, explicit values about high achievement and high supportiveness); (6) 'stick to the knitting' (that is, stay with tasks and markets where there is the expertise); (7) simple form, lean staff; (8) simultaneous loose–tight properties (that is, elements of both centralization and decentralization). Peters and Waterman provide only anecdotal evidence that the cultures of successful companies do indeed have these attributes, although they argue their case with some persuasiveness.

In Chapter 1 we discussed the urgency with which successive generations searched for the One Best Way of leadership. Peters and Waterman's work and the massive attention which it has gained may be seen as a resurgence of such thinking. If there were indeed to be just One Best Culture for organizations, the task of leadership would be substantially clarified. However, scrutiny of the book reveals it to be an amalgam of very general prescriptions (such as 'A Bias for Action') and very specific examples (such as 'Managing by Wandering Around'). While the general prescriptions might prove fairly widely applicable, the specific ones are much less likely to do so. One way of summarizing the problem is to say that Peters and Waterman, like many leadership researchers, have confounded together what is to be done and how it is to be done. Even at the level of what is to be done, evidence marshalled by Hitt and Ireland (1987) indicates that Peters and Waterman's prescriptions are either incomplete or wrong. They examined the recent economic performance of the firms identified as excellent by Peters and Waterman. These firms did no better than a random sample of other firms. Drawing on survey data collected from a wide sample of firms some years earlier, Hitt and Ireland were able to show that the firms which had been particularly successful scored high on only one of the four qualities advocated by Peters and Waterman for which they had measures. This was the fostering of leaders and innovators. In line with the emphasis of the present book Hitt and Ireland emphasize that one should not expect all the success criteria for a large organization to be positively correlated with one another. They report that the firms showing best performance on economic criteria were of medium rather than large size, and grew by way of acquisitions rather than by internal growth. It could be that some of the qualities delineated by Peters and Waterman are more important in organizations seeking to maintain a large market share, rather than to grow.

It is interesting that the one quality advocated by Peters and Waterman which did find some support in Hitt and Ireland's study was the role of leadership in creating a culture of excellence. Their chapter on this topic is devoted to the theme of autonomy and entrepreneurship. The internal entrepreneur is portrayed as a 'champion' who seeks and is given the responsibility and support to proceed with a major project. Support in this sense tends not to mean large amounts of explicit resources. Instead, it particularly involves other more senior people who provide a role model for 'championing' and who protect a champion from risk-minimizing organizational pressures. While one emphasis is on technical initiative and direct responsibility with a product or customer, internal entrepreneurs must also garner resources, as well as motivate and direct subordinates. Part of the idea of entrepreneurship is that formal responsibility may be more constructive for motivating subordinates than are the organizational rules that might substitute for it.

The internal entrepreneur idea is developed in greater detail in a study of the internal corporate venturing process (Burgelman, 1983). A new product idea must be championed through two 'core processes' and two 'overlaying processes'. The core processes involve defining the technical nature of the product and its potential user and gaining support to pursue it. Overlaying processes require the integration of the product with the organization's strategy and the establishment of a permanent product-based department for it. The role of a leader in these processes is indicated, but as in the Peters and Waterman discussion, the leader's role in motivating and encouraging subordinates is not developed. Thus while the idea of entrepreneurial leadership has been pointed to as an issue in strategic management, it has not been developed in the context of the leadership literature.

The type of entrepreneurship discussed by Peters and Waterman (1982) and by Burgelman (1983) indicates that their implicit view of leadership is once more an individualistic one. That has also been true of the popular interpretation of what they are saying. The implication of the Peters books is seen as being that if an organization does not have a culture of excellence, the task of leadership is to change that culture to ensure that it does. The title of Kilmann et al.'s (1985) book, *Gaining Control of the Corporate Culture*, reflects this emphasis. Schein's analysis should give us cause to wonder how easily such a thing might be done even if it were desirable. His view, much more consistent with a contingency theory viewpoint, would indicate that the task of leadership is to start with an intimate knowledge of the existing culture, and to explore ways in which that culture might change toward one which is compatible with the organization's current circumstance. The history of attempts at organizational development is full of examples indicating that such change is likely to be slow and uncertain. Pettigrew (1985), for example, gives a detailed analysis of attempts within the British firm ICI to make changes in the culture of four of their divisions over 20 years. In the 1960s Shell Oil sought to modify their organizational culture by adopting a document outlining a new philosophy of management, deriving from work by the Tavistock Institute (Hill, 1971). By 1980, little sign of lasting changes was visible (Blackler and Brown, 1980). Published case studies do exist of organizations within which major changes in culture have been successfully accomplished (Marrow, Bowers and Seashore, 1967) and shown to persist (Seashore and Bowers, 1970), but they are rare.

The creation of changes in organizational culture may not depend so much upon externally administered programmes of training and consultancy as upon the cumulative impact of day-to-day events. Indeed, Greiner (1972) has argued that the progressive evolution of an organization over time will be punctuated by a series of somewhat predictable revolutions. In his model, an initial phase of creativity is succeeded by a crisis of leadership. This is succeeded by a phase of direction, which in due course creates a crisis of autonomy. A further series of phases and crises is foreseen. Organizational leadership may thus entail not so much the creation of change, but the anticipation of crises and the construction of cultures which are best adapted to handling them. Schein's list of five mechanisms no doubt captures some of how this can occur, but his list lacks coherence for our present purpose. The problem is that Schein presents the items on his list as crucial, but provides no basis upon which one could judge whether he has or has not selected the appropriate items for inclusion. Since the listing is based upon a wealth of practical experience, it has substantial plausibility. What is needed is a theoretical framework which would explain to us why those particular items are crucial ones. In a similar manner, we have so far argued in this chapter that Burns's formulation of the leadership process is preferable to those of more individualist writers without providing a full explanation of why this should be so.

The missing theoretical element in our discussion of both Schein and Burns is that of leadership as the management of meaning. Pfeffer (1981b) gives a concise formulation of such a viewpoint. He sees organizations as systems of wholly or partly shared meanings. Meanings may be subdivided between what the organization is seen as being *for* – in other words, its goals, ideologies and values – and how the organization believes those purposes are to be accomplished. The distinction parallels that made by Misumi (1985) between the generalized functions of leaders and the specific means by which those functions may be accomplished. Pfeffer argues that some organizations are much more fully agreed about their goals or ideology than others, but that in any event it is relatively difficult for organizations or people to change their goals. Much easier is the making of changes in belief about how a particular goal might be accomplished. Pfeffer sees the role of leaders in organizations to be in influencing the meanings and values placed on particular ways of approaching goals. In similar vein Pondy (1978) asserts that:

> the effectiveness of a leader lies in his ability to make activity meaningful for those in his role set – not to change behaviour but to give others a sense of understanding what they are doing and especially to articulate it so they can communicate about the meaning of their behavior . . . If in addition the leader *can put it into words* then the meaning of what the group is doing becomes a *social* fact . . . This dual capacity . . . to make sense of things *and* to put them into language meaningful to large numbers of people gives the person who has it enormous leverage. (1978: 94–5)

This conception of leadership provides a framework for comprehending Schein's list of five mechanisms whereby leaders influence organizational culture. The mechanisms have to be seen as particularly potent ways of influencing the meanings organizations place upon events. In a similar manner, this conception of leadership requires the inclusion of followers, peers, superiors and rule systems as well as leaders, since meaning can only rarely be unilaterally defined. A good deal of managerial success in influencing subordinates as intended is likely to rest upon intimate knowledge of subordinates' goals and their beliefs as to how those goals may be accomplished. Burns cites the views of Chairman Mao Dze Tung on the value of such knowledge:

> We should never pretend to know what we don't know, we should not feel afraid to ask and learn from people below, and we should listen carefully to the views of the cadres at the lower levels. Be a pupil before you become a teacher; learn from the cadres at the lower levels before you issue orders. (Burns, 1978: 238)

However, Burns's conception of charismatic influence, like that of most other writers on charisma, also has a paternalistic element. He presumes that the leader knows better than the followers what the followers really want, even if they do not know it. The basic task of leadership is thus in a rather literal sense consciousness-raising. As Burns puts it: 'But the fundamental process is a more elusive one; it is in large part, *to make conscious what lies unconscious among followers'* (1978: 40; emphasis in the original).

Pfeffer's view is that the role of leadership in organizations may be largely but not entirely restricted to symbolic actions, whose purpose is the management of meanings placed upon events by organization members. He sees actual behaviours of organization members as more readily predictable upon the basis of 'external' objective qualities such as technology, size, market forces and so forth. The two systems, symbolic and behavioural, are seen as only loosely coupled. Such a dualistic mode of thinking is certainly consistent with findings showing more reliable links between leader style and job attitudes than between leader behaviour and productivity. However, it invites us to draw a line between 'real' external social events and their contextual meaning which we have argued against in earlier chapters. There is an undeniable reality to the physical characteristics of people and the physical motions and sounds which constitute social and organizational behaviour. The range of meanings which can be attributed to these behaviours, although not entirely unlimited, appears to be far broader than the range of meanings attributable to events which do not involve people. For example, intricate differences in the meanings attached to sounds are evident in language. Cross-cultural analyses of language (Pike, 1967) struggle to identify correspondences between symbols representing apparently transcultural physical events. Tremendous difficulty surrounds the identification of shared meanings attached even to such universally shared events as the procurement of food for a primary social unit. As we have seen, Hofstede (1980) has proposed that certain dimensions of meaning are universally applicable to the study of organizational behaviour, but he does not address the question of what events generate these meanings in different cultures.

It is clear that at least the greater proportion of meanings attributed to social behaviour can only be considered as real by those who share frameworks for imputing meaning. If we take as given the constraints of the physical world and of a particular cultural context, the event management model suggests that meanings will not be consensually defined even by the leader's role set. The rhetoric of leaders engaged in the management of meaning includes frequent references to external events which organization members *agree to define as real*. The leader's role in representing realities external to the work group to the members of that group is also frequently crucial as we shall see in Chapter 9.

It may be more fruitful to recast Pfeffer's discussion in terms which avoid the risk that his distinction between the symbolic and the behavioural is a culture-bound one. Within a large cultural group there may well exist a substantially consensual belief system. Let us take as an example the ideological belief that it is right and proper to regulate the growth or decline of organizations on the basis of a cash economy. The consequences which flow from this consensus are that certain artefacts, such as balance sheets, are treated as real, objective or the 'bottom-line'. This in turn leads to a wide variety of actions, individual or collective, which are seen as contributing to the economic health of the organization. These include investment decisions, hirings, firings and many other management actions. Now suppose that in that same large cultural group there exists no consensus that all individuals have a pre-ordained right to a happy life. The consequences of this lack of consensus would be that each individual who values happiness would need to explore their own ways of accomplishing it. To organizations, such actions would be individualistic and subjective. The organization would need to make provision for the management of these actions in so far as they threatened the accomplishment of their 'real' goals.

This detour into hypothetical examples serves to argue that most of organizational life is socially constructed, even if in one or another cultural group we choose to treat certain events as more real than others. If one accepts the views of Pfeffer (1981b) and others that the management of meaning is indeed a central task of leaders, then certain other distinctions which we have explored in this chapter lose their value. For instance, the proposition that charismatic leadership is qualitatively distinct from transactional leadership or routine administration reduces to a division between the category of value consensus within which each type of leadership operates. The charismatic leader would be one who successfully articulates some type or other of 'vision' (Bennis and Nanus, 1985). The transactional leader would operate instead within a more limited, pre-established and pragmatic set of values.

Management writers and Chief Executive Officers not infrequently advocate the accomplishment of consensus upon some crucial value within their organization. It may be that the failure of many programmes of organizational development occurs precisely because they do not acknowledge the inevitability of conflicting frameworks of meaning within a large organization. The failure by Shell Oil to popularize a philosophy of management from the top down has already been mentioned. Beyer (1981) reviews a range of studies indicating that where groups exist within an organization with conflicting values, the prospects for effective decision-making may be enhanced. Indeed, organizations which have cultures based on low conflict and high commitment may require leadership which reduces the risk of 'groupthink' (Janis, 1972) or excessively conformist thinking. Not all types of conflict will necessarily be beneficial though. Other failures to create organizational change have occurred where specialist organizational development groups espoused humanistic values at odds with technocratic values favoured by more powerful groups within the organization. The prospects for change will be much enhanced where value consensus is to some degree established, and some basis exists for debating how better to accomplish those values.

One of the best-established rituals whereby organizations signal either the wish or the opportunity for change is by the replacement of a senior manager. The new appointee can be seen as a prestigious type of change agent. Nicholson (1984) has advanced a theory of work role transitions. His model differentiates the types of change which may occur after the incumbent in a work role changes, as a function of personality and of organizational characteristics. The theory has been tested upon a sample of 1700 British managers (Nicholson and West, 1987; West, 1987). Self-reported role innovation was found to be a function of the amount of discretion afforded by the new job, a prior history of innovation, and in the case of those converting to a new type of role, the support available from others. Thus there is some evidence of the ability of individual leaders to institute change, even in the absence of larger scale programmes of organizational training or change.

Among North American researchers, studies of leadership succession have been rather few, perhaps because the topic falls between the preoccupations of organization theorists and the more individualistic leadership researchers. Gouldner (1954) used a study of managerial succession to explore some of the inadequacies of theories of bureaucracy. He showed how the initiatives of the newly appointed manager of a gypsum mine provided an alternative meaning framework to that in use among the 'Old Bunch' of his predecessor's subordinates. The old bunch maintained a view of the period of indulgency under the former manager which Gouldner labels as the 'Rebecca Myth'. Everything under the old regime was seen as having been good, and everything new was bad. This interpretive framework led to substantial resistance to change among the workforce. Conflict between the two frameworks was handled by the new manager through the use of various political processes. Gouldner's analysis goes well beyond the study of superior–subordinate relations, showing how Peele, the new manager, had to establish new meaning frameworks with numerous other parties. These included head office executives, local labour union leaders, the predecessor's wife, employees' wives, and the established system of organizational rules. New meanings were negotiated in the course of implementing major organizational changes. The installation of new equipment allowed Peele to promote potential supporters and simultaneously to augment their power. The ambiguities of the newly introduced technology permitted Peele a quite Machiavellian concealment of his purpose through which he could put into position those who would sustain his type of meaning framework. The methods used by Peele may cause us to reflect upon coercive styles of leadership, and we shall now do this.

Leaders as power-holders

There exists in much of the literature on leadership and organization an implicit assumption that leaders are valued and constructive members of their organization. On the whole this volume has, until this point, made a similar tacit assumption. Such an assumption on the part of academics and others who write about leadership may in itself be evidence of the effectiveness of leaders in the skill upon which this chapter focuses – the management of meaning. It is of course not true that everyone admires leaders. Values about leaders and what is or is not admired in them varies from culture to culture as Hofstede's (1980) work has shown, and varies also within the subcultures of the academic world. By drawing more heavily upon the sociological study of organizations we might readily cast leaders in a less attractive role (Salaman, 1979). Having commenced this chapter with a return to the conceptions of Weber, we now retrace our steps further still to ideas closer to those of Machiavelli.

To put it in another way, our analysis of leadership to this point has tacitly assumed that while subordinates and others may interpret events somewhat differently, they do concede that the leader has the right to manage the meaning of events. Discussions of social power usually portray social influence types ranging from consensual to coercive. If we are to sustain our portrayal of leadership as the management of meaning, we must show its applicability to types of leadership at all points on that spectrum. French and Raven (1959) proposed that social power may rest upon five different bases, which they termed reward power, coercive power, legitimate power, expert power and referent power. This typology has proven popular with many writers, but as Podsakoff and Schriesheim (1985) point out, the manner in which researchers have sought to measure these differing types of power leaves much to be desired. In particular, the most frequently used measures have an inbuilt assumption that if one type of power is operative in a situation, the other types of power must be absent. This is plainly implausible, and it could indeed be the case that a charismatic leader style could rest upon elements of all five types of social power. More recent theories of types of power such as that of House (1984, 1988), are also vulnerable to the criticism that the typologies they employ are arbitrarily constructed. In this case four power bases are differentiated, charismatic, expertise, authority and political influence. In both classifications, some of the bases of power are clearly those which can only operate where there is a shared perception between leader and follower of the meaning of the actions in which they are participating. For instance, referent (that is, friendship) power, authority or legitimate power, expertise or expert power, and reward power are all plausibly interpretable in this manner. The more interesting power bases for the present purpose are the remaining ones, that is, the concept of coercive power in the French and Raven model and political influence in the House model. Coercive power is defined in terms of the power to punish, and the difficulty of sustaining a separate definition of it is illustrated by the evident fact that responses to coercion will vary greatly depending upon whether the person using coercive power is seen as having the legitimate authority to administer punishment or not. The classic study relevant to this issue is the much-debated work by Milgram (1974), who required his experimental subjects to administer what appeared to be increasingly dangerous shocks to a 'learner' in a psychology experiment. Since no reasons for carrying through this procedure were provided to the subject, the study gives a relatively clear picture of some of the dynamics of coercive influence. Yet even within this setting it can be shown that whether or not the experimenter succeeds in coercing the subject into continuing to administer shocks depends upon the meaning of the situation to the subject. In one condition of the experiment, Milgram provided the subject with two assistants who were supposed to assist in the administration of the shocks. It was found that when these assistants refused to continue, the subject almost always also gave up. Thus the supposedly implacable coercive power of the experimenter turns out to be redefinable where others are present who act in ways which question that power. Recent studies in Holland by Meeus and Raaijmakers (1986) have shown that even where there are no third parties present the power of a coercive experimenter may be undermined by additional information. In their study, refusal of the experimenter's instructions was much increased by the information that a previous experimental subject had taken legal action against the experimenters. Such findings are reminiscent of those reported in Chapter 3 showing that leaders moderate their responses toward subordinates depending upon the information they have about them. However, they have not been systematically integrated with the leadership research literature.

One might argue that in the laboratory experiments discussed above, the experimenters were not in possession of 'real' coercive power, in the sense of the sanctions available to leaders in industry or the military. The point we are making, however, is that the realness of coercive power in non-experimental settings is very frequently buttressed by consensual definitions of the legitimacy of the actions undertaken. In settings such as industrial disputes where one or another party acts in a manner which is not consensually defined as legitimate, that action itself is likely to be the subject of further dispute. We shall discuss the management of conflict more fully in the next chapter.

House's fourth type of power, political influence, describes a process whereby leaders may accomplish their ends in a more indirect manner through control of information and contacts with others. It is perhaps not surprising that French and Raven omitted it from their list, since practitioners of political influence are frequently adept at concealing what has occurred. Here indeed may be an instance of the exercise of leadership without the existence of shared meanings between leader and follower. If one seeks to discover how such political influence may be wielded, the best guide is provided by the studies of Christie and Geis (1970). These authors devised questionnaire measures of the orientations toward political influence advanced by Machiavelli. They found that those who scored high on their Machiavellianism questionnaire were indeed adept at getting their way in a wide variety of settings. However, they failed to find any systematic differences between the behaviour shown by Machiavellians and others. They concluded that Machiavellians may not differ from others so much in what they do as in when they do it, and how they read the needs of a particular situation and use it to their advantage. Thus even this style of leadership requires an acute awareness of others, which enables Machiavellians to redefine the situation in a manner which suits their covert ends.

It can therefore be argued that all types of power and influence do rest upon the existence of shared meanings, even if some of those meanings may change in the course of the influence process. This discussion of types of power has underlined the arbitrariness of current classifications of types of power. They confound the possession of power with the manner in which it may be employed in specific cultures or organizations. It may be more fruitful in concluding this chapter to look at work which treats power in a more unitary manner. Kipnis (1976) has undertaken a series of analyses of power-holders. In line with the thinking of attribution theorists he shows that the influence mode selected by power-holders is a product of their own power needs, perception of the target and the history of previous transactions with that target. In contrast to House's (1984) model Kipnis does not seek to specify the circumstances under which each type of influence might prove effective. His interest is limited to predicting the circumstances under which each mode will be selected. Coercive means of influence, for instance, are seen as more likely to be selected where the power-holder has reason to believe that influence will be difficult or impossible. Such an approach is more consistent with the model of the leader's choice of actions advanced in Chapter 4, since it allows that 'effectiveness' may be defined quite differently by the various interested parties.

A novel aspect of Kipnis's model is that it then goes on to consider the impact upon power-holders of the repeated exercise of power. He reasons that where power-holders see themselves as successful in their influence attempts, they will gradually become contemptuous of those whom they have influenced. This will be particularly true where influence has been based more upon coercive means. The sentiment is much the same as the classic assertion by Lord Acton that 'Power tends to corrupt and absolute power corrupts absolutely.' Kipnis supports this view with a series of laboratory studies in which it is found that the more strongly power-holders perceive themselves as the source of influence, the more they disparage the target of their influence. Over time therefore power-holders who exercise coercive power are likely to become more distant from the targets of their influence. This will make it more difficult for them to influence those targets in other ways, and this in turn will lead to selection of still more coercive means of influence on future occasions. The commendable manner in which the Kipnis model incorporates the time variable might seem to suggest that all influence processes are likely to become more coercive as time passes. However, one is only likely to make such a prediction if considering the power-holder–target-person dyad in isolation. As we have argued earlier, it is more fruitful to view leaders as focal persons in a role set. Pressures toward distance and the use of coercion are often counterweighed by pressures from other members of one's role set to maintain and develop collaborative relations within the organization. For instance, a leader's superior may make it clear that the leader is expected to maintain adequate morale among subordinates.

Although this chapter has returned to the 'classical' emphasis of leadership theory, namely the downward flow of influence from leader to follower, it has done so in a manner which lays much more emphasis upon the two-way nature of this flow. The area within which it has been least easy to develop this type of analysis has been that where relations are characterized by coercion and conflict. There are other aspects of leadership experience wherein the management of conflict is rather more frequent, and we consider these in the next chapter. The burden of the present chapter has been that the leader's exercise of power resides in the ability to transmit influence by way of the network of meanings which constitutes the organization's culture. Like other aspects of culture, such meanings are deeply rooted and amenable only to gradual change.

9
Leadership as Negotiation

As we have seen, most conceptions of leadership have envisaged the leader acting as an autonomous individual in relation to one or more less powerful subordinates. Some analyses do consider the constraints on the leader from above by distinguishing incremental, discretionary or 'choice' leadership from that which is required or demanded (Katz and Kahn, 1965/1978; Hunt and Osborn, 1982; Stewart, 1982a). The event management model extends this view by pointing out the alternative sources of meaning which create conflict in its most basic form, namely alternative versions of what constitutes social reality. When any one event is under scrutiny, the active or implicit negotiation of meaning must be considered at two points as described in Chapters 4 and 6. On the one hand, formal leaders negotiate an interpretation of events upon which their *own* actions can be based. On the other hand, they then engage in processes of negotiating meanings with *others* and attempting to influence their actions. In this sense, all leadership actions are conflictual. This analysis may prove most readily applicable to leaders' relations with their colleagues, but we start by examining the more general notion of leadership as the management of conflict.

The negotiation of order

The concept of a negotiated order appears to have been developed independently by researchers on both sides of the Atlantic. It first appears in the early work of Strauss (1978), who developed it in the course of studies of psychiatric hospitals in the late 1950s. He used the term to convey the notion that behaviour in such settings was indeed ordered rather than chaotic, but that social interaction involved a continual negotiation and renegotiation of the manner in which those present would relate to one another. In his 1978 book he draws on case studies of factories and argues that the concept is equally applicable there. Kelvin (1969) also treats order as a fundamental concept. An ordered set of interpersonal relationships is not necessarily, in Kelvin's view, a static or rigid state. What he has in mind is more that order exists where those involved have a clear sense of the meaning of the transactions in which they are engaged. Kelvin then proposes that the leader in any setting is 'the individual who contributes most to the creation and maintenance of order in the group'. Unlike many of the theorists discussed earlier, both Strauss and Kelvin clearly fall within the symbolic interactionist research tradition initiated by G.H. Mead (1934). In Mead's view the meanings of events or of symbols are in no way fixed or immutable, but are continually defined and redefined through the actions and reactions of those concerned.

These ideas have been picked up and developed by Morley and Hosking (1984) and Hosking and Morley (1988). They argue that the group and organizational settings within which leadership occurs are almost never characterized by consensus. Within groups there is frequently competition between individuals as to who shall be most powerful. This will also occur within organizations, but in addition there will also be competition between the various groups which comprise the overall organization. Following Tajfel's (1981) theory of intergroup relations, they see these processes as inescapable, since the establishment of an adequate social identity rests upon the making of social comparisons between oneself and relevant others or groups. This lack of consensus will not be random, but will be explicable in terms of the contexts within which the various groups and individuals are located.

It follows from this type of analysis that leadership ability is best thought of as an attribute bestowed upon an individual in respect of certain skills of creating and maintaining meaning. Hosking and Morley attempt to specify what these skills might be. Clearly, the relevant skills are not simply those of achieving consensus with others, since conflict is seen as endemic. They propose instead that effective leadership entails the *interlocking of means*. In other words, effective leaders work upon the basis that what they wish to achieve and what others in the organization wish to achieve are to some degree interlocked. By observing the specific nature of particular interlocking elements in the system, they are able to act upon those elements in ways which advance their goals and values. In particular, leaders need to be on the lookout for opportunities and for threats. Opportunities may occur to build networks of collaborative relationships, which will yield information of no immediate relevance, but which may prove crucial in meeting some later threat. Network building may be accomplished through actions which make others' tasks easier while making one's own no more difficult. Threats are events which may overwhelm the previously established order. What is required here is adequate information to anticipate threats, and the flexibility necessary to provide new interpretations of what has happened and what must now be done.

The Hosking–Morley model bears some resemblance to those of theorists such as Pfeffer and Pondy who, as we saw in Chapter 8, consider the management of meaning to be crucial to the leadership role. However, Hosking and Morley give much more weight than others to leadership as a process of negotiation between leaders and their environments. While Pfeffer and Pondy lay a good deal of emphasis upon the way in which leaders *give* new meanings to events for their followers, Hosking and Morley go beyond dyadic analysis to underline the multiple-party nature of meaning-making processes. They propose that in order to be more able to define the meanings of events in ways which others accept, leaders require an acute observational sensitivity and wide networks from which to draw information. Like negotiators in wage bargaining, leaders need to know enough to anticipate the reactions of the various other parties. By so doing they can establish collusive linkages which transcend the continuing differences in the perspectives of themselves and their role sets. This type of model is intended to apply to relations between leaders and all their constituencies. However, its merit is likely to be particularly apparent in the instance of colleague relationships, so that we now focus more directly upon these. This is not simply because Hosking and Morley stress negotiation as the basis for leadership, but also because they argue that excessive emphasis upon the leader's superior–subordinate relationships has led to a woeful neglect of lateral relationships.

Colleague relationships

Clearly there are some leaders for whom relationships with colleagues are not particularly important, and for whom neither cooperation nor conflict will be salient. However, the frequency with which Stewart's (1976) studies identified managers with a 'hub' pattern of relationships indicates that much more attention is required to how managers relate to their colleagues. The restrictiveness of the prior emphasis upon the leader's style toward subordinates lies in the fact that that style will frequently be determined by the nature of the leader's own relations with colleagues and superiors. Consider the following case study:

> Nancy Pfizer is the manager in charge of small fan production. Her production costs have far exceeded budget because of a plastic blades shortage causing stops and starts in production. In calling her counterpart in parts fabrication, she learns that they have in stock a large supply of discontinued metal blades from a previous model fan. Nancy calls her boss, vice-president for manufacturing, to inquire whether she can make use of these substitute fan blades.
>
> The VP-Manufacturing, Hal Cohen, says he'll have to check this out. He contacts the head of engineering to ask whether he'll approve this change. The engineering manager says he'll have to call his technical subordinate who knows that equipment first-hand. 'He'll be able to assess whether

performance or user safety could be affected.' Cohen then calls the sales office responsible for getting these fans to distributors to tell them of the likely change. They must also approve. Their reaction is one of great anxiety. The sales manager says she can't approve this without the OK of her boss, the VP of sales, and they may want market research to run some tests on whether consumers will be loath to buy metal versus plastic blades (and, of course, hurt her sales targets for the coming months).

When the sales manager reaches her VP, she is told that the substitute is acceptable only if manufacturing agrees that no metal bladed fans will be produced for delivery after June 15, because that is when advertising will be distributing a new catalog and magazine advertisements for the company's fans.

The sales manager negotiates that concession from Cohen, and then Cohen is told by engineering to go ahead as long as an extra lock washer is placed on the blade guard to make it unlikely that the guard would accidentally fall off and expose rotating metal blades. Cohen then calls Pfizer and tells her to add the lock washers to the manufacturing procedures and to be sure to finish production of metal bladed fans by June 1. (Sayles, 1979: 73-4)

As Sayles comments, the complexity of these procedures is reduced by the fact that in this case all relations appear cooperative. Nonetheless the centrality of lateral relationships between colleagues in managerial roles is clearly illustrated. The implications of these relationships for subordinates' perceptions of their manager's behaviour have been entirely disregarded in traditional research on leaders and subordinates. In this particular case five lateral communications are referred to, compared with only two upward ones and three downward ones. A more systematic study by Landsberger (1961) showed that among six British middle managers, over 40 per cent of communication was with colleagues. Sayles argues that to class all lateral relationships together as a single entity is also misleading. He notes that one of the things which frequently makes lateral relationships difficult is a lack of clarity as to the nature of the relation between the two parties. Lateral relationships may stem from work flow, service provision, technical or other advice, auditing, a right of veto over others' activities, or liaison. Rather frequently the meaning or nature of a relationship may be defined differently by the various parties. Different departments may seek to establish that their representatives have the right to make demands upon other departments. Success in establishing such influence will make it easier for managers of the more influential departments to meet their own priorities and those of their subordinates. But success is by no means assured by establishing the desired influence structure: a departmental manager may alienate colleagues to a degree which makes their own work impossible. Thus the manager's need will be to negotiate the resources or assistance which are required, but to do so in a manner where the meanings attached to the negotiations by all parties ensure the continuance of the relationship.

Empirical studies of managers' relations with their colleagues are few and far between. Salancik, Calder, Rowland, Leblebici and Conway (1975) report a study within an insurance office. The subordinates of 11 supervisors were asked to make ratings of their supervisors on various scales. They made ratings both of how they saw the supervisor's behaviour and of how they would like the supervisor to behave. Correlations were computed between actual and preferred behaviour. Salancik et al. then show that the supervisors who came nearest to behaving as their subordinates might wish were those who had to coordinate work with only one or two other departments. Those who came least near were those who had to coordinate with as many as eight other departments. The rank ordering of number of departments to coordinate with and failure to meet subordinates' wishes was almost perfect.

This study does not provide any measure of how supervisors did actually relate to those in other departments, but it does support the view of the leader's role as necessarily conflictual. At least in these circumstances if the leader satisfies one constituency, this necessarily frustrates others. If we can find further instances of such results, it will serve to underline the perils of evaluating leader effectiveness solely on the basis of subordinate perceptions. In the insurance firm, it may very well have been the case that coordination of different departments' work was more crucial to the survival of the organization than the maximization of subordinate satisfaction. Osborn and Hunt (1974) studied lateral relationships within a very different type of organization. They asked 39 managers within an institution for the mentally retarded how one should relate to colleagues on the same level. It was found that those managers who favoured active approaches and feedback to colleagues were also the managers whose subordinates were most satisfied. However, there was no link between the managers' preferred lateral relationships and ratings of subordinates' performance. Some caution is needed in interpreting these findings since the managers provided their own statements of preferred lateral relationship style and we know nothing of how such styles were perceived by their actual colleagues. Nonetheless, we find that in this study also there is a divergence between attention to colleagues and subordinate performance. Furthermore, it was found that there *was* a link between preferred lateral relationships and measures of system performance. Another study linking lateral relationships and performance criteria is reported by Graen and Scandura (1987). They showed that the quality of LMX relationships between information systems professionals and their users in other departments was linked to ratings of project process effectiveness. In a similar manner, Tjosvold (1986) showed that among employees of a municipal engineering department in Canada, those who saw their goals as highly interdependent with their peers were more satisfied. However, in these two studies no reference is made to concurrent relations with subordinates and the measures of performance are not clearly distinguished from the assessments of lateral relationships.

A much more extensive sample of colleague relationships is included in the study by Heller and Wilpert (1981) which was discussed in Chapter 2. A sample of 808 middle and senior managers in many types of organizations were asked to characterize their 'decision-making style' towards colleagues. In doing so they used the same five alternatives which were employed in other questions concerning their subordinates. Heller and Wilpert found that decision-making with colleagues was reported as much less participative than with subordinates. The categories 'own decision without explanation' and 'own decision with explanation' were much more frequently used with colleagues, whereas consultation and joint decision-making were less frequent. Heller and Wilpert suggest that this may be due to power struggles and promotion rivalries between colleagues. It may also be the case that superiors and subordinates within the same department have more similar priorities than do managers of different departments. They might therefore be more trusting of one another. Unfortunately, Heller and Wilpert do not provide further analyses of their colleague data, as they did for their subordinate data, so that no further light is shed on how decision-styles toward colleagues are selected, nor on what are their consequences. They do, however, show that just as with subordinates, there are substantial cultural differences in the decision-styles reported by their sample. British managers were the least likely to use collaborative decision-making with their colleagues, whereas American, French and Spanish managers were more likely to do so.

A detailed study of 25 purchasing agents, whose work is almost entirely oriented toward lateral relationships, is reported by Strauss (1962). Five categories of tactics were identified. These were classified as: rule-oriented, rule-evading, personal-political, educational and organizational-interactional. Strauss indicates that most agents used all these tactics on occasion, but selected which to employ depending upon their assessment of the circumstances. The most frequent tactics were the application of rules in order to regulate the demands of others, and the trading of favours based upon personal friendship. The most striking thing about this typology lies in its resemblance to the more recent versions of leadership contingency theories, such as that of House (1984). Both House and Strauss see the actor selecting one or other influence mode depending upon a series of perceptions of the relative power of oneself and the other party. Erez, Rim and Keider (1986) also provide data on the manner in which managers select influence strategies to suit particular circumstances. Among a sample of 206 Israeli managers, they found that the most frequently reported influence strategies *towards* colleagues were those which the researchers categorize as predominantly strong or powerful tactics, namely, rationality, assertiveness, blocking, sanctions, upward appeals and use of coalitions. However, when a similar sample were asked what influence strategies were received by them *from* colleagues, the most frequently reported were weak or low power tactics, namely, manipulation, exchange and passive blocking. Thus an equivalent set of influence attempts are quite differently labelled by those who initiate and those who receive such attempts. The labels assigned serve to emphasize one's own power and to devalue that of the other party.

The image of lateral relationships which emerges from almost all of the studies we have reviewed is one of difficulty, complexity and cautiousness. In the absence of organizational constraints, colleagues would no doubt find it easy enough to relate to one another. The difficulties which arise do so because each party represents a separate series of interests. Organizations frequently spell out rules and procedures which are to be used to regulate such conflicts. However, it is not unusual for adroit negotiators to covertly use other sources of meaning for interpreting and acting during the conflict, while openly appealing to legitimized rules and procedures to outmanoeuvre their opponents (Hickson et al., 1986). In the case of complex decision-making at senior levels in organizations, there may be so many parties to a decision that it becomes valuable for organizations to systematically analyse who are all the 'stakeholders' of each of the possible courses of future action (Mason and Mitroff, 1981). For our purpose the crucial issue is to analyse how the fact that one is representing others affects one's behaviour as a leader.

The representative role

One of the clearest conceptualizations of leadership as representation is that proposed by Likert (1961), in his 'linkpin' theory of organization. Likert saw an organization as a hierarchy of overlapping groups, wherein each member of each group acts as a representative of the other groups to which they concurrently belong. Thus a foreman acts as the representative of management when relating to workers, but as a representative of workers when relating to management. A salesman will represent the company to customers, but will also represent customers to other departments within the company.

Given the fact that a great deal of organizational life is conducted upon the basis of representation, one might hope that the massive research literature concerning bargaining and negotiation would illuminate this issue. Unfortunately, the individualistic emphasis of much American research in this field has led to the neglect of representation as a key variable. The great majority of research studies are concerned with two individuals bargaining with one another, with little or no reference to any broader constituency (Rubin and Brown, 1975; Pruitt, 1981). The word 'negotiation' has rather more of an implication of representation than does 'bargaining', but there is no consistency in the literature as to how the two terms have been employed. Morley and Stephenson (1977) make a more straightforward distinction between interpersonal bargaining and collective bargaining. A further difficulty with many studies has been their short-term nature, whereas negotiators in real settings almost always have to interpret negotiations in the context of past history and in anticipation of possible futures.

McGrath (1966) proposes a 'tripolar' model of collective bargaining whereby the bargainer is subject to R forces, A forces and C forces. R (Reference) forces constrain negotiators to adhere to their own group's position. A (Agreement) forces encourage negotiators to yield ground to their opponent. C (Community) forces are derived from the broader social system, and encourage the accomplishment of integrative solutions. From a more individualistic perspective, Pruitt (1981) proposes that the negotiator has three options, which parallel those of McGrath: competitive behaviour, unilateral concession and coordinative behaviour.

A series of experimental studies has shown that where negotiators are representing a constituency, their behaviour is more competitive than in individual bargaining. In some studies, subjects were told that they represented a group which would determine how much of the winnings would be given to the subject (Benton, 1972), while in others they were told that they were accountable to their group and would be either watched by them or required to meet them after negotiation was complete (Klimoski and Ash, 1974). It appears that either of these manipulations is able to produce the effect of enhanced competitiveness. Benton and Druckman (1974) told half of their subjects that their constituents wanted them to bargain 'hard and aggressively', while the other half were told that their constituents wanted them to 'stress compromise'. Subjects in the hard and aggressive condition acted similarly to those who were given no information as to their constituents' wishes. This implies that at least within the confines of this type of experiment, subjects assume that their constituents want them to be hard and aggressive. Carnevale, Pruitt and Britton (1979) and Carnevale, Pruitt and Seilheimer (1981) showed in a similar way that surveillance by one's constituents, whether visual or verbal, enhanced negotiators' wishes to look tough.

The pro-management bias of much of organizational psychology is emphasized by the scarcity of studies of trade union leadership and representation. A notable exception to this is the series of studies by Batstone, Boraston and Frenkel (1977). Basing their research upon a conception of negotiated order, they compared the effectiveness of those shop stewards whom they designated as 'leaders' and those whom they designated as 'populists'. Populists regarded themselves as delegates of the workforce, whereas leaders saw themselves as representatives. Leaders were more effective gaining benefits for their members. In doing so they were less likely to resort to strike action, more likely to guide their actions through reference to previously established union rules and principles, and more likely to have wide networks of contacts including those with management. These contacts enabled them to be well informed, to try out the feasibility of ideas and to reach informal agreements. The parallels with managerial leadership are clear.

The studies of both managers and union leaders provide a rather vivid picture of the pressures upon negotiators who are also representatives. They need to find ways both of accomplishing their task goals of obtaining a good bargain, and also of maintaining adequately harmonious relations with those to whom they must continue to relate. We consider now how far such processes may be analysed in terms of the concepts which proved useful in our earlier consideration of superior–subordinate relationships.

Universals and specifics in the negotiating role

In Chapter 7 we explored the usefulness of Misumi's (1985) distinction between the general functions of leadership and the specific behaviours which can give expression to those functions in a given context. As we have argued above, leaders as negotiators also need to fulfil certain general functions. Indeed the functions required of negotiators as expressed in general terms sound remarkably similar to Misumi's leadership functions. Effective negotiators need to satisfy the task or performance function of obtaining an adequate bargain, and they need to satisfy the interpersonal or maintenance function of preserving effective collaborative relations. The thrust of Misumi's distinction between the general and the specific is to suggest that these functions will be fulfilled in different ways in different settings.

Studies of the process whereby negotiators arrive at agreements are less numerous than those which look simply at the outcome of bargaining. Those studies which have been made also vary widely in whether they choose to study specific behaviours from minute to minute, or more general issues of overall strategy (Morley, 1986). Several researchers have been influenced by the case studies of industrial bargaining in the USA reported by Douglas (1962). Douglas distinguishes between what she calls 'interparty' and 'interpersonal' climates in negotiations. Effective negotiation is seen as a progression from an initial heavy emphasis upon the interparty demands of each protagonist, towards a cautious use of interpersonal linkages in first reconnoitring what may be possible and later agreeing upon possible compromises. If Douglas's model is correct, timing is a key element in negotiation, and a crucial issue would be how each party signals to the other their readiness to move towards the later stages of negotiation. Since not all disputes are resolved to the satisfaction of both parties, it may well be that the Douglas model gives an idealized view of negotiation. Nonetheless, it can be equally interesting to know whether negotiations which have an unsatisfactory outcome do so because of failure by one or other party to read correctly the signals given by the other.

Morley and Stephenson (1977) made detailed observations of a series of industrial negotiations within two British firms. The Douglas model received substantial support, with marked increases in the later stages of negotiation in procedural suggestions and accepting comments. Blind judges of tape recordings were less able to detect whether particular statements had been made by union or management in later stages than they were in the early stages. Of more interest in terms of the Misumi model is that Morley and Stephenson report that the atmosphere of the two negotiations was entirely different. In one company a controlled and orderly debate occurred with all remarks addressed to the chair. In the other a spontaneous, sometimes chaotic discussion occurred. We must presume that in either case the parties were familiar with the manner in which such negotiations were customarily conducted in their organization and knew how to use the format to accomplish their goals.

The management of conflict between colleagues is rarely handled in such a structured manner as are industrial negotiations. However, the variation in specific procedures employed can vary equally greatly. Hickson et al. (1986) describe one case of top management decision-making in which two directors fought a bitter struggle over several years. The directors each obtained separate estimates of the costs and benefits of a new project and sought to undermine the other. In another case, a decision to build a new plant was reached in a single meeting on the basis of information and costings which had been prepared and digested in advance of the meeting. Clearly one of these procedures was more effective than the other, but in less glaringly contrasted cases the effectiveness of different procedures will have more to do with how well they fit an existing organizational culture than with externally applicable criteria of effectiveness. A study of 56 decisions in three Dutch organizations was reported by the DIO International Research Team (1983). In line with the literature on negotiation, they found it necessary to distinguish four phases of decision-making: start-up, developmental, finalization and implementation. Conflict was greatest within the developmental phase and high participation at this stage was associated with high satisfaction with the ultimate outcome. This was not true for the other phases. The researchers argue that only by subdividing the different phases of decision-making is it possible to begin to see relationships between how decisions are made and their ultimate effectiveness.

Specific procedures for handling conflict will vary not only in terms of organizational culture but of national culture. Takahashi and Takayamagi (1985) studied decision-making within Japanese organizations. They found that, of 133 decisions, 18 were made through conference-debate, 41 by the senior manager and the remaining 74 through the procedures of informal peer consultation known in Japan as 'nemawashi'. This study will be discussed more fully in Chapter 10. Porat (1970) compared performance on the same simulated negotiation exercise by managers from five European countries. Differences were found in the planning and negotiating strategies used within each country. In Spain, both parties sought a settlement close to the community average. In Britain, managers sought to minimize costs, while union negotiators sought to achieve the community average. In Sweden and Denmark, negotiators gave less forethought to what might be the strategy of the other party, and perhaps because of this took longer in their bargaining and departed further from their previously planned strategy. In each of these four countries, negotiators favoured a package deal. However, in Switzerland negotiators preferred to set maxima and minima to be achieved on each issue separately. Porat suggests that these variations in strategy are to some extent explicable in terms of the prevailing climate of industrial relations in each of these countries during the 1960s. Given a standardized negotiation format, managers in each country gave that format meaning in terms of their own current experience.

Although the lateral relationships of managers have been much neglected, this chapter has sought to show that these relationships can be fruitfully studied using the same concepts as have been proposed for the study of superior–subordinate relations. In both cases the leader has certain general functions to fulfil and the cultural context defines how these may be best accomplished. In individualistic cultures, one's obligations to peers are not very clearly delineated, and this may account for the relative lack of attention to peer relationships by Western leadership researchers. In collectivist cultures, influence processes which Western researchers identify as conformity may be more salient. However, while most Western researchers have seen conformity as a restriction of the individual's liberty, in collective cultures peer relationships will provide the basis for the individual's identity. In Western cultures, individual leaders very frequently have less power over their colleagues than over their subordinates, and this dictates a somewhat different choice of specific influencing behaviours. Not all leaders are necessarily in conflict with their peers, but the management of the conflicts which do occur are more problematic because the bases for obtaining quick compliance are not available. Leaders have still less power over their own superiors, but they do nonetheless need to influence them. In the next chapter we examine the choices, individual and collective, which are open to them.

10
Upward Influence

The connotations which the word 'leadership' carries, at least in English, make it difficult to think of the exercise of upward influence as integral to leadership effectiveness. Yet from the time of Pelz's (1952) classic study it has been clear that leaders who are able to influence their superiors are also more likely to have influence over their subordinates. Pelz found that where supervisors in the Detroit Edison Company felt they had high influence with their own boss, subordinates' responses to participative leadership styles were more positive. While there is no reason to assume that such a linkage might always be present, it is highly plausible that subordinates' response to their leaders will be qualified by their perceptions of whether or not those leaders have any influence with higher management.

The implicit connotations of the concept of leadership go further than this. The general assumption that leadership entails a downward flow of influence not only causes us to give little attention to the leader's relation to the boss. It also makes it likely that if we do find that the leader has high influence with the boss we shall assume that this is something granted by the boss rather than stemming from the efforts of the leader to build such influence. To put it another way, if leaders have high upward influence we may see that as their good fortune, whereas if they do not we may assume that there is relatively little which they can do about it. This chapter will explore the view that these expectations about leadership are valid only for certain cultures. In particular, in Western cultures, leadership is seen as a set of individualistic actions. In consequence, upward influence is also seen as comprising a rather limited set of options open to the individual leader. It may be that by examining actions of leaders in more collective cultures we can gain a broader sense of the options, including also the possibility of collective actions by leaders. We start, however, with a consideration of the individualistic options.

Individual strategies

The individual leader who seeks to influence those at higher levels in the organization faces in an acute form the dilemmas discussed in the last chapter. Their power is likely to be inferior to that of the other party, so that in the case of direct conflict they are likely to be defeated. Of course, it may quite often be that a superior is willing to accept subordinate influence. The initial focus of this chapter is upon situations where this is not so. Sayles (1979) provides a case study originally reported by William F. Whyte of how a skilled manager faced up to such a situation within a US corporation:

> Wes Walsh . . . came in under a works manager widely known in the company for his type of autocratic control. Furthermore the offices of the two men were within a hundred feet of each other, so that although the boss was also responsible for other plants in the area, he could keep a close watch over Walsh. Nevertheless, Walsh was able to manage his plant very much according to his own notions, with little interference from above. How did he do it?
>
> The previous superintendent had been constantly at swords' points with the works manager. He advised Walsh to keep away from the manager's office. 'The less you see of that son of a bitch, the better you'll get along.' Though Walsh and his predecessor were good friends, Walsh decided to disregard this advice. If it hadn't worked for his predecessor, why should it work for him? Instead, Walsh saw to it that he had frequent contacts with the boss, and contacts that were initiated primarily by Walsh himself. He would drop in, with apparent casualness, to report progress or to seek the works manager's approval on some minor matter, carefully selected so that the boss could hardly veto it. Walsh was getting his boss used to saying yes to him!
>
> Major matters required longer interaction between the men, carefully prepared and staged. Consider the problems of the materials-reprocessing unit. With increasing volume of production going through the plant, it had become apparent to Walsh – as indeed it had to his predecessor – that this unit was inadequate for current requirements. It was too slow in operation and too limited in capacity. This condition seriously hampered production and created a storage problem in the plant. Materials awaiting reprocessing were strewn about in the operating area.
>
> Walsh's first step was to propose to the boss that he pick a time when he could spend a couple of hours with Walsh in the plant, so that they could look over some of the problems the plant was facing. The manager set the time and the two men spent the hours together on an inspection tour. To some extent the physical conditions the works manager saw spoke for themselves, but Walsh also supplemented these visual clues with an account of the way in which the inadequacies of the materials-reprocessing unit hampered his operation. The boss had to agree that the condition was undesirable. Eventually he asked, 'What do you propose?'
>
> Walsh was ready with a carefully worked out proposal for the purchase of a new type of reprocessing unit at a cost of $150 000. After a brief discussion of the impact of a new machine on costs and production, the works manager authorized the purchase. It is noteworthy that essentially the same proposal had been made more than once to the works manager by Walsh's predecessor. Made no doubt in a different form and fitting into a different pattern of interpersonal relationships, the good idea had received simply a flat rejection. (Sayles, 1979: 117–18)

While Walsh's specific actions might not have proved effective in all circumstances, his strategy for establishing upward influence is clear. He used a procedure of ingratiation to build up his power base over time. He gradually extended the range of issues over which he took the initiative, while not threatening his boss as he did so.

Porter, Allen and Angle (1981) provide a more extensive analysis of upward influence. They propose that all the modes of influence available in downward or lateral influence are also available to those seeking to exert upward influence. However, the probabilities of success are different, so that different types of influence will be the most frequently employed ones. They distinguish persuasion, manipulative persuasion and manipulation. These three influence modes differ in the degree to which it is acknowledged that an influence attempt is occurring. In persuasion, the influence attempt is overt and is likely to be based upon qualities of the influence agent such as expertise, prestige or prior trustworthiness. In manipulative persuasion the influence agent acknowledges that an influence attempt is occurring, but conceals the true objective of the attempt. For instance the influence agent might argue in favour of a particular policy, knowing that if that policy were implemented certain desired things would ensue, where these consequences were not known to the target of influence. In the third mode of influence, which Porter, Allen and Angle term manipulation, both the goal of influence and the fact that an influence attempt is occurring are concealed. This may be accomplished by withholding information whose disclosure might lead to undesirable decisions. Alternatively, where disclosure is inevitable the influence agent may seek to bury the damaging information in a mass of less important or irrelevant data. Porter, Allen and Angle found both of these manipulative strategies frequently reported in a survey of 30 small to medium-sized firms. Schlit and Locke (1982) report interviews with subordinates and with a separate set of superiors concerning successful and unsuccessful attempts at upward influence. In these samples, rational presentation of information was said to be much the most frequent mode of influence employed. The differences in findings of the two studies is probably accounted for by the fact that Schlit and Locke's subjects were much younger and had been with their organizations for a median period of only three years.

The essence of manipulation and of manipulative persuasion is that the influence agent seeks to be not found out. This exacerbates the difficulty of studying such forms of influence. Within an organization it may be important to the influence agent that some deception remain secret for a considerable time, perhaps until a desired promotion has been accomplished. Furthermore, as illustrated in the Wes Walsh case, an act of manipulation may need to be preceded by an extended period of ingratiation. Laboratory studies of the effects of ingratiation and manipulation can only hope to capture the strategies people use and their short-term effects. Jones and Pittman (1982) summarize twenty years of experimental research on ingratiation. They distinguish ingratiation, or the attempt to influence others to like one, from other strategies such as self-promotion, which they define as an attempt to influence others to see one as competent. Ingratiators in low power positions are found to engage in more conformity, more doing of favours, more attempts to show themselves in a positive light and more flattery of superiors than do those in equal power positions. However, the exercise of each of these tactics is bounded by the fact that excessive use of them will reveal their self-seeking purpose. Jones and Pittman note that the acceptability of these tactics varies from one setting to another.

In presenting the findings of Jones and Pittman, a distinction has been introduced between strategy and tactics. Jones and Pittman see the strategic purpose of all the types of self-presentation which they discuss as being the augmenting or maintaining of one's power in a relationship. They see the tactics to be preferred as varying from one culture or situational context to another. Their analysis thus parallels Misumi's distinction discussed earlier between the general and specific functions of leadership behaviour. Jones and Pittman suggest that the individualistic climate of American business may be more tolerant of ingratiation tactics than other sectors of US society. The survey data reported in Porter, Allen and Angle (1981) suggest that manipulation of information is a more widespread tactic: managers may enhance their reputations through the benefits of their indirect influence. Alternatively, it could be that respondents were more willing to acknowledge manipulation of information than other tactics which they may also have employed.

The willingness of manipulators to admit that they manipulate may be more of a problem in some cultures than others. Oksenberg (1971) attempted to test the Western view that the Chinese are more manipulative than Westerners. Using English and Cantonese versions of the Christie and Geis Machiavellianism scale, she found that Westernized Chinese students scored higher than did non-Westernized students. However, it would be rash to conclude very much from this. The Machiavellianism scale makes no distinction between strategy and tactics, and its items may well favour Western tactics rather than Chinese ones. As Yang (1986) points out the Machiavellianism scale has a different factor structure with Chinese respondents than it does with Western ones. A more fruitful approach is to study the ingratiation tactics which are favoured by different cultural settings.

Pandey (1986) proposes that ingratiation tactics are particularly important in situations of inequality, deprivation, limited resources and sociopolitical uncertainty. While he suggests that these conditions are widespread in many non-Western countries, his own studies are from India. Subjects in Pandey's studies report that ingratiation tactics are expected rather than deviant within the samples studied. Furthermore, in addition to the four tactics identified in the United States by Jones and Pittman, four further tactics were found to be important. These were self-degradation, emphasizing one's dependency upon the superior, name dropping, and opportunistic change as the situation changes. Further studies by Pandey have shown that where ingratiating tactics are used in India, the supervisor responds more positively. Bystanders perceived non-ingratiators more positively, but they saw ingratiators as better adjusted. Pandey and Bohra (1984) show that while ingratiation may be the tactic of choice in certain organizations in India, Indians may nonetheless prefer to avoid such organizations where that is possible. No range of studies equivalent to those by Pandey is available from any other non-American country. We therefore know little about how much ingratiation tactics vary from culture to culture. It is notable, however, that within a society as diverse as India, Pandey did not find substantial differences from one sample to another.

The individualistic strategies for upward influence outlined above are all predicated upon the wish of the influence agent to preserve or advance their own interests. They lay a disproportionate emphasis upon covert forms of influence and, with the exception of the Schlit and Locke study, give the impression that no superior ever willingly listens to communication from below. Most probably this imbalance arises because researchers think of upward influence which is willingly accepted as an instance of participative decision-making. In other words, in line with our earlier argument, they assume that the initiative for the process must have come from above rather than below. There are other notable omissions from the literature on upward influence. Both the surveys by Porter, Allen and Angle (1981) and that by Schlit and Locke (1982) focus upon the processes of communication between subordinate and superior. They thereby neglect other possibilities, such as the use of indirect communication. For instance, in the type of situation envisaged by the Graen leadership model, upward influence attempts may frequently be channelled through the subordinate with whom the leader has a strong vertical dyad linkage. These surveys also neglect other widespread practices, such as the lobbying of influential third parties.

In recent years a new type of attempted upward influence has emerged, which has become known as 'whistle-blowing'. Here the influence agent is so incensed by some moral or political outrage that they decide to abandon all caution and make it public, whatever the consequent risk to themselves. This may be done anonymously or publicly, but anonymity may often prove hard to preserve. Research into this phenomenon has thus far focused predominantly upon the circumstances that lead individuals to undertake a course of action which holds such substantial dangers for them (Near and Miceli, 1987). The broader question of whether or not whistle-blowing does succeed in terminating the injustices or outrages to which it is addressed has not been satisfactorily answered. We may expect that the effectiveness of whistle-blowing, like that of the various other strategies, will depend upon the cultural and organizational context within which it occurs. Most particularly we may expect that the success of this supremely individualistic strategy will rest upon the degree to which it recruits collective support both within and outside the organization where it occurs. It is time then to examine more collectivist strategies.

Collective strategies

One of the more disabling dichotomies of Western thought about organizations is that between lateral relationships and vertical relationships. One instance of this was the early organization theorists' stress on the difference between staff and line relationships. Another has been the divergence between social psychologists who think of leadership as a process of downward social influence and conformity as a process of lateral, peer influence. What makes such distinctions possible at all is our individualist ways of thinking. If we seek to understand the processes which occur within organizations in a collectivist society such as Japan, we are immediately in difficulty. Observers of Japanese society and of Japanese work organizations identify the small group as the basic unit. Such a group within a work organization will comprise a superior and a set of colleagues who will exercise a collective responsibility for the tasks assigned to their group (Smith, 1984). To analyse superior–subordinate relations in such a setting while ignoring peer relationships would be absurd. Since the Western authors of this book have inevitably fallen into the trap just outlined, by constructing separate chapters focused upon lateral and vertical relationships, there is some arbitrariness entailed in deciding where in the book to locate consideration of influence processes in Japanese organizations.

Misumi (1984) has given a concise account of the manner in which Japanese organizations succeed in being both hierarchical and peer-oriented. A characteristic decision-making procedure in many Japanese organizations is that known as *ringi*. Under this procedure proposals for future actions are initiated by junior members of the organization, circulated to their colleagues for approval and then submitted to the superior, who most typically approved the proposal. Decision-making procedures are not necessarily so smooth as this outline implies, but their goal is to arrive at consensus decision-making. In order to ensure that colleagues will indeed approve the proposal, extensive informal consultation known as *nemawashi* may be needed. The essence of this process is conveyed by the literal meaning of the word in Japanese: pruning and preparing the roots of a plant before transplanting it. The nearest English language equivalent, that of acquiring information 'on the grapevine', does not have the same implication of future action. Where such consultations indicate a lack of consensus, substantial delays and reformulations of the proposal before it is circulated may be necessary. Nor is it the case that the first the superior knows of the proposal is when the *ringi*-proposal lands on his desk. Often the subordinate may seek to anticipate what type of proposal the superior might wish to see formulated. On occasion the superior may even spell out informally what is required. However, where this is done the face-saving myth will be preserved that the proposal comes from the subordinate. This enables the proposal to be discussed and amended during the process of *nemawashi* without embarrassment to the superior.

The description of this type of decision-making runs the risk of portraying Japanese organizations simply as more participative than Western ones. As we have stated, Japanese organizations are not only peer-oriented but also hierarchical. The Japanese language makes it impossible to address someone without indicating whether they are regarded as having status which is superior, equal or inferior to one's own. The deference required towards one's superiors is a strong obligation. Thus the *ringi* procedure should be thought of not simply as a search procedure for innovation, but as a way of coming up with ideas and proposals which are likely to please the superior and to show him due deference.

Japanese organizations therefore provide a classic illustration of upward influence based not upon ingratiation and deception, but upon a collective sharing of responsibility. While some authors have argued that Japanese organizations are rapidly becoming more similar to those in the West (Marsh and Mannari, 1976), the recent survey by Takahashi and Takayamagi (1985) found 56 per cent of decisions still made through *nemawashi* rather than by the senior manager. Misumi (1984) cites data from a study by Takamiya in 1961 indicating that 82 per cent of firms were using the *ringi* procedure. It appears possible that what has happened is that the relatively formalized *ringi* procedure is in decline, while its essential component of *nemawashi* continues to find a use. Furthermore, other decision-making procedures with an equally collective basis have become increasingly popular. The best known of these is the Quality Circles movement. Initially seen as a 'modern' American innovation to replace old-fashioned procedures such as *ringi*, quality circles have put down much firmer roots in Japan than they have ever had in the West.

Many Japanese organizations take pride in recounting how many million suggestions for work improvements have been generated from quality circles composed of their shop-floor workers. The integration of vertical and lateral relations in Japanese organizations is illustrated by the way in which supervisors normally attend quality circle meetings, whereas in Western quality circles more emphasis is often placed on voluntary attendance and independence from supervision. It is clearly no simple matter to disentangle the high incidence of upward influence in Japanese organizations from a complex web of cultural and historical components. For present purposes it may be sufficient to assert that the exercise of upward influence is an integral part of the collective obligations of the Japanese work group to one another. The Japanese language has no indigenous word for leadership, most probably because it is self-evident that junior members of the group will show deference to their seniors. It is equally self-evident that they will show loyalty to their peers. Comparative surveys have shown that Japanese men lead the world in their commitment to work and the responsibilities which it entails (Meaning of Working International Team, 1987). Similarly, surveys have shown that a large sample of Japanese organizations reported wider power-sharing and upward influence than did samples of US and European organizations (Nonaka and Okamura, 1984). How far such collective responsibility will survive current pressures in Japan towards greater individualism remains to be seen.

One clue is provided by the existence of organizations in the West which do espouse a policy of collective upward influence. These are organizations which are participatively managed. Our concern here is not with the effect of participatory leader styles on subordinates, but rather with the effect of subordinate participation upon the superior. Manz and Sims (1987) debate, for instance, whether it is not paradoxical to appoint leaders to an organization which is based upon what they term 'self-management', a usage of the phrase which differs from that in this book. In the manufacturing organization which they studied, work teams prepare their own budget, undertake quality control, assign jobs, handle problems with machines and cope with team problems such as absenteeism. They have an elected team leader. Manz and Sims found that the team coordinators, who were the next level in seniority above the team leaders, had a role of providing encouragement. They encouraged teams to reward themselves for good performance, to be critical of failures to set performance goals, to evaluate whether these were achieved and to anticipate and rehearse future actions. While this list is rather different from that of leaders in more typical Western organizations, it nonetheless suggests that the team coordinators were engaging in substantial downward influence intended to maintain the existing organizational culture. This may prove to be essential where an organization seeks to create a culture which is less deeply rooted in existing national culture than is that of many Japanese organizations. Indeed it is not wholly clear from the Manz and Sims study how much upward influence work teams had: they clearly had been granted substantial autonomy, but overall strategy remained in the hands of senior management.

Similar ambiguities attend attempts to use the Japanese idea of quality circles within Western organizations. Steel and Shane (1986) reiew studies of how successful these have been. While many Western writers have written enthusiastically about the impact of this innovation, only two studies are yet available which compare changes occurring in comparable groups who are and are not participating in quality circles. Steel et al. (1985) found significant improvements where quality circles were introduced into a maintenance organization, but some deterioration in a hospital. No changes attributable to quality circles were found in the other study, which took place in three Navy organizations (Steel and Shane, 1986). Steel and Shane conclude that the impact of quality circles is in no sense automatic. It depends on such factors as the culture of the organization, what is asked of the circles and how long they continue. Thus a collective form of upward influence will only accomplish results if it is integrated into a compatible cultural context. As Hazama (1979) makes clear, there are a variety of ways of relating to one another collectively. Baseball and the tug-of-war are both collective team sports. But in baseball individual performances and roles are differentiated and each person's performance is assessed separately. In the tug-of-war the roles of team members are interchangeable. Some may contribute more than others, but only the overall team performance may be readily evaluated. Hazama proposes that Japanese work organization is much closer to the tug-of-war model.

Thus far, this chapter has contrasted manipulative or competitive individual strategies with collaborative collective ones. A third option should not be overlooked, namely that of competitive collective strategies. Such strategies have a good deal in common with the individual strategies discussed earlier, but they gain power from the involvement of suitably selected allies. Brager and Holloway (1978) distinguish campaigns from contests, on the basis of how much overlap there is in the positions of the two parties. Contests between subordinates and their superiors are unlikely, except in the instance of a whistle-blower who attracts some allies. Such contests may often finish up with the whistle-blower outside the organization and the contest being fought in the courts. Campaigns are more likely where a group of subordinates set out to amend some aspect of organizational policy. In this case they are often able to legitimize their campaign by pointing to the overlap in goals between themselves and superiors and to argue that the dispute is not about goals but about how goals shall be accomplished. If this basis can be established, the subordinate group are quite often able to exert some power by virtue of their collective access to networks of relevant information. Resnick (1980) argues that such campaigns require very careful analysis and planning, in order that appropriate tactics may be selected. He proposes that one should never fight a battle if there is a chance of losing it, a guiding principle which was clearly also important to Wes Walsh in his individual campaign.

Two types of influence?

The various writers who have discussed upward influence have proposed a variety of classifications of both the strategies and the tactics which may contribute towards effective upward influence. There are few strong connections between the various classifications. Furthermore, there is little consistency between writers in their understanding of what is to be thought of as strategy and what as tactics. Nonetheless, there does exist in most formulations the implicit assumption that power is a unitary variable, and that the less of it one has the more limited is the range of tactics which have any chance of success. A radical departure from this view has been put forward by the French psychologist Moscovici (1976). He proposes that if we are to understand the processes of social influence, we must distinguish what he initially termed majority influence from minority influence. In the context of the present discussion, 'majority' need not imply a numerical majority, but rather one or more persons with relatively high power. Similarly, 'minority' is to be interpreted as having low power. Minorities may be numerically outnumbered, but that is not the essential quality which defines them. Moscovici proposes that majority influence rests upon the power to reward or punish and that the effect which it creates is one of compliance. The exercise of real or anticipated majority power is direct.

By contrast, Moscovici sees minorities as exercising power in an indirect manner. The effects they accomplish are not compliance, but what he calls conversion. If conversion occurs the process will be slow and dependent upon the use of appropriate tactics by the minority. These tactics are those which will ensure that although the minority's views are overtly rejected by the majority, they are gradually established within the majority's view as an established viewpoint, and one which indirect measures will show that they take into account. The principal effective minority tactic identified by Moscovici is that of consistency. He argues that where a minority takes up a position which is consistent over time this induces others to believe that their position has some validity, even though the majority overtly rejects it. Numerous examples can be cited from history and contemporary politics where a consistently expressed minority view has subsequently become the policy of the majority.

Empirical studies undertaken by Moscovici and all of those who have subsequently tested his formulation take the form of laboratory studies of conformity. A minority of group members are instructed to give responses on a judgement task or an opinion scale which are counternormative. The majority group members are found to change their judgements, particularly where indirect measures are used (Moscovici, 1980). In terms of the conventional demarcations of topics within social psychology, these are studies of conformity rather than of leadership. How, one might ask, can these studies tell us anything about upward influence, if there are no power differentials represented within the experimental designs used? It is true that within Moscovici's own experiments, power differentials are represented only by the number of subjects making up the majority and the minority groups. Further studies by Mugny (1982) in Switzerland have employed a different procedure. Here opinion judgements are used which are known in advance to represent majority and minority viewpoints within Swiss society. Numerous tests have now been made of the minority influence hypothesis on both sides of the Atlantic (Maass and Clark, 1984). It appears that minorities in these types of experiments do frequently exert influence, sometimes indirectly, upon the majority. The results concerning consistency as the basis for such influence are rather more mixed. Some researchers in the USA have proposed that, following Hollander's earlier 'idiosyncrasy credit' model of leadership, early conformity by the minority will enhance their later influence with the majority. Some support was found for this view (Bray, Johnson and Chilstrom, 1982). Others have proposed that it is not simply the behavioural style of minority members which affects their influence but also the type of minority status a person has and whether the setting is one which favours innovation (Maass and Clark, 1984). For instance, a 'double minority' member (for example, someone who is both foreign and a woman) is found less influential than a single minority member (such as someone who is either foreign *or* a woman).

These findings suggest that, like the other research fields considered in this book, this research area has need of a distinction between the general and the specific functions of behaviour. The research tradition initiated by Moscovici has established that minorities in general do have some influence upon majorities. This effect had been overlooked by earlier researchers, perhaps partly because it was less conspicuous than are majority effects, but also because the dominant paradigm within US research into conformity considered only majority effects. Moscovici's success is thus an illustration of the operation of his own theory. However, when it comes to the question of the specific behaviours by which minorities achieve their effect the findings are more diverse. There is no reason why consistency, for instance, should always be construed by majorities in the same manner. In one setting consistency might appear evidence of conviction and honesty. In a second it could be seen as pig-headed, stupid or ignorant. To understand why particular minorities achieve their effect we should need to study their cultural setting, just as we would in the case of other aspects of leadership. The most recent research in this field (Moscovici, Mugny and Avermaet, 1985) shows wide variation in why different researchers think that minorities can achieve influence. Some see the effect as attributable to the social support they are able to give one another, either in reality or through the perception of the majority that those who agree so much must have a strong basis for their view. Others propose that minorities achieve influence because they are willing to tolerate continuing conflict on a topic they feel strongly about, whereas the more indifferent majority have a lesser willingness to continue conflict. Both of these are plausible and their importance may prove to vary by context.

The proposition that there are two fundamental forms of social influence is thus not well supported. There is no reason to analyse upward or lateral influence in terms of concepts which are different from those applicable to downward influence. The distinctiveness of upward influence lies in the constricted range of one's choices as to possible tactics. Furthermore, some writers are less optimistic than Moscovici about the prospects for substantial and lasting amounts of upward influence (Ng, 1980). We have considered already the classic formulation by Michels (1962) of the process whereby initially democratic organizations move toward autocracy. Rather similar recent findings are reported by Eccles (1981) who studied a factory which became a worker cooperative. The former trade union convenors became the effective management. Their lack of expertise pushed them toward an increasingly autocratic stance and they lost the confidence of the workforce.

The Dutch researcher Mulder (1975) has formulated a theory of 'power distance reduction', which arises partly from laboratory experiments and partly from field studies of Yugoslavian enterprises. He proposes that where representatives of a lower power group are given membership of a high power group, they inevitably compare themselves with other group members and find themselves deficient in relevant skills. The consequence of this is that far from reducing power differentials, the differentials are increased. Mulder suggests that this has frequently happened within works councils in Holland and Yugoslavia. Ng (1980) questions what he sees as the individualistic emphasis of the Mulder model. In line with the earlier sections of this chapter, he argues that more substantial equalization of power may prove possible where collective rather than individual action occurs. Thus the value of Moscovici's work may prove to be not his emphasis upon different types of influence, but his emphasis upon the manner in which a minority of two or more have a greater potential for influence than does a single individual.

11
Leadership Reconstructed

In the second half of this book, a view of leadership processes has been presented which stresses the manner in which leadership is interrelated with the context within which it arises. In this final chapter, we consider first how far such a view does or does not depart from more orthodox formulations. We then move on to the question of the practical implications of the view we have advanced.

When is a contingency theory not a contingency theory?

In a certain sense, once the notion of One Best Way of Leadership is discarded, all subsequent leadership theories must be contingency theories. That is, they must make some statement about what are the circumstances which affect the behaviour and effectiveness of leaders. In that sense, this book outlines a whole series of contingency theories. What are customarily thought of as contingency theories appear in Chapter 2. They are distinguishable from later versions by the fixed and static manner in which they envisage interactions occurring between leader and situation. The Fiedler model, for instance, treats LPC as a fixed entity which interacts with situational circumstances such as task structure in a fixed and predictable manner. Later contingency theories such as path–goal theory envisage more complex interactions between variables, for example on account of moderator variables. However, the static nature of the assumed interactions remains unchanged.

The cognitive revolution in psychology is reflected in Chapters 3 and 4. Here we see that the contingencies which regulate relations between leaders and followers are mediated by perceptual processes. The leader's environment is by no means a fixed and static entity. Leaders may construe it in a variety of ways, depending upon such things as the degree to which their attention is engaged by it, the reasons they invoke for what they perceive as happening, and their own particular motives at the time. In order to encompass the complexity of these processes, cognitive theorists have constructed models solely of what goes on within the leader. Such models no longer claim to be able to predict how the leader will act, except in so far as conscious behavioural intentions can be assumed to correspond to behaviour. They are process models, which tell us *how* the leader handles information, and what inferences leaders or others will draw from any particular circumstance. We might consider them as theories of perceptual contingency. Researchers in this tradition have encountered the same difficulty as did the older school of contingency theorists, namely the problem of how to select dimensions along which to classify events. The most active school at present is made up of those who have drawn upon achievement-oriented attribution theories, deriving originally from the work of Weiner et al. (1971). There is no apparent strong reason why variables such as success, failure, effort and ability should be the basis of such contingency models. They have certainly been shown to have some importance, but others which are less readily manipulable in short-term experiments may be equally important in mediating perceptual contingency. These may well include schemas which operate outside the level of the perceiver's awareness. As Weick (1976) and others have emphasized, *post hoc* rationalization of decisions and behaviour choices by leaders is at least as significant as conscious information processing.

The model of leadership advanced in Chapters 5 to 10 does not seek to resolve the difficulties faced by perceptual contingency theorists directly. Indeed there are good reasons to believe that the difficulties are insoluble in the form in which perceptual contingency theories present them. Instead, a different approach is attempted, which places the leader in a social context. Within this framework, all events have multiple potential meanings. Leaders (and everyone else) must constantly choose from which of a series of possible sources they will derive event meaning. Over time such choices become substantially routinized, to the point where some leaders expect that certain sources are most potent and active in defining meaning, whereas others may be for the most part disregarded. Nonetheless, leaders will be aware that each of the persons or groups who serve as definers of event *meaning* for them are also, among other things, definers of leadership *effectiveness* for them. Leaders must thus guide their actions so as to satisfy the evaluations of all members of their role set to some minimal degree.

Within work organizations, such satisficing will have two relatively distinct aspects, a task aspect and a relationship aspect. Such a distinction avoids the arbitrariness of aspects selected by perceptual contingency theorists, since it is based upon a simple logical pro-position. Where an organization of people is created for the purpose of carrying through some task, there are necessarily two aspects of organizational process, task-oriented ones and relationship-oriented ones, although all organizational events will carry implications both for the task and for relationships. Task-oriented aspects derive ultimately from an organization's linkages with external parties. Relationship-oriented aspects directly concern relationships with organization members. Reminiscent though it is of old-style contingency theories, this binary split is preferable to more recent proposals to analyse leadership behaviour into much larger numbers of categories, because the recent proposals make a confusion between *what* leaders need to do, and *how* they set about doing it in any particular context. Even the six problem areas into which aspects of events are organized in Chapter 6 are likely to have an importance in a given context which is only relatively high or relatively low, despite their applicability to organizations in general.

It is consideration of the context which differentiates our usage of the task and relationship dimensions from that of earlier researchers. They saw task or relationship orientation as fixed attributes of leader style. We see them as ways that leaders, followers and often observers make sense out of their experience of more specific actions. Every leader must struggle with the need to adapt their behaviour to forms which will be experienced by others in the role set in the manner intended. The English language does not lend itself readily to the process whereby leaders adapt their behaviour to the flow of events. Verbs have either active or passive overtones, where what is required is a word which avoids either of these. Leaders who are described as adapting their behaviour to the circumstance are by implication weak or passive in the face of others. If we say instead that leaders 'select' the behaviour suited to the circumstance, the implication becomes more powerful and controlling, with some suggestion that the leader takes little note of others' views. The metaphor we have adopted in the later chapters is that of negotiation, since that implies some kind of equality between the parties. The term is not ideal either, however, because it carries an overtone of overt, conscious bargaining. As the cognitive researchers have shown there is no reason to expect that all or even most of such processes occur at the level of conscious choice or judgement. Furthermore there is no reason why all such negotiation need necessarily influence someone to change. As the more radical critics have pointed out leadership may sometimes have a symbolic function which legitimates and makes sense of things as they are.

The event management model of leadership arises not only from an abstract theoretical position, but from the value-base of the authors. It provides a basis for interpreting, without overinterpreting, the function of symbolic organizational activities and of discussion, argumentation and influence attempts. Such processes do often have reward and punishment elements, upon which earlier behaviourist theorists preferred to focus. However, the perspective presented here is based on a belief that the behaviourist techniques of controlled experiment, 'objective' observation, and strictly structural modelling of organizational phenomena will only prove useful as a supplement to systems models which include both leaders and their role sets and which acknowledge the role of cognition.

The model can be summarized as a series of six propositions:

1 Sources of event meaning direct the leader's attention towards or away from various aspects of the work situation, thereby affecting what is seen and not seen, the conscious construction of events, and the tacit context which frames those events.

2 Sources of event meaning provide alternative schemas within which the leader can interpret events and link them to other events, in the past, present or future.

3 Sources of event meaning affect the relative salience of attitudes or schemas which determine the meaning placed on events.

4 Sources of event meaning determine the relative weight given to the elements used for explaining the causes of events and what information will be sought about those events.

5 Sources of event meaning determine the behavioural choice processes by which leadership actions are selected.

6 Sources of event meaning provide the context-rich vocabulary within which leadership actions are expressed.

The model as it stands is not directly open to empirical test. Its function is more of a heuristic one, suggesting aspects of leadership which need fuller exploration. Is our model too a contingency model? It has in common with perceptual contingency models an emphasis upon the manner in which the leader's actions are a function of the way in which events are construed. It suggests, however, that the more fully a leader leans upon one source of event meaning, and is judged effective by that source, the less likely it is that other sources will also find them effective. If it were necessary to force the model into one or another category, it has more in common with 'One Best Way' theories, in so far as it argues that what effective leaders must do is to take adequate care of two aspects of their role in relation to all members of their role set. Like Blake and Mouton (1964) it asserts that the overall strategy of management is the same in every setting. Also like Blake and Mouton it sees that the tactics for achieving that goal are highly variable. However, Blake and Mouton have used their insight to develop training programmes which identify and label the optimal '9,9' strategy. In contrast, we believe it more important to develop the skills of diagnosing and using the differing tactics which are appropriate responses to events that occur in each cultural or organizational context.

The neglect of self-management

This book has perpetuated one of the greatest errors of omission in the field of leadership study by giving little attention to the processes whereby leaders rely upon themselves as sources of strength or support. As was proposed by the fifth and most radical remedy for the ailing field of leadership in Chapter 3, we may be subject to the influence of leaders from above much less than we think. If we are indeed on our own to some substantial degree, self-management becomes a key issue. Treatments of the topic tend to appear in books on managerial stress, but not in the context of theorizing about leadership. Even where there is evidence of others' influence upon us, as Tsui's (1984b) study showed, the greatest divergence in her sample was between managers' expectations of themselves and others' expectations of them. Such a conflict indicates that under many circumstances, leaders have no option but to rely upon themselves as a source of event meaning. To do otherwise is to risk becoming a pawn in the hands of one's role set. This need is allowed for in the event management model, through what is there termed self-management. Management of oneself could be seen as the central element in the process of leadership. It may be, as we have argued, that leaders need to listen to and negotiate with their sources of event meaning, but still more importantly, they need to know when to listen to them and when not to. Like the skilled driver of a car, they need to know when to attend to crucial signals, and when it is in order to attend to something else. We have seen that the life of most managers is a constant succession of 'attention-interrupt' signals, so that the management of oneself in the face of overload is often critical.

Some findings relevant to this issue were obtained in the classic study of role conflict undertaken by Kahn et al. (1964). They showed that experienced role conflict was sometimes attributable to the incompatibility of demands from one's role set and sometimes to a lack of personal skills or attributes which might be required either in a specific role or more generally in any managerial role. The most frequent mode of coping with role conflict was found to be withdrawal from communication with the parties whose demands were not being met. Kahn et al. see withdrawal as a short-term solution which makes likely a more acute conflict in the longer run. Where organizational procedures made communication unavoidable, it was found that managers who were most vulnerable to conflict were those who were neurotic, introverted, rigid and status-oriented. Such findings are likely to prove culturally relative. For instance, one could imagine circumstances under which flexible people rather than rigid ones are likely to be the most stressed. We also have very little firm information about the incidence of role conflict within collective cultures. It is likely that in such settings, even more than was the case with Tsui's Californian data, that the principal conflict will be that between oneself as leader and the entire role set.

Much of the literature on stress within organizations has utilized mechanistic conceptions of empirically specifiable stressors acting upon specified types of individual. Such formulations ignore the cyclical process which we have emphasized, whereby the meanings of events experienced by role occupants are constructed through a process of negotiation (Handy, 1985). To apply such thinking to the exercise of self-management by the individual leader, we need to see self-management neither as a set of personal skills or qualities, nor as something which certain organizational structures permit, but as an instance of person–situation interaction. In other words, the leaders who are able to exercise self-management will be those who can define clear meanings both for the situational pressures they face and for the specific actions which will be effective in coping with them in that setting. One should not exclude the possibility that under certain circumstances, leaders might conclude that the most effective coping strategy would be to leave a situation which was beyond their power to change.

While individualistic self-management remains an under-researched topic, collective schemes of self-management have received extensive attention. Some recent researchers do indeed use the term 'self-management' (Manz and Sims, 1987), but much more widely used terms have been participative decision-making, autonomous work groups, industrial democracy and so forth. There is no scope within this book to review this literature in any detail, although some aspects of it have been touched on in earlier chapters. Wagner and Gooding (1987) report a meta-analysis of 70 studies of participation. They found no overall average effect of participation and attributed differences found in the various studies to differences in the research measures used. As Locke and Schweiger (1979) comment, much of the confusion between researchers in this area has arisen because of a neo-behaviouristic assumption that work groups who have autonomy would always be expected to react in the same way. Thus the way forward for researchers in this area, as we have argued it is for students of leadership also, is to attend to context and culture and the manner in which it defines and redefines the meaning of participation. Participation in a Japanese work team, a Yugoslav Workers' Council, an autonomous work group in the Volvo car plant or a 'self-managed' US software house are only in the broadest sense the same thing.

This is partly because in each of these settings the negotiated meanings of participation will vary according to the past and present relationships of those involved. Equally important, however, are the supra-organizational demands and constraints which delimit participation in different countries. Governmental legislation, for instance, falls outside of what would ordinarily be thought of as leadership. Comparative studies of industrial democracy in different European countries have nonetheless shown that such legislation has a major effect on the nature and meaning of participation in different countries (IDE International Research Group, 1981). As an example of such effects, Drenth and Koopman (1983/4) describe the Dutch system of *werkoverleg*. This is 'a system of regular and formalised consultation between a superior and his subordinates as a group, aimed at participation in and influence upon decision-making, especially with respect to their own work situation'. In effect, the 1983 Dutch Works Council Act requires that all parties view workplace events as having aspects affecting workers' lives as well as the more traditional ways of viewing workplace events. A second-order collaborative process is thus imposed upon leaders which legitimizes the negotiation of meaning by upward influence (Koopman et al., 1981). A further example can be drawn from recent developments in mainland China (Peterson, in press). In seeking to apply Misumi's PM leadership theory within China, the project directors found themselves required to add a third dimension to their leadership measures. This dimension referred to the leader's moral character, and reflects such questions as how much the leader adheres to Party Policy, which includes specifications of how leaders should relate to subordinates. Here also, therefore, is an instance of the manner in which the interpretations put upon events are part and parcel of their cultural context. While this book has striven to avoid describing leaders as wholly autonomous individuals, more remains to be done in showing the degree to which 'self-management', whether it be individual or collective, can occur only within a culture which gives that notion meaning.

Organizations which seek to create a culture within which individuals may use self-management will need to attend both to structural determinants of culture and to the skills of those whom they recruit. If this has been adequately done, the goal of leadership training then becomes the development of the situationally specific attributes which enable managers to choose best how to cope with their particular dilemmas. Let us consider how this may best be done.

The training of leaders

Not only researchers and theorists but other individuals stand to benefit from an understanding of their roles within the many organizations which comprise their environment. Autonomy and choice are sometimes paradoxical concomitants of the knowledge of external constraint. Formal training as well as social learning in less-structured settings can be carried out effectively only when we understand the processes of personal and organizational change. It is apparent from the past few decades that such changes are not guaranteed by any amount of training. Training only begins to have some chance of success when it has some clearly thought-out purpose which is shared by those who are to be trained.

It will be apparent from our analysis that we see effective leadership training not as a matter of inculcating appropriate styles, but of training for choice. As Hosking and Morley (1988) emphasize, leaders do rather frequently have the requisite social skills to carry through the processes of influence and negotiation. What they lack is the ability to 'find their way around', or develop the network of contacts which give them the necessary know-how. Only when this is accomplished can they exercise their existing social skills to best advantage. Leaders therefore often need to learn how to choose which sources of information or demands upon them to attend to, and how to choose which specific behaviours would stand the best chance of implementing their intentions. They will learn a good deal about such things when they join the organization and are exposed to its socialization processes (Van Maanen and Schein, 1979). But the way in which these processes of socialization are carried through by most organizations is likely to teach more about the demands and constraints upon one than about the choices. Marshall and Stewart (1981a, b) asked a sample of British middle managers how much choice they experienced in their jobs. The majority of respondents indicated that they were not often conscious of choosing how to act. They saw whether or not they had choice as something which was largely fixed for them by external constraints. They were mostly not dissatisfied with this situation. A minority of the sample reported being much more aware of choice processes, and these were the ones who also thought more actively about planning their own career progress. The studies by cognitive psychologists reviewed in Chapter 4 should caution us against concluding that because most managers are not often aware of choices they do not in fact make many choices. Their choices may indeed be predominantly programmed ones.

A first priority in leadership training might therefore be to increase trainees' awareness that even the decision to operate upon the basis of choices which are largely programmed ones is itself an implicit act of choice. In many circumstances it may also be the right choice, but the purpose of training should be to subject this to systematic review. Stewart (1982b) presents a series of simple exercises designed to help managers identify who are the people they most need to influence and what choices are open to them in doing so. The exercises are constructed at the level of diagnosing one's goals and strategies, and then move on to the more specific level of how one might implement choices within the existing demands and constraints.

If the implementation of strategy is dependent upon a clear knowledge of existing organizational culture, it follows that most valid training will need to be conducted within specific organizations. Training for groups drawn from a heterogeneous range of organizations may have value at a more general level in raising awareness of the possible range of ways of being a leader. Schein and Bennis (1964) proposed that 'learning how to learn' was a key element in successful human relations training. In a similar way, learning how to choose would be important here. But this is unlikely to have a lasting impact unless more specific connections can be made with the organization's unique culture. An element connecting the training of individuals with the culture of many organizations is that nomination of an individual to attend a particular course is treated as a symbolic statement that the individual will be promoted in the near future. In such circumstances, the impact of the course may have little to do with its content.

The past twenty years have seen a decreasing emphasis by trainers upon management development, and its replacement by greater investment in organizational development. This reflects an increased awareness of the need to make better connections between a specific organizational culture or problem and the use of resources to act upon it. We have discussed in Chapter 7 Schein's ideas as to how organizational culture may be diagnosed. Such diagnoses are likely to generate the maximum likelihood of creating change where they are arrived at by members of the organization themselves. This diagnostic work is best aided by the skills which Schein (1987) defines as process consultation. By this he means the feeding back to a group of observations or queries about the processes whereby they interact with one another or with third parties. It is interesting that in the first edition of Schein's book, which appeared in 1969, he sees process consultation as a set of skills to be employed by external consultants. In the second edition he argues that these skills are of equal use to line managers. The evolution in Schein's ideas most probably parallels the evolution of culture within those large US corporations who have invested in training over the same period. The specific procedures which will prove effective are most unlikely to be the same around the world, or even within organizations having different cultures in the same country. One admirable quality of those who practise organizational development has been their willingness to give public accounts of their failures as well as their successes (e.g. Mirvis and Berg, 1977), which enables some cumulative learning to occur in a field which is well provided with pitfalls. Lindsay and Dempsey (1983) give an account of 'ten painfully learned lessons', which derive from their experience as Americans running management training in mainland China. Steele (1977), who is also American, reports an equal lack of success in winning the confidence of British business firms. In each of these cases communication between consultant and client went awry, and differences in culturally determined ways of rectifying misunderstandings seemingly prevented the situations from being retrieved.

These general comments about the training of leaders should not be read as implying any specific focus for particular training programmes. Effective training always arises out of some diagnosed need, and the suggestions above would need adaptation to the specific circumstances identified. Once such a focus was determined, a wide variety of established training procedures could be useful in diagnosing culture, identifying choices and rehearsing alternative solutions. It might appear that these proposals concerning leadership training no longer approximate what in time past has been thought of as leadership training. They are nonetheless a clear consequence of ceasing to think of leaders individualistically and of locating them instead within their context. Furthermore, the proposals allow the possibility that leaders and their contexts constantly redefine one another, rather than simply coexist. Contrasting strategies, such as that advanced by followers of the Fiedler contingency theory, propose matching leaders to their appropriate context or else training them to change their environment (Fiedler and Chemers, 1984). Recent studies by Jago and Ragan (1987) indicate that the 'Leader Match' manual fails to classify more than 75 to 80 per cent of leaders to the context specified as appropriate for them by Fiedler's contingency theory. Even if Leader Match were successful in assigning people in the manner specified by the theory, we should still have the problem that, as we saw in Chapter 2, the behaviour of high and low LPC leaders does in fact vary by situation. An altogether safer procedure is therefore to employ training methods which enable the meanings placed on the behaviours of leaders and their role set to be assessed *in situ* by those whom it affects.

Leadership in a multicultural world

The implicit assumption of the previous section was that within most organizations there exists an adequately consensual culture which defines the meaning of events. This is at best a convenient myth, since many organizations are segmented between groups based on social class, who place rather different meanings on events. Most usually, these polarized sets of meanings do not encounter one another directly, due to a series of intermediate levels in the power hierarchy who buffer each culture from the other.

There is a range of increasingly frequent circumstances under which differing sets of cultural assumptions do collide within the same organization. These include situations where multinational firms set up subsidiaries in foreign countries, and situations where organizations merge or acquire ownership of one another. Numerous anecdotes are available of the misunderstandings which rather often arise under such circumstances. More systematic studies indicate that with adequate selection and training, the incidence of such problems may be at least reduced. Tung (1982, 1987) reports a survey of the preparations for expatriate assignments by multinationals and of their outcome. She found that a substantially higher proportion of US expatriate managers than European or Japanese ones were judged by their employers to have failed and were recalled from their assignment. In each sample the extent of prior training was linked to the failure rate. Among the reasons she cites for the higher failure rate among US multinationals are shorter assignments, more short-term evaluation procedures, less language training, less comprehensive overseas support, shorter experience of multinational operation and higher job mobility within the USA. Adler (1981) found that for Canadian expatriate managers the return home was the more stressful transition, since little overt attention was paid to it by the organization and little interest was expressed in the potential value to the organization of the multicultural experience which the manager had acquired.

Multinationals differ in the manner in which they seek to manage differences between host-country culture and the culture of the multinational itself. IBM is particularly well known as a company that seeks to create a climate which transcends national boundaries. Some British firms stand at the opposite end of the spectrum, granting substantial autonomy to subsidiaries and exerting only financial controls. Studies by Negandhi (1985) show that US multinationals within six developing countries use many more 'advanced' management techniques than do locally owned firms. This was true also for European and Japanese multinationals in these countries.

The majority of recent studies of multinationals concern the performance of Japanese firms in Western countries (Smith and Misumi, 1989). Such studies quickly make clear that the widespread Western myth that there is one single style of Japanese management has no basis: Japanese companies vary in culture just as much as do Western ones. Takamiya and Thurley (1985), for instance, studied four electronics plants in Britain, two of them Japanese-owned, one locally owned and one US-owned. One of the Japanese-owned plants was said to be much more 'people-oriented' in contrast to the 'task-oriented' climate at the other. The authors found the Japanese plants to be more successful, and concluded that this was due not to more advanced technology, but to superior production management techniques, more flexible working practices, single union representation and better interdepartmental cooperation. These findings are particularly interesting since they suggest that some of the collectivism which characterizes Japanese culture has found expression within the two British plants studied. In case studies of a broader sample of Japanese plants in Britain, White and Trevor (1983) indicate that such accomplishments are by no means always found. Japanese banks, for instance, with a predominantly middle-class workforce have had much more difficulty in establishing systems of collective responsibility than have several of the electronics firms who have recruited predominantly working-class employees from areas with strong community spirit. Where a procedure is not readily assimilable within Western culture, the Japanese may continue using it among themselves, at the risk of creating later misunderstandings. Trevor (1983) cites some Japanese-owned British companies where the *ringi* decision procedure was used by the Japanese, but British managers within the plant were not aware of this. Other firms have successfully incorporated British managers into *ringi*.

Studies by Pascale in the USA also show that Japanese multi-nationals have been selective in the manner in which they have transposed company culture to a US context. In fact, Pascale (1978) and Pascale and Maguire (1980) found as many differences between Japanese firms in the USA and Japanese firms in Japan as there were between American firms in the USA and Japanese firms in Japan. The evidence suggests that those Japanese multinationals who have done well in the West have been those who have kept their strategy firmly in mind, but have adapted their practices to take account of the meanings placed on behaviours in Western countries. The substantial amount of prior training for expatriate Japanese managers which was reported by Tung no doubt aids this process.

The clash of cultural expectations brought about by mergers and acquisitions is likely to be at least as acute as that caused by crossing national boundaries. This is because they are frequently determined by financial considerations with little thought given to the compatibility of the organizational cultures concerned. In contrast, the setting up of foreign subsidiaries often follows extensive planning and preparation. Furthermore the victors of takeover battles are likely to be critical of existing organizational culture and to believe that it must be changed, either coercively or in some other way. Walter (1985) proposes that these dynamics will be strongest in the case of takeovers by firms with highly similar production or distribution systems and less acute in the cases of mergers with one's suppliers or takeovers by holding companies. Buono, Bowditch and Lewis (1985) studied a merger between two adjacent savings banks. The nickname of the Chief Executive of the first bank was 'The Buddha' while that of the second was 'Dennis the Menace'. In line with this, the culture of Bank A was people-oriented, while that of Bank B was more task-centred. Members of both banks were initially favourable, but after what became known as the 'Christmas massacre', when some redundancies were announced, members of Bank A became disillusioned and the culture of Bank B came to be dominant.

This brief exposition of the problem facing multinationals and others confronted by divergent cultures indicates that the heterogeneity of organizational culture makes more acute the problems addressed earlier in this chapter. Such organizations will have greater need than most of consultancy and training designed to clarify choices and work out how those choices are to be implemented. It is precisely in such circumstances that the suggestions of Meindl, Ehrlich and Dukerich (1985), that leadership is no more than a romantic myth, are least likely to be true. The making and remaking of cultures is a hard business.

In concluding your reading of our book we ask you, the reader, to consider which constituency in the domain of leadership and leadership research you identify with. Reflecting upon this may provide some guidance as to which aspects of our presentation will have been most readily assimilable to your own position. Our own world views lead us to see our presentation as fair-minded, if not entirely neutral. Your own cultural interpretive frameworks may well lead you to an alternative evaluation. We leave you with the paradox, that if this is so, it would constitute some kind of evidence in favour of the type of model we have presented.

References

Abdel-Halim, A.A. (1981) 'Personality and Task Moderators of Subordinate Responses to Perceived Leader Behavior', *Human Relations*, 34: 73-88.

Abdel-Halim, A.A. (1983a) 'Effects of Task and Personality Characteristics on Subordinate Responses to Participative Decision-Making', *Academy of Management Journal*, 26: 477-84.

Abdel-Halim, A.A. (1983b) 'Power Equalization, Participative Decision-Making and Individual Differences', *Human Relations*, 36: 683-704.

Ackerson, L. (1942) *Children's Behavior Problems: Relative Importance and Inter-correlations Among Traits*. Chicago: University of Chicago Press.

Adler, N.J. (1981) 'Re-Entry: Managing Cross-Cultural Transitions', *Group and Organization Studies*, 6: 341-56.

Adler, N.J., R. Doktor, and S.G. Redding (1986) 'From the Atlantic to the Pacific Century: Cross-Cultural Management Reviewed', *Journal of Management*, 12: 295-318.

Alderfer, C.P. (1972) *Existence, Relatedness and Growth*. New York: Free Press.

Al-Gattan, A.R. (1985) 'Test of the Path–Goal Theory in the Multinational Domain', *Group and Organization Studies*, 10: 429-46.

Allan, P. (1981) 'Managers at Work: A Large-Scale Study of the Managerial Job in New York City Government', *Academy of Management Journal*, 24: 613-19.

Argyle, M., G. Gardner and F. Cioffi (1958) 'Supervisory Methods Related to Productivity, Absenteeism and Labour Turnover', *Human Relations*, 11: 289-304.

Arvey, R.D. and J.M. Ivancevich (1980) 'Punishment in Organizations: A Review, Propositions and Research Suggestions', *Academy of Management Review*, 5: 123-32.

Ashour, A.S. (1973) 'The Contingency Model of Leadership Effectiveness: An Evaluation', *Organizational Behavior and Human Performance*, 9: 335-55, 369-76.

Ashour, A.S. and G. Johns (1983) 'Leader Influence Through Operant Principles: A Theoretical and Methodological Framework', *Human Relations*, 36: 603-26.

Avolio, B. and B.M. Bass (1988) 'Charisma and Beyond: Research Findings on Transformational and Transactional Leadership', pp. 29-49 in J.G. Hunt, B.R. Baliga, H.P. Dachler and C.A. Schriesheim (eds), *Emerging Leadership Vistas*. Boston, MA: Lexington.

Ayman, R. and M.M. Chemers (1983) 'Relationship of Supervisory Behavior Ratings to Work Group Effectiveness and Subordinate Satisfaction among Iranian Managers', *Journal of Applied Psychology*, 68: 338-41.

Bales, R.F. and P. Slater (1955) 'Role Differentiation in Small Social Groups', pp. 259-306 in T. Parsons, R.F. Bales and E.A. Shils (eds), *Family, Socialisation and Interaction Process*. Glencoe, IL: Free Press.

Barnard, C. (1938) *The Functions of the Executive*. Cambridge, MA: Harvard University Press.

Barnlund, D.C. (1962) 'Consistency of Emergent Leadership in Groups with Changing Tasks and Members', *Speech Monographs*, 29: 45-52.

Bass, B.M. (1965) *Organizational Psychology*. Boston: Allyn and Bacon.

Bass, B.M. (1985) *Leadership and Performance Beyond Expectations*. New York: Free Press.

Bass, B.M. and P.C. Burger (1979) *Assessment of Managers: An International Comparison.* New York: Free Press.

Bass, B.M., D.A. Waldman, B.J. Avolio and M. Bebb (1987) 'Transformational Leadership and the Falling Dominoes Effect', *Group and Organization Studies*, 12: 73–87.

Batstone, E., I. Boraston and S. Frenkel (1977) *Shop Stewards in Action.* Oxford: Basil Blackwell.

Bennis, W.G. and B. Nanus (1985) *Leaders: the Strategies for Taking Charge.* New York: Harper & Row.

Benton, A.A. (1972) 'Accountability and Negotiation between Group Representatives', *Proceedings of the 80th Annual Convention of the American Psychological Association*, 227–8.

Benton, A.A. and D. Druckman (1974) 'Constituent's Bargaining Orientation, and Intergroup Negotiations', *Journal of Applied Social Psychology*, 4: 141–50.

Berry, J.W. (1980) 'Introduction to Methodology', pp. 1–28 in H.C. Triandis and R.W. Brislin (eds), *Handbook of Cross Cultural Psychology, Volume 2.* Boston, MA: Allyn and Bacon.

Bettman, J.R. (1979) *An Information Processing Theory of Consumer Choice.* Reading, MA: Addison-Wesley.

Beyer, J.M. (1981) 'Ideologies, Values and Decision-Making Organizations', pp. 166–202 in P.C. Nystrom and W.H. Starbuck (eds), *Handbook of Organizational Design, Volume 2: Remodeling Organizations and their Environments.* Oxford: Oxford University Press.

Biddle, B.J. and E.J. Thomas (1966) *Role Theory: Concepts and Research.* New York: Wiley.

Bizman, A. and S. Fox (1984) 'Managers' Perception of the Stability of Workers' Positive and Negative Behaviors', *Journal of Applied Psychology*, 63: 40–3.

Blackler, F. and C. Brown (1980) *Whatever Happened to Shell's New Philosophy of Management?* London: Saxon House.

Blake, R.R. and J.S. Mouton (1964) *The Managerial Grid.* Houston: Gulf.

Blake, R.R. and J.S. Mouton (1982) 'Theory and Research for Developing a Science of Leadership', *Journal of Applied Behavioral Science*, 18: 275–92.

Blanchard, K. and S. Johnson (1982) *The One Minute Manager.* New York: William Morrow.

Blau, G.J. (1985) 'Relationship of Extrinsic, Intrinsic and Demographic Predictors to Various Types of Withdrawal Behavior', *Journal of Applied Psychology*, 70: 442–50.

Blau, P.M. and W.R. Scott (1963) *Formal Organizations: A Comparative Approach.* London: Routledge & Kegan Paul.

Bond, M.H. and K.K. Hwang (1986) 'The Social Psychology of Chinese People', pp. 213–66 in M.H. Bond (ed.), *The Psychology of the Chinese People.* Hong Kong: Oxford University Press.

Bowers, D.G. (1963) 'Self-esteem and the Diffusion of Leadership Style', *Journal of Applied Psychology*, 47: 135–40.

Bowers, D.G. (1975) 'Hierarchy, Function and the Generalizability of Leadership Practices', pp. 167–80 in J.G. Hunt and L.L. Larson (eds), *Leadership Frontiers.* Kent, OH: Kent State University Press.

Bowers, D.G. and S.E. Seashore (1966) 'Predicting Organizational Effectiveness With a Four-Factor Theory of Leadership', *Administrative Science Quarterly*, 11: 238–63.

Brager, G. and S. Holloway (1978) *Changing Human Service Organizations: Politics and Practice.* New York: Free Press.

Bray, D.W., R.J. Campbell and D.L. Grant (1974) *Formative Years in Business: A Long-Term A T and T Study of Managerial Lives*. New York: Wiley.

Bray, R.M., D. Johnson and J.T. Chilstrom (1982) 'Social Influence by Group Members with Minority Opinions', *Journal of Personality and Social Psychology*, 34: 78–88.

Brayfield, A.H. and W.H. Crockett (1955) 'Employee Attitudes and Employee Performance', *Psychological Bulletin*, 52: 396–424.

Broussine, M. and Y. Guerrier (1985) *Surviving as a Middle Manager*. London: Croom Helm.

Bryman, A. (1986) *Leadership and Organizations*. London: Routledge & Kegan Paul.

Bryman, A., M. Bresnen, J. Ford, A. Beardsworth and T. Keil (1987) 'Leader Orientation and Organizational Transience: An Investigation Using Fiedler's LPC Scale', *Journal of Occupational Psychology*, 60: 13–20.

Buono, A.F., J.L. Bowditch and J.W. Lewis (1985) 'When Cultures Collide: The Anatomy of a Merger', *Human Relations*, 38: 477–500.

Burgelman, R.A. (1983) 'A Process Model of Internal Corporate Venturing in the Diversified Major Firm', *Administrative Science Quarterly*, 28: 223–44.

Burns, J.M. (1978) *Leadership*. New York: Harper & Row.

Bussom, R.S., L.L. Larson and W.M. Vicars (1982) 'Unstructured, Nonparticipant Observation and the Study of Leaders' Interpersonal Contacts', pp. 31–49 in J.G. Hunt, U. Sekaran and C.A. Schriesheim (eds), *Leadership: Beyond Establishment Views*. Carbondale, IL: Southern Illinois University Press.

Calder, B.J. (1977) 'An Attribution Theory of Leadership', pp. 179–204 in B.M. Staw and G.R. Salancik (eds), *New Directions in Organizational Behavior*. Chicago: St. Clair.

Carlson, S. (1951) *Executive Behavior*. Stockholm: Stromberg.

Carlyle, T. (1907) *Heroes and Hero Worship*. Boston: Adams (first published 1841).

Carnevale, P.J.D., D.G. Pruitt and S.D. Britton (1979) 'Looking Tough: the Negotiator under Constituent Surveillance', *Personality and Social Psychology Bulletin*, 5: 118–21.

Carnevale, P.J.D., D.G. Pruitt and S. Seilheimer (1981) 'Looking and Competing: Accountability and Visual Access in Integrative Bargaining', *Journal of Personality and Social Psychology*, 40: 111–20.

Cartwright, D. and A. Zander (eds) (1953) *Group Dynamics: Research and Theory*. New York: Harper & Row.

Carver, C.S. and M.F. Scheier (1981) *Attention and Self-Regulation: a Control Theory Approach to Human Behaviour*. New York: Springer-Verlag.

Carver, C.S. and M.F. Scheier (1982) 'Control Theory: A Useful Conceptual Framework for Personality-social, Clinical and Health Psychology', *Psychological Bulletin*, 92: 111–35.

Chemers, M.M. and G.J. Skrzypek (1972) 'Experimental Test of the Contingency Model of Leadership Effectiveness', *Journal of Personality and Social Psychology*, 24: 171–7.

Chomsky, N. (1959) 'Review of *Verbal Behavior*, by B.F. Skinner', *Language*, 35: 26–58.

Christie, R. and F. Geis (1970) *Studies in Machiavellianism*. New York: Academic Press.

Cohen, M.D., J.G. March and J.P. Olsen (1972) 'A Garbage Can Model of Organizational Choice', *Administrative Science Quarterly*, 17: 1–25.

Cooke, R.A. and D.M. Rousseau (1981) 'Problems of Complex Systems: A Model of System Problem Solving Applied to Schools', *Education Administration Quarterly*, 17 (3): 15–41.

Cooper, R. (1966) 'Leader's Task Relevance and Subordinate Behaviour in Industrial Work Groups', *Human Relations*, 19: 57–84.

Cornelius, E.T. and F.B. Lane (1984) 'The Power Motive and Managerial Success in a

Professionally-Oriented Service Industry Organization', *Journal of Applied Psychology*, 69: 32–9.

Crouch, A. and P.W. Yetton (1988) 'The Management Team: An Equilibrium Model of Manager and Subordinate Performance', pp. 107–27 in J.G. Hunt, B.R. Baliga, H.P. Dachler and C.A. Schriesheim (eds), *Emerging Leadership Vistas*. Boston, MA: Lexington.

Cummings, T. (1978) 'Self-Regulating Work Groups: A Sociotechnical Synthesis', *Academy of Management Review*, 3: 625–34.

Curry, J.P., D.S. Wakefield, J.L. Price and C.W. Mueller (1986) 'On the Causal Ordering of Job Satisfaction and Organizational Commitment', *Academy of Management Journal*, 29: 847–58.

Dachler, H.P. (1984) 'On Refocussing Leadership from a Social Systems Perspective of Management', pp. 100–8 in J.G. Hunt, D.M. Hosking, C.A. Schriesheim and R. Stewart (eds), *Leaders and Managers: International Perspectives on Managerial Behavior and Leadership*. Oxford: Pergamon.

Dansereau, F.G., Graen and W. Haga (1975) 'A Vertical Dyad Linkage Approach to Leadership Within Formal Organizations: A Longitudinal Investigation of the Role-Making Process', *Organizational Behavior and Human Performance*, 13: 46–78.

Darley, J.M. and R.H. Fazio (1980) 'Expectancy Confirmation Processes Arising in the Social Interaction Sequence', *American Psychologist*, 35: 867–81.

Deal, T.E. and A.A. Kennedy (1982) *Corporate Cultures*. Reading, MA: Addison-Wesley.

DIO International Research Team (1983) 'A Contingency Model of Participative Decision-making: An Analysis of 56 Decisions in Three Dutch Organizations', *Journal of Occupational Psychology*, 56: 1–18.

Dobbins, G.H. and S.J. Zaccaro (1986) 'The Effects of Group Cohesion and Leader Behavior on Subordinate Satisfaction', *Group and Organization Studies*, 11: 203–19.

Douglas, A. (1962) *Industrial Peacemaking*. New York: Columbia University Press.

Drenth, P.J.D. and P.L. Koopman, (1983/4) 'Experience with "Werkoverleg" in the Netherlands: Implications for Quality Circles', *Journal of General Management*, 9: 57–73.

Eccles, T. (1981) *Under New Management: The Story of Britain's Largest Worker Cooperative – its Successes and Failures*. London: Pan.

Eden, D. (1984) 'Self-Fulfilling Prophecy as a Management Tool: Harnessing Pygmalion', *Academy of Management Review*, 9: 64–73.

Eden, D. and U. Leviatan (1975) 'Implicit Leadership Theory as a Determinant of the Factor Structure Underlying Supervisory Behavior Scales', *Journal of Applied Psychology*, 60: 736–41.

Eden, D. and G. Ravid (1982) 'Pygmalion Versus Self-Expectancy: Effects of Instructor- and Self-Expectancy on Trainee Performance', *Organizational Behavior and Human Performance*, 30: 351–64.

Edwards, R.C. (1979) *Contested Terrain: The Transformation of the Workplace in the Twentieth Century*. New York: Basic Books.

Erez, M., Y. Rim and I. Keider (1986) 'The Two Sides of the Tactics of Influence: Agent vs. Target', *Journal of Occupational Psychology*, 59: 25–39.

Evered, R. (1983) 'The Language of Organizations: the Case of the Navy', pp. 125–44 in L.R. Pondy, P.J. Frost, G. Morgan and T.C. Dandridge (eds), *Organizational Symbolism*. Greenwich, CT: JAI.

Farris, G.F. and D.A. Butterfield (1972) 'Control Theory in Brazilian Organizations', *Administrative Science Quarterly*, 17: 574–85.

Fayol, H. (1949) *General Industrial Management*. London: Pitman (first published 1916).

Feldman, J.M. (1981) 'Beyond Attribution Theory: Cognitive Processes in Performance Appraisal', *Journal of Applied Psychology*, 66: 127–48.

Ferris, G.R. (1985) 'Role of Leadership in the Employee Withdrawal Process', *Journal of Applied Psychology*, 70: 777–81.

Fiedler, F.E. (1967) *A Contingency Theory of Leadership Effectiveness*. New York: McGraw-Hill.

Fiedler, F.E. (1978) 'The Contingency Model and the Dynamics of the Leadership Process', pp. 59–112 in L. Berkowitz (ed.), *Advances in Experimental Social Psychology, Volume 11*. New York: Academic Press.

Fiedler, F.E. and M.M. Chemers (1984) *Improving Leadership Effectiveness: the LEADER MATCH Concept*. Revised edition, New York: Wiley.

Fiedler, F.E. and J.E. Garcia (1987) *New Approaches to Effective Leadership: Cognitive Resources and Organizational Performance*. New York: Wiley.

Field, R.H.G. (1979) 'A Critique of the Vroom–Yetton Contingency Model of Leadership Behavior', *Academy of Management Review*, 4: 249–57.

Field, R.H.G. (1982) 'A Test of the Vroom–Yetton Normative Model of Leadership', *Journal of Applied Psychology*, 67: 523–32.

Fineman, S. and R. Payne (1981) 'Role Stress – A Methodological Trap?', *Journal of Occupational Behaviour*, 2: 51–64.

Fisher, C.D. and R. Gitelson (1983) 'A Meta-analysis of the Correlates of Role Conflict and Ambiguity', *Journal of Applied Psychology*, 68: 320–33.

Fleishman, E. (1953) 'The Description of Supervisory Behavior', *Personnel Psychology*, 37: 1–6.

Fleishman, E.A. and E.F. Harris (1962) 'Patterns of Leadership Behavior Related to Employee Grievances and Turnover', *Personnel Psychology*, 15: 43–56.

Fleishman, E.A. and J. Simmons (1970) 'Relationship Between Leadership Patterns and Effectiveness Ratings in Israeli Foreman', *Personnel Psychology*, 23: 169–72.

Foti, R.J., S.L. Fraser and R.G. Lord (1982) 'Effects of Leadership Labels and Prototypes on Perceptions of Political Leaders', *Journal of Applied Psychology*, 67: 326–33.

French, J.R.P. Jr. and B.H. Raven (1959) 'The Bases of Social Power', pp. 150–67 in D. Cartwright (ed.), *Studies in Social Power*. Ann Arbor, MI: Institute for Social Research, University of Michigan.

Galbraith, J. (1973) *Designing Complex Organizations*. Reading, MA: Addison-Wesley.

Galton, F. (1870) *Hereditary Genius*. New York: Appleton.

Geertz, C. (1973) *The Interpretation of Cultures*. New York: Basic Books.

Georgopoulos, B.S. (1972) 'The Hospital as an Organization and Problem-Solving System', pp. 9–48 in B.S. Georgopoulos (ed.), *Organizational Research on Health Institutions*. Ann Arbor, MI: Institute for Social Research.

Georgopoulos, B.S. and R.A. Cooke (1979) 'Working Conceptual–Theoretical Framework for the Study of Hospital Emergency Services', Working Paper. Ann Arbor, MI: Institute for Social Research.

Gergen, KJ. (1973) 'Social Psychology as History', *Journal of Personality and Social Psychology*, 26: 309–20.

Gioia, D.A. and H.P. Sims (1985) 'On Avoiding the Influence of Implicit Leadership Theories in Leader Behaviour Descriptions', *Educational and Psychological Measurement*, 45: 217–32.

Goldthorpe, J.H., D. Lockwood, F. Bechhofer and J. Platt (1968) *The Affluent Worker: Industrial Attitudes and Behaviour*. London: Cambridge University Press.

Gouldner, A.W. (1954) *Patterns of Industrial Bureaucracy*. New York: Free Press.

Graen, G. (1976) 'Role-making Processes in Complex Organizations', pp. 1201–45 in M.D. Dunnette (ed.), *Handbook of Industrial and Organizational Psychology*. Chicago: Rand McNally.

Graen, G., K. Alvares, J.B. Orris and J.A. Martella (1972) 'Contingency Model of Leadership Effectiveness: Antecedent and Evidential Results', *Psychological Bulletin*, 74: 285–96.

Graen, G.B. and J.F. Cashman (1975) 'A Role-Making Model of Leadership in Formal Organizations: A Developmental Approach', pp. 143–65 in J.G. Hunt and L.L. Larson (eds), *Leadership Frontiers*. Kent, OH: Kent State University Press.

Graen, G.B., J.F. Cashman, S. Ginsburgh and W. Schiemann (1978) 'Effects of Linking-pin Quality upon the Quality of Working Life of Lower Participants: A Longitudinal Investigation of the Managerial Understructure', *Administrative Science Quarterly*, 22: 491–504.

Graen, G.B., R.C. Liden and W. Hoel (1982) 'Role of Leadership in the Employee Withdrawal Process', *Journal of Applied Psychology*, 67: 868–72.

Graen, G., M.A. Novak and P. Sommerkamp (1982) 'The Effects of Leader–Member Exchange and Job Design on Productivity and Satisfaction: Testing a Dual Attachment Model', *Organizational Behavior and Human Performance*, 30: 109–31.

Graen, G.B. and T.A. Scandura (1987) 'Toward a Psychology of Dyadic Organizing', pp. 175–208 in L.L. Cummings and B.M. Staw (eds), *Research in Organizational Behavior, Volume 9*. Greenwich, CT: JAI Press.

Graumann, C.F. (1986) 'Power and Leadership in Lewinian Field Theory: Recalling an Interrupted Task', pp. 83–100 in C.F. Graumann and S. Moscovici (eds), *Changing Conceptions of Leadership*. Heidelberg: Springer.

Graumann, C.F. and S. Moscovici (eds) (1986) *Changing Conceptions of Leadership*. Heidelberg: Springer.

Green, S.G. and R.C. Liden (1980) 'Contextual and Attributional Influences on Control Decisions', *Journal of Applied Psychology*, 65: 453–8.

Green, S.G. and T.R. Mitchell (1979) 'Attributional Processes of Leaders in Leader–Member Interactions', *Organizational Behavior and Human Performance*, 23: 429–58.

Greene, C.N. (1979) 'Questions of Causation in the Path–Goal Theory of Leadership', *Academy of Management Journal*, 22: 22–41.

Greene, C.N. and P.M. Podsakoff (1981) 'Effects of Withdrawal of a Performance-Contingent Reward on Supervisory Influence and Power', *Academy of Management Journal*, 24: 242–4.

Greiner, L.E. (1972) 'Evolution and Revolution as Organizations Grow', *Harvard Business Review*, 50: 37–46.

Gronn, P.C. (1983) 'Talk as the Work: The Accomplishment of School Administration', *Administrative Science Quarterly*, 28: 1–21.

Haire, M., E.F. Ghiselli and L.W. Porter (1966) *Managerial Thinking: An International Study*. New York: Wiley.

Hambleton, R.K. and R. Gumpert (1982) 'The Validity of Hersey and Blanchard's Theory of Leader Effectiveness', *Group and Organization Studies*, 7: 225–42.

Handy, J.A. (1986) 'Considering Organizations in Organizational Stress Research: A Rejoinder to Glowinkowski and Cooper and to Duckworth', *Bulletin of the British Psychological Society*, 39: 205–9.

Harrell, A.M. and M.J. Stahl (1981) 'A Behavioral Decision Theory Approach for Measuring McClelland's Trichotomy of Needs', *Journal of Applied Psychology*, 66: 242–4.

Harrison, R. (1972) 'When Power Conflicts Trigger Team Spirit', *European Business* (Spring): 27–65.

Hazama, H. (1979) 'Characteristics of Japanese Style Management', *Japanese Economic Studies*, 6: 110–73.

Heilmann, M.E., H.A. Hornstein, J.H. Cage and J.K. Herschlag (1984) 'Reactions to Prescribed Leader Behavior as a Function of Role Perspective: The Case of the Vroom–Yetton Model', *Journal of Applied Psychology*, 69: 50–60.

Heller, F.A. and B. Wilpert (1981) *Competence and Power in Managerial Decision-Making*. Chichester: Wiley.

Hersey, P. and K.H. Blanchard (1982) *Management of Organizational Behavior: Utilising Human Resources*. Englewood Cliffs, NJ: Prentice-Hall.

Hickson, D.J., R.J. Butler, D. Cray, G.R. Mallory and D.C. Wilson (1986) *Top Decisions: Strategic Decision-making in Organizations*. Oxford: Basil Blackwell.

Hickson, D.J., C.R. Hinings, C.A. Lee, R.J. Schneck and J.M. Pennings (1971) 'A Strategic Contingencies Theory of Intraorganizational Power', *Administrative Science Quarterly*, 16: 216–29.

Hill, P. (1971) *Towards a New Philosophy of Management*. London: Gower.

Hirsch, P.M. and J.A.Y. Andrews (1983) 'Ambushes, Shootouts and Knights of the Round Table: The Language of Corporate Takeovers', pp. 145–56 in L.R. Pondy, P.J. Frost, G. Morgan and T.C. Dandridge (eds), *Organizational Symbolism*. Greenwich, CT: JAI Press.

Hitt, M.A. and R.D. Ireland (1987) 'Peters and Waterman Revisited: the Unended Quest for Excellence', *Academy of Management Executive*, 1: 91–8.

Hofstede, G. (1980) *Culture's Consequences: International Differences in Work-related Values*. Beverly Hills, CA: Sage.

Hollander, E.P. (1964) *Leaders, Groups and Influence*. New York: Oxford University Press.

Hollander, E.P. (1979) 'Leadership and Social Exchange Processes', pp. 103–18 in K.J. Gergen, M.S. Greenberg and R.H. Willis (eds), *Social Exchange: Advances in Theory and Research*. New York: Winston–Wiley.

Homans, G.C. (1961) *Social Behaviour: its Elementary Forms*. Harcourt, Brace: New York.

Horne, J.H. and Lupton, T. (1965) 'The Work Activities of "Middle" Managers', *Journal of Management Studies*, 2: 14–33.

Hosking, D.M. and Morley, I. (1988) 'The Skills of Leadership', pp. 80–106 in J.G. Hunt, B.R. Baliga, H.P. Dachler and C.A. Schriesheim (eds), *Emerging Leadership Vistas*. Boston, MA: Lexington.

House, R.J. (1971) 'A Path–Goal Theory of Leader Effectiveness', *Administrative Science Quarterly*, 16: 321–38.

House, R.J. (1977) 'A 1976 Theory of Charismatic Leadership', pp. 189–207 in J.G. Hunt and L.L. Larson (eds), *Leadership: The Cutting Edge*. Carbondale, IL: Southern Illinois University Press.

House, R.J. (1984) 'Power in Organizations: A Social Psychological Perspective', Unpublished paper, Faculty of Management, University of Toronto.

House, R.J. (1987) 'The "All Things in Moderation" Leader', *Academy of Management Review*, 12: 164–9.

House, R.J. (1988) 'Power and Personality in Complex Organizations', pp. 305–57 in B.M. Staw (ed.), *Research in Organizational Behavior, Volume 10*. Greenwich CT: JAI Press.

House, R.J. and M.L. Baetz (1979) 'Leadership: Some Empirical Generalizations and

New Research Directions', pp. 341–423 in B.M. Staw (ed.), *Research in Organizational Behavior, Volume 1.* Greenwich, CT: JAI Press.

House, R.J. and G. Dessler (1974) 'The Path–Goal Theory of Leadership: Some Post Hoc and A Priori Tests', pp. 29–55 in J.G. Hunt and L.L. Larson (eds), *Contingency Approaches to Leadership.* Carbondale IL: Southern Illinois University Press.

House, R.J. and T.R. Mitchell (1974) 'Path–Goal Theory of Leadership', *Journal of Contemporary Business,* 3: 81–97.

Howell, J.P. and P.W. Dorfman (1981) 'Substitutes for Leadership: Test of a Construct', *Academy of Management Journal,* 24: 714–28.

Howell, J.P., P.W. Dorfman and S. Kerr (1986) 'Moderator Variable in Leadership Research', *Academy of Management Review,* 11: 88–102.

Hunt, J.G. and R.N. Osborn (1982) 'Toward a Macro-oriented Model of Leadership: An Odyssey', pp. 196–221 in J.G. Hunt, U. Sekaran and C.A. Schriesheim (eds), *Leadership: Beyond Establishment Views.* Carbondale, IL: Southern Illinois University Press.

IDE International Research Group (1981) *Industrial Democracy in Europe.* Oxford: Oxford University Press.

Ilgen, D.R. and W.A. Knowlton, Jr. (1980) 'Performance Attributional Effects on Feedback from Superiors', *Organizational Behavior and Human Performance,* 25: 441–56.

Ilgen, D.R., T.R. Mitchell and J.W. Fredrickson (1981) 'Poor Performers: Supervisors' and Subordinates' Responses', *Organizational Behavior and Human Performance,* 27: 386–410.

Isenberg, D.J. (1981) 'Some Effects of Time Pressure on Vertical Structure and Decision-Making Accuracy in Small Groups', *Organizational Behavior and Human Performance,* 27: 119–34.

Ivancevich, J.M. (1983) 'Contrast Effects in Performance Evaluation and Reward Practices', *Academy of Management Journal,* 26: 465–76.

Jacobs, T.O. (1970) *Leadership and Exchange in Formal Organization.* Alexandria, VA: Human Resources Research Organization.

Jago, A.G. (1981) 'An Assessment of the Deemed Appropriateness of Participative Decision-Making for High and Low Hierarchical Levels'. *Human Relations,* 34: 379–96.

Jago, A.G. and J.W. Ragan (1987) 'The Trouble with LEADER MATCH is that it doesn't Match Fiedler's Contingency Model', *Journal of Applied Psychology,* 71: 555–9.

Jago, A.G. and V.H. Vroom (1980) 'An Evaluation of Two Alternatives to the Vroom–Yetton Normative Model', *Academy of Management Journal,* 23: 347–55.

James, L.R. and J.F. White (1983) 'Cross-Situational Specificity in Managers' Perceptions of Subordinate Performance, Attributions, and Leader Behaviors', *Personnel Psychology,* 36: 809–56.

Janis, I.L. (1972) *Victims of Groupthink: a Psychological Study of Foreign Policy Disasters and Fiascoes.* Boston: Houghton Mifflin.

Jones, E.E. and T.S. Pittman (1982) 'Toward a General Theory of Strategic Self-Presentation', pp. 231–62 in J. Suls (ed.), *Psychological Perspectives on the Self, Volume 1.* Hillsdale, NJ: Erlbaum.

Kahn, R.L., D.M. Wolfe, R.P. Quinn, J.D. Snoek and R.A. Rosenthal (1964) *Organizational Stress: Studies in Role Conflict and Ambiguity.* New York: Wiley.

Katerberg, R. and P.W. Hom (1981) 'Effects of Within-Group and Between-Group Variation in Leadership', *Journal of Applied Psychology,* 66: 218–23.

Katz, D. and R. Kahn (1965) *The Social Psychology of Organizations*. New York: Wiley (Second edition, 1978).

Kay, B.R. (1963) 'Perception and Prescription of the Supervisory Role: A Rolecentric Interpretation', *Occupational Psychology*, 36: 219–27.

Kelley, H.H. (1972) 'Attribution in Social Interaction', pp. 1–23 in E. Jones, D. Kanouse, H. Kelley, R. Nisbett, S. Valins and B. Weiner (eds), *Attribution: Perceiving the Causes of Behavior*. Morristown, NJ: General Learning Press.

Kelley, H.H. (1973) 'The Processes of Causal Attribution', *American Psychologist*, 28: 107–28.

Kelvin, P. (1969) *The Bases of Social Behaviour: an Approach in terms of Order and Value*. London: Holt, Rinehart and Winston.

Kennedy, J.K. (1982) 'Middle LPC Leaders and the Contingency Model of Leadership Effectiveness', *Organizational Behavior and Human Performance*, 30: 1–14.

Kenny, D.A. and S.J. Zaccaro (1983) 'An Estimate of Variance Due to Traits in Leadership', *Journal of Applied Psychology*, 68: 678–85.

Kerr, S., K.D. Hill and S.G. Broedling (1986) 'The First-Line Supervisor: Phasing Out or Here to Stay?', *Academy of Management Review*, 11: 103–17.

Kerr, S. and J.M. Jermier (1978) 'Substitutes for Leadership: Their Meaning and Measurement', *Organizational Behavior and Human Performance*, 22: 375–403.

Kerr, S. and C. Schriesheim (1974) 'Consideration, Initiating Structure and Organizational Criteria – An Update of Korman's 1966 Review', *Personnel Psychology*, 27: 555–68.

Kiesler, S. and L. Sproull (1982) 'Managerial Response to Changing Environments: Perspectives on Problem Sensing from Social Cognition', *Administrative Science Quarterly*, 27: 548–70.

Kilmann, R.H., M.J. Saxton and R. Serpa (1985) *Gaining Control of the Corporate Culture*. San Francisco: Jossey-Bass.

Kipnis, D. (1976) *The Powerholders*. Chicago: University of Chicago Press.

Kipnis, D., S. Schmidt, K. Price and C. Stitt (1981) 'Why Do I Like Thee: Is It Your Performance or My Orders?', *Journal of Applied Psychology*, 66: 324–8.

Klimoski, R.J. and R.A. Ash (1974) 'Accountability and Negotiation Behaviour', *Organizational Behavior and Human Performance*, 11: 409–25.

Knowlton, W.A. and T.R. Mitchell (1980) 'Effects of Causal Attributions on a Supervisor's Evaluation of Subordinate Performance', *Journal of Applied Psychology*, 65: 459–66.

Koopman, P.L., P.J.D. Drenth, F.B.M. Bus, A.J. Kruyswijk and A.F.M. Wierdsma (1981) 'Content, Process and Effects of Participative Decision-Making on the Shop Floor: Three Cases in the Netherlands', *Human Relations*, 34: 657–76.

Korman, A.K. (1966) 'Consideration, Initiating Structure and Organizational Criteria – A Review', *Personnel Psychology*, 19: 349–62.

Kotter, J.P. (1982) *The General Managers*. New York: Free Press.

Landsberger, H.A. (1961) 'The Horizontal Dimension in a Bureaucracy', *Administrative Science Quarterly*, 6: 298–332.

Larson, J.R., Jr. (1982) 'Cognitive Mechanisms Mediating the Impact of Implicit Theories of Leader Behavior on Leader Behavior Ratings', *Organizational Behavior and Human Performance*, 29: 129–40.

Larson, J.R., Jr. (1984) 'The Performance Feedback Process: A Preliminary Model', *Organizational Behavior and Human Performance*, 29: 42–76.

Lawler, E.E. (1973) *Motivation in Work Organizations*. Monterey, CA: Brooks/Cole.

Lawrence, P.R. and Lorsch, J.W. (1967) *Organization and Environment: Managing*

Differentiation in Work Organizations. Cambridge, MA: Graduate School of Business, Harvard University.

Lewin, K., R. Lippitt and R.K. White (1939) 'Patterns of Aggressive Behaviour in Experimentally Created Social Climates', *Journal of Social Psychology,* 10: 271–99.

Liden, R.C. and G.B. Graen (1980) 'Generalizability of the Vertical Dyad Linkage Model of Leadership', *Academy of Management Journal,* 23: 451–65.

Liden, R.C. and T.R. Mitchell (1983) 'The Effects of Group Interdependence on Supervisor Performance Evaluations', *Personnel Psychology,* 36: 289–99.

Likert, R. (1961) *New Patterns of Management.* New York: McGraw-Hill.

Lindsay, C.P. and B.L. Dempsey (1983) 'Ten Painfully Learned Lessons About Working in China: the Insights of Two American Behavioral Scientists', *Journal of Applied Behavioral Science,* 19: 265–76.

Locke, E.A. and D.M. Schweiger (1979) 'Participation in Decision-Making: One More Look', pp. 265–340 in B.M. Staw (ed.), *Research in Organizational Behavior, Volume 1.* Greenwich, CT: JAI Press.

Lord, R.G., C.L. de Vader and G.M. Alliger (1986) 'A Meta-Analysis of the Relation Between Personality Traits and Leadership Perceptions: An Application of Validity Generalization Procedures', *Journal of Applied Psychology,* 71: 402–10.

Lord, R.G. and M.C. Kernan (1987) 'Scripts as Determinants of Purposive Behaviour in Organizations', *Academy of Management Review,* 12: 265–77.

Lord, R.G. and J.E. Smith (1983) 'Theoretical, Information Processing, and Situational Factors Affecting Attribution Theory Models of Organizational Behaviour', *Academy of Management Review,* 8: 50–60.

Lowin, A., W.J. Hrapchak and M.J. Kavanagh (1969) 'Consideration and Initiating Structure: An Experimental Investigation of Leadership Traits', *Administrative Science Quarterly,* 14: 238–53.

Luthans, F. and D.L. Lockwood (1984) 'Toward an Observation System for Measuring Leader Behavior in Natural Settings,' pp. 117–41 in J.G. Hunt, D.M. Hosking, C.A. Schriesheim and R. Stewart (eds), *Leaders and Managers.* New York: Pergamon Press.

Maass, A. and R.D. Clark (1984) 'Hidden Impact of Minorities: Fifteen Years of Minority Influence Research', *Psychological Bulletin,* 95: 428–50.

McCall, M.W. and M.M. Lombardo (eds) (1978) *Leadership: Where Else Can We Go?* Durham, N.C.: Duke University Press.

McClelland, D. (1961) *The Achieving Society.* New York: Van Nostrand Reinhold.

McClelland, D. (1975) *Power: The Inner Experience.* New York: Irvington.

McClelland, D.C. and R.E. Boyatzis (1982) 'Leadership Motive Pattern and Long-Term Success in Management', *Journal of Applied Psychology,* 67: 737–43.

McElroy, J.C. (1982) 'A Typology of Attribution Leadership Research', *Academy of Management Review,* 7: 413–17.

McGrath, J.E. (1966) 'A Social Psychological Approach to the Study of Negotiation', pp. 101–34 in R.W. Bowers (ed), *Studies on Behavior in Organizations: a Research Symposium.* Athens, GA: University of Georgia Press.

Machiavelli, N. (1977) *The Prince* (tr. R.M. Adams). New York: Norton (first published 1513).

Machin, J.L.J. (1980) *The Expectations Approach: Improving Managerial Communication and Performance.* New York: McGraw-Hill.

Machin, J.L.J. and C.H.S. Tai (1983) 'A Communication-based Methodology for Research into and Development of Management Control Systems', pp. 193–226 in E.A. Lowe and J.L.J. Machin (eds), *New Perspectives in Management Control.* London: Macmillan.

Mann, R.D. (1959) 'A Review of the Relationships Between Personality and Performance in Small Groups', *Psychological Bulletin*, 56: 241–70.

Mannheim, B.F., Y. Rim ånd G. Grinberg (1967) 'Instrumental Status of Supervisors as Related to Workers' Perceptions and Expectations', *Human Relations*, 20: 387–97.

Manz, C.C. (1986) 'Self-leadership: Toward an Expanded Theory of Self-Influence Processes in Organizations', *Academy of Management Review*, 11: 585–600.

Manz, C.C. and H.P. Sims Jr. (1980) 'Self-Management as a Substitute for Leadership: A Social Learning Theory Perspective', *Academy of Management Review*, 3: 361–7.

Manz, C.C. and H.P. Sims (1987) 'Leading Workers to Lead Themselves: the External Leadership of Self-Managing Work Teams', *Administrative Science Quarterly*, 32: 106–28.

March, J.G. and H.A. Simon (1958) *Organizations*. New York: Wiley.

Markus, H. and R.B. Zajonc (1985) 'The Cognitive Perspective in Social Psychology', pp. 137–230 in G. Lindzey and E. Aronson (eds), *Handbook of Social Psychology, Volume 1: Theory and Method*. New York: Random House.

Marrow, A.J., D.G. Bowers and S.E. Seashore (1967) *Management by Participation*. New York: Harper & Row.

Marsh, R.M. and H. Mannari (1976) *Modernisation and the Japanese Factory*. Princeton, NJ: Princeton University Press.

Marshall, J. and A. McLean (1985) 'Exploring Organisation Culture as a Route to Organisational Change', pp. 2–20 in V. Hammond (ed.), *Current Research in Management*. London: Frances Pinter.

Marshall, J. and R. Stewart (1981a) 'Managers' Job Perceptions: Part 1 – Their Overall Frameworks and Working Strategies', *Journal of Management Studies*, 18: 177–89.

Marshall, J. and R. Stewart (1981b) 'Managers' Job Perceptions: Part 2 – Opportunities for and Attitudes to Choice', *Journal of Management Studies*, 18: 263–75.

Martin, J., M.S. Feldman, M.J. Hatch and S.B. Sitkin (1983) 'The Uniqueness Paradox in Organizational Stories', *Administrative Science Quarterly*, 28: 438–53.

Martinko, M.J. and W.L. Gardner (1982) 'Learned Helplessness: An Alternative Explanation for Performance Deficits', *Academy of Management Review*, 7: 195–204.

Martinko, M.J. and W.L. Gardner (1984a) 'The Observation of High-Performing Educational Managers: Methodological Issues and Managerial Implications', pp. 142–62 in J.G. Hunt, D.M. Hosking, C.A. Schriesheim and R. Stewart (eds), *Leaders and Managers*. New York: Pergamon Press.

Martinko, M.J. and W.L. Gardner (1984b) 'The Behavior of High-Performing Educational Managers: An Observational Study', Unpublished report, Department of Management, Florida State University, Tallahasee FL.

Martinko, M.J. and W.L. Gardner (1987a) 'The Leader/Member Attribution Process', *Academy of Management Review*, 12: 235–49.

Martinko, M.J. and W.L. Gardner (1987b) 'Structured Observation of Managerial Work: A Replication and Synthesis', Paper presented at the Annual Meeting of the Academy of Management, New Orleans, August 1987.

Maruyama, M. (1982) 'New Mindscapes for Future Business Policy and Management', *Technology Forecasting and Social Change*, 21: 53–76.

Maslow, A.H. (1954) *Motivation and Personality*. New York: Harper & Row.

Mason, R.O. and I.I. Mitroff (1981) *Challenging Strategic Planning Assumptions: Theory, Cases and Techniques*. New York: Wiley.

Matsui, R., R. Osawa and T. Terai (1975) 'Relations Between Supervisory Motivation and the Consideration and Structure Aspects of Supervisory Behaviour', *Journal of Applied Psychology*, 60: 451–4.

Matsui, T. and Y. Ohtsuka (1978) 'Within-Person Expectancy Theory Predictions of Supervisory Consideration and Structure Behaviour', *Journal of Applied Psychology*, 128–31.

Mawhinney, T.C. (1980) 'Stogdill on Punishment and Punitive Aspects of Leadership: A Response to Sims', *Academy of Management Review*, 5: 605–6.

Mead, G.H. (1934) *Mind, Self and Society*. Chicago: University of Chicago Press.

Meade, R.D. (1967) 'An Experimental Study of Leadership in India', *Journal of Social Psychology*, 72: 35–43.

Meaning of Working International Team (ed.) (1987) *The Meaning of Work: An International View*. New York: Academic Press.

Meeus, W.H.J. and Q.A.W. Raaijmakers (1986) 'Administrative Obedience: Carrying Out Orders to Use Psychological–Administrative Violence', *European Journal of Social Psychology*, 16: 311–24.

Meindl, J.R. and S.B. Ehrlich (1987) 'The Romance of Leadership and the Evaluation of Organizational Performance', *Academy of Management Journal*, 30: 91–109.

Meindl, J.R., S.B. Ehrlich and J.M. Dukerich (1985) 'The Romance of Leadership', *Administrative Science Quarterly*, 30: 78–102.

Meyer, J.W. (1984) 'Organizations as Ideological Systems', pp. 186–205 in T.J. Sergiovanni and J.B. Corbally (eds), *Leadership and Organizational Culture*. Urbana, IL: University of Illinois Press.

Michels, R. (1962) *Political Parties: A Sociological Study of the Oligarchical Tendencies of Modern Democracies* (tr. E. & C. Paul). New York: Crowell–Collier (first publ. 1915).

Milgram, S. (1974) *Obedience to Authority*. New York: Harper & Row.

Mill, J.S. (1973) *A System of Logic* (ed. J.M. Robson). *Collected Works of John Stuart Mill, Volumes 7 and 8*. Toronto: University of Toronto Press (first published 1872).

Miller, E.J. and A.K. Rice (1967) *Systems of Organization: The Control of Task and Sentient Boundaries*. London: Tavistock.

Mills, P.K. (1983) 'Self-Management: Its Control and Relationship to Other Organizational Properties', *Academy of Management Review*, 8: 445–53.

Mills, P.K. and B.Z. Posner (1982) 'The Relationship Among Self-Supervision, Structure, and Technology in Professional Service Organizations', *Academy of Management Journal*, 25: 437–43.

Miner, J.B. (1975) 'The Uncertain Future of the Leadership Concept: An Overview', pp. 197–208 in J.G. Hunt and L.L. Larson (eds), *Leadership Frontiers*, Kent, OH: Kent State University Press.

Miner, J.B. (1978) 'Twenty Years of Research on Role-Motivation Theory of Managerial Effectiveness', *Personnel Psychology*, 31: 739–60.

Miner, J.B. (1982) 'The Uncertain Future of the Leadership Concept: Revisions and Clarifications', *Journal of Applied Behavioral Science*, 18: 293–308.

Miner, J.B. and D.P. Crane (1981) 'Motivation to Manage and the Manifestation of a Managerial Orientation in Career Planning', *Academy of Management Journal*, 24: 626–33.

Mintzberg, H. (1973) *The Nature of Managerial Work*. New York: Harper & Row.

Mintzberg, H. (1979) *The Structuring of Organizations*. Englewood Cliffs, NJ: Prentice-Hall.

Mintzberg, H. (1982) 'If You're not Serving Bill and Ben, Then You're Not Serving Leadership', pp. 239–59 in J.G. Hunt, U. Sekaran and C.A. Schriesheim (eds), *Leadership: Beyond Establishment Views*. Carbondale, IL: Southern Illinois University Press.

Mintzberg, H. (1983) *Power In and Around Organizations*. Englewood Cliffs, NJ: Prentice-Hall.

Mirvis, P.H. and D.N. Berg (1977) *Failures in Organizational Change and Development: Cases and Essays for Learning*. New York: Wiley.

Mischel, W. (1968) *Personality and Assessment*. New York: Wiley.

Misumi, J. (1984) 'Decision-making in Japanese Groups and Organizations', pp. 525–40 in B. Wilpert and A. Sorge (eds), *International Yearbook of Organizational Democracy, Volume 2*. Chichester: Wiley.

Misumi, J. (1985) *The Behavioral Science of Leadership* (ed. M.F. Peterson). Ann Arbor, Michigan: University of Michigan Press.

Misumi, J. and M.F. Peterson (1985) 'The Performance-Maintenance (PM) Theory of Leadership: review of a Japanese Research Program', *Administrative Science Quarterly*, 30: 198–223.

Mitchell, T.R. (1974) 'Expectancy Models of Job Satisfaction, Occupational Preference, and Effort: A Theoretical, Methodological, and Empirical Appraisal', *Psychological Bulletin*, 81: 1053–77.

Mitchell, T.R. and L.S. Kalb (1981) 'Effects of Outcome Knowledge and Outcome Valence on Supervisors' Evaluations', *Journal of Applied Psychology*, 604–12.

Mitchell, T.R. and L.S. Kalb (1982) 'Effects of Job Experience on Supervisor Attributions for a Subordinate's Poor Performance', *Journal of Applied Psychology*, 67: 181–8.

Mitchell, T.R. and R.C. Liden (1982) 'The Effects of the Social Context on Performance Evaluations', *Organizational Behavior and Human Performance*, 29: 241–56.

Mitchell, T.R. and R.E. Wood (1980) 'Supervisor's Responses to Subordinate Poor Performance: A Test of an Attributional Model', *Organizational Behavior and Human Performance*, 25: 123–38.

Mobley, W.H. (1977) 'Intermediate Linkages in the Relationship between Job Satisfaction and Employee Turnover', *Journal of Applied Psychology*, 62: 237–40.

Morey, N.C. and F. Luthans (1985) 'Refining the Displacement of Culture and the Use of Scenes and Themes in Organizational Studies', *Academy of Management Review*, 10: 219–29.

Morley, I.E. (1986) 'Negotiating and Bargaining', pp. 303–24 in O. Hargie (ed.), *A Handbook of Communication Skills*. London: Croom-Helm.

Morley, I.E. and D.M. Hosking (1984) 'Decision-making and Negotiation', pp. 71–92 in M. Gruneberg and T. Wall (eds), *Social Psychology and Organizational Behaviour*. Chichester: Wiley.

Morley, I.E. and G.M. Stephenson (1977) *The Social Psychology of Bargaining*. London: Allen and Unwin.

Moscovici, S. (1976) *Social Influence and Social Change*. New York: Academic Press.

Moscovici, S. (1980) 'Toward a Theory of Conversion Behavior', pp. 209–39 in L. Berkowitz (ed.), *Advances in Experimental Social Psychology, Volume 13*. New York: Academic Press.

Moscovici, S., G. Mugny and E. Avermaet (eds) (1985) *Perspectives on Minority Influence*. Cambridge: Cambridge University Press.

Mugny, G. (1982) *The Power of Minorities*. London: Academic Press.

Mulder, M. (1975) 'Reduction of Power Differences in Practice: The Power Distance Theory and Its Implications', pp. 79–94 in G. Hofstede and M.S. Kassem (eds), *European Contributions to Organization Theory*. Assen, Holland: Van Gorcum.

Near, J.P. and M.P. Miceli (1987) 'Whistle-Blowers in Organizations: Dissidents or Reformers?', pp. 321–68 in L.L. Cummings and B.M. Staw (eds), *Research in Organizational Behavior, Volume 9*. Greenwich, CT: JAI Press.

Nebeker, D.M. and T.R. Mitchell (1974) 'Leader Behaviour: An Expectancy Theory Approach', *Organizational Behavior and Human Performance*, 11: 355–67.

Needham, J. (1978) *The Shorter Science and Civilisation in China, Volume 1*. Cambridge: Cambridge University Press.

Negandhi, A.R. (1985) 'Management Strategies and Policies of American, German and Japanese Multinational Corporations', *Management Japan*, 18: 12–20.

Nelson, P.D. (1964) 'Similarities and Differences Among Leaders and Followers', *Journal of Social Psychology*, 63: 161–7.

Ng, S.H. (1980) *The Social Psychology of Power*. London: Academic Press.

Nicholson, N. (1984) 'A Theory of Work Role Transitions', *Administrative Science Quarterly*, 29: 172–91.

Nicholson, N. and M.A. West (1987) *Managerial Job Change*. Cambridge: Cambridge University Press.

Nisbett, R.E. and L. Ross (1980) *Human Inference*. Englewood Cliffs, NJ: Prentice-Hall.

Nisbett, R.E. and T.D. Wilson (1977) 'Telling More Than We Can Know: Verbal Reports on Mental Processes', *Psychological Review*, 84: 231–59.

Nonaka, I. and A. Okamura (1984) 'A Comparison of Management in American, Japanese and European Firms (1)', *Management Japan*, 17: 23–39.

Ogilvie, J.R. and N. Schmitt (1979) 'Situational Influences on Linear and Non-Linear Use of Information', *Organizational Behavior and Human Performance*, 23: 292–306.

Oksenberg, L. (1971) 'Machiavellianism in Traditional and Westernised Chinese Students', pp. 92–8 in W.W. Lambert and R. Weisbrod (eds), *Comparative Perspectives on Social Psychology*. Boston, MA: Little, Brown.

O'Reilly, C.A. III and B.A. Weitz (1980) 'Managing Marginal Employees: The Use of Warnings and Dismissals', *Administrative Science Quarterly*, 25: 467–84.

Osborn, R.N. and J.G. Hunt (1974) 'An Empirical Investigation of Lateral and Vertical Leadership at Two Organizational Levels', *Journal of Business Research*, 2: 209–21.

Pandey, J. (1986) 'Sociocultural Perspectives on Ingratiation', pp. 205–29 in B.A. Maher and W.B. Maher (eds), *Progress in Experimental Personality Research, Volume 14*. Orlando, FL: Academic Press.

Pandey, J. and K.A. Bohra (1984) 'Ingratiation as a Function of Organizational Characteristics and Supervisory Styles', *International Review of Applied Psychology*, 33: 381–94.

Parsons, T., R.F. Bales and E.A. Shils (eds) 1953) *Working Papers in the Theory of Action*. Glencoe, IL: Free Press.

Pascale, R.T. (1978) 'Communication and Decision-making across Cultures: Japanese and American Comparisons', *Administrative Science Quarterly*, 23: 91–109.

Pascale, R.T. and M.A. Maguire (1980) 'Comparison of Selected Work Factors in Japan and the United States', *Human Relations*, 33: 433–55.

Pavett, C.M. and A.W. Lau (1983) 'Managerial Work: The Influence of Hierarchical Level and Functional Speciality', *Academy of Management Journal*, 26: 170–7.

Payne, J.W., M.L. Braunstein and J.S. Carroll (1978) 'Exploring Predecisional Behavior: An Alternative Approach to Decision Research', *Organizational Behavior and Human Performance*, 22: 17–44.

Payne, R. and D.S. Pugh (1976) 'Organization Structure and Climate', pp. 1125–73 in M.D. Dunnette (ed.), *Handbook of Industrial and Organizational Psychology*. Chicago: Rand McNally.

Pelz, D.C. (1951) 'Leadership Within a Hierarchical Organization', *Journal of Social Issues*, 7: 49–55.

Pelz, D.C. (1952) 'Influence: a Key to Effective Leadership in the First-line Supervisor', *Personnel* (November): 3–11.

Pence, E.C., W.C. Pendleton, G.H. Dobbins and J.A. Sgro (1982) 'Effects of Causal Explanations and Sex Variables on Recommendations for Corrective Actions Following Employee Failure', *Organizational Behavior and Human Performance*, 29: 227–40.

Pereira, D. (1986) 'Factors Associated with Transformational Leadership in an Indian Engineering Firm', Paper given to 21st International Congress of Applied Psychology, Jerusalem.

Perrow, C. (1970) *Organizational Analysis: a Sociological View*. London: Tavistock.

Peters, L.H., D.D. Hartke and J.T. Pohlmann (1985) 'Fiedler's Contingency Theory of Leadership: An Application of the Meta-Analysis Procedures of Schmidt and Hunter', *Psychological Bulletin*, 97: 274–85.

Peters, T.J. and N. Austin (1985) *A Passion for Excellence*. New York: Random House.

Peters, T.J. and R.H. Waterman (1982) *In Search of Excellence: Lessons from America's Best Run Companies*. New York: Harper & Row.

Peterson, M.F. (1979) 'Problem-appropriate Leadership in Hospital Emergency Units', Unpublished doctoral dissertation, Ann Arbor, MI, University of Michigan.

Peterson, M.F. (1985) 'Experienced Acceptability: Measuring Perceptions of Dysfunctional Leadership', *Group and Organization Studies*, 10: 447–77.

Peterson, M.F. (in press) 'Organization Development Programs in Japan and China. Based on the Performance-Maintenance (PM) Theory of Leadership', *Organizational Dynamics*.

Peterson, M.F., H. Maiya and C. Herreid (1987) 'Field Application of Japanese PM Leadership Theory in Two US Service Organizations', Unpublished manuscript, College of Business, Texas Tech. University, Lubbock TX.

Peterson, M.F., P.B. Smith and M.H. Tayeb (1987) 'Development and Use of English-Language Versions of Japanese PM Leadership Measures in Electronics Plants', Proceedings of the Annual Meeting of the Southern Management Association, New Orleans, November 1987.

Pettigrew, A. (1979) 'On Studying Organizational Cultures', *Administrative Science Quarterly*, 24: 570–81.

Pettigrew, A. (1985) *The Awakening Giant: Continuity and Change at Imperial Chemical Industries*. Oxford: Basil Blackwell.

Pfeffer, J. (1977) 'The Ambiguity of Leadership', *Academy of Management Review*, 2: 104–12.

Pfeffer, J. (1981a) *Power in Organizations*. Marshfield, MA: Pitman.

Pfeffer, J. (1981b) 'Management as Symbolic Action: The Creation and Maintenance of Organizational Paradigms', pp. 1–52 in L.L. Cummings and B.M. Staw (eds), *Research in Organizational Behavior, Volume 3*. Greenwich, CT: JAI.

Pfeffer, J. and G.R. Salancik (1975) 'Determinants of Supervisory Behavior: A Role Set Analysis', *Human Relations*, 28: 139–54.

Phillips, J.S. (1984) 'The Accuracy of Leadership Ratings: A Cognitive Categorization Perspective', *Organizational Behavior and Human Performance*, 33: 125–38.

Phillips, J.S. and R.G. Lord (1981) 'Causal Attributions and Perceptions of Leadership', *Organizational Behavior and Human Performance*, 28: 143–63.

Phillips, J.S. and R.G. Lord (1982) 'Schematic Information Processing and Perceptions of Leadership in Problem-Solving Groups', *Journal of Applied Psychology*, 67: 486–92.

Pike, K.L. (1967) *Language in Relation to a Unified Theory of the Structure of Human Behaviour* (Second edition). The Hague: Mouton.

Podsakoff, P.M. (1982) 'Determinants of a Supervisor's Use of Rewards and Punishments: A Literature Review and Suggestions for Further Research', *Organizational Behavior and Human Performance*, 29: 58–83.

Podsakoff, P.M. and C.A. Schriesheim (1985) 'Field Studies of French and Raven's Bases of Power: Critique, Reanalysis and Suggestions for Future Research', *Psychological Bulletin*, 97: 387–411.

Podsakoff, P.M., W.D. Todor and R. Skov (1982) 'Effects of Leader Contingent and Noncontingent Reward and Punishment Behaviors on Subordinate Performance and Satisfaction', *Academy of Management Journal*, 25: 810–21.

Pondy, L.R. (1978) 'Leadership is a Language Game', pp. 88–99 in M.W. McCall Jr. and M.M. Lombardo (eds), *Leadership: Where Else Can We Go?* Durham, NC: Duke University Press.

Pondy, L.R., P.J. Frost, G. Morgan and T.C. Dandridge (eds) (1983) *Organizational Symbolism*. Greenwich, CT: JAI.

Porat, A.M. (1970) 'Cross-cultural Differences in Resolving Union–Management Conflict Through Negotiations', *Journal of Applied Psychology*, 54: 441–51.

Porter, L.W., R.W. Allen and H.L. Angle (1981) 'The Politics of Upward Influence in Organizations', pp. 109–49 in L.L. Cummings and B.M. Staw (eds), *Research in Organizational Behavior, Volume 3*. Greenwich, CT: JAI Press.

Pruitt, D.G. (1981) *Negotiation Behavior*. New York: Academic Press.

Resnick, H. (1980) 'Tasks in Changing the Organization from Within', pp. 200–16 in H. Resnick and R.J. Patti (eds), *Change from Within: Humanising Social Welfare Organisations*. Philadelphia, PA: Temple University Press.

Rice, R.W. (1978) 'Construct Validity of the Least Preferred Coworker Score', *Psychological Bulletin*, 85: 1199–237.

Rice, R.W. (1981) 'Leader LPC and Follower Satisfaction: A Review', *Organizational Behavior and Human Performance*, 28: 1–25.

Roethlisberger, F.J. (1945) 'The Industrial Foreman: Master and Victim of Doubletalk', *Harvard Business Review*, 23: 283–94.

Roethlisberger, F.J. and W.J. Dickson (1939) *Management and the Worker*. Cambridge, MA: Harvard University Press.

Ross, M. and G.J.O. Fletcher (1985) 'Attribution and Social Perception', pp. 73–122 in G. Lindzey and E. Aronson (eds), *Handbook of Social Psychology, Volume 2: Special Fields and Applications*. New York: Random House.

Rubin, J.Z. and B.R. Brown (1975) *The Social Psychology of Bargaining and Negotiation*. New York: Academic Press.

Rush, M.C. and L.L. Beauvais (1981) 'A Critical Analysis of Format-Induced Versus Subject-Imposed Bias in Leadership Ratings', *Journal of Applied Psychology*, 66: 722–7.

Rush, M.C., J.S. Phillips and R.G. Lord (1981) 'Effects of a Temporal Delay in Rating on Leader Behavior Descriptions: A Laboratory Investigation', *Journal of Applied Psychology*, 66: 442–50.

Rush, M.C., J.C. Thomas and R.G. Lord (1977) 'Implicit Leadership Theory: A Potential Threat to the Internal Validity of Leader Behavior Questionnaires', *Organizational Behavior and Human Performance*, 20: 93–110.

Russell, B. (1961) 'Physics and Neutral Monism', pp. 607–14 in R.E. Egner and L.E. Denonn (eds), *The Basic Writings of Bertrand Russell: 1903–1959*. London: Allen and Unwin.

Sadler, P.J. (1970) 'Leadership Style, Confidence in Management and Job Satisfaction', *Journal of Applied Behavioral Science*, 6: 3–20.

Salaman, G. (1979) *Work Organizations: Resistance and Control.* London: Longman.

Salancik, G.R., B.J. Calder, K.M. Rowland, H. Leblebici and M. Conway (1975) 'Leadership as an Outcome of Social Structure and Process: A Multidimensional Analysis', pp. 81–101 in J.G. Hunt and L.L. Larson (eds), *Leadership Frontiers.* Columbus, OH: Kent State University Press.

Salancik, G.R. and J. Pfeffer (1978) 'A Social Information Processing Approach to Job Attitudes and Task Design', *Administrative Science Quarterly*, 23: 224–53.

Sashkin, M. and R.M. Fulmer (1988) 'A New Framework for Leadership: Vision, Charisma and Culture Creation', pp. 51–65 in J.G. Hunt, B.R. Baliga, H.P. Dachler and C. A. Schriesheim (eds), *Emerging Leadership Vistas.* Boston, MA: Lexington.

Sashkin, M. and H. Garland (1979) 'Laboratory and Field Research in Leadership: Integrating Divergent Streams', pp. 64–87 in J.G. Hunt and L.L. Larson (eds), *Cross-Currents in Leadership.* Carbondale IL: Southern Illinois University Press.

Sayles, L.R. (1964) *Managerial Behavior.* New York: McGraw-Hill.

Sayles, L.R. (1979) *Leadership: What Effective Managers Really Do and How They Do It.* New York: McGraw-Hill.

Scandura, T.A., G.B. Graen and M.A. Novak (1986) 'When Managers Decide Not to Behave Autocratically: An Investigation of Leader–Member Exchange and Decision Influence', *Journal of Applied Psychology*, 71: 579–86.

Schein, E.H. (1985) *Organizational Culture and Leadership: A Dynamic View.* San Francisco: Jossey-Bass.

Schein, E.H. (1987) *Process Consultation, Volume 2: Some Lessons for Managers and Consultants.* Reading, MA: Addison-Wesley.

Schein, E.H. and W.G. Bennis (1964) *Personal and Organizational Change Through Group Methods.* New York: Wiley.

Schlit, W.K. and E.A. Locke (1982) 'A Study of Upward Influence in Organizations', *Administrative Science Quarterly*, 27: 304–16.

Schneider, J. and J.O. Mitchell (1980) 'Functions of Life Insurance Agency Managers and Relationships with Agency Characteristics and Managerial Tenure', *Personnel Psychology*, 33: 795–808.

Schneider, W. and R.M. Shiffrin (1977) 'Controlled and Automatic Human Information Processing: I. Detection, Search, and Attention', *Psychological Review*, 84: 1–66.

Schriesheim, C.A. and A.S. De Nisi (1981) 'Task Dimensions as Moderators of the Effects of Instrumental Leadership: A Two Sample Replicated Test of Path–Goal Leadership Theory', *Journal of Applied Psychology*, 66: 589–97.

Schriesheim, C.A. and S. Kerr (1977) 'Theories and Measures of Leadership: A Critical Appraisal of Current and Future Directions', pp. 9–45 in J.G. Hunt and L.L. Larson (eds), *Leadership: The Cutting Edge.* Carbondale, IL: Southern Illinois University Press.

Schriesheim, J.F. and C.A. Schriesheim (1980) 'A Test of the Path–Goal Theory of Leadership and Some Suggested Directions for Future Research', *Personnel Psychology*, 33: 349–70.

Seashore, S.E. and D.G. Bowers (1970) 'Durability of Organizational Change', *American Psychologist*, 25: 227–33.

Shapira, Z. and R.L.M. Dunbar (1980 'Testing Mintzberg's Managerial Roles Classification Using an In-Basket Simulation', *Journal of Applied Psychology*, 65: 87–95.

Sheridan, J.E., D.J. Vredenburgh and M.A. Abelson (1984) 'Contextual Model of Leadership Influence in Hospital Units', *Academy of Management Journal*, 27: 57–78.

Shiffrin, R.M. and W. Schneider (1977) 'Controlled and Automatic Human Information

Processing: II. Perceptual Learning, Automatic Attending, and a General Theory', *Psychological Review*, 84: 127–90.

Shiflett, S.C. (1973) 'The Contingency Model of Leadership Effectiveness: Some Implications of its Statistical and Methodological Properties', *Behavioral Science*, 18: 429–40.

Sims, H.P., Jr. (1977) 'The Leader as a Manager of Reinforcement Contingencies: An Empirical Example and a Model', pp. 121–37 in J.G. Hunt and L.L. Larson (eds), *Leadership: The Cutting Edge*. Carbondale, IL: Southern Illinois University Press.

Sims, H.P., Jr. (1980) 'Further Thoughts on Punishment in Organizations', *Academy of Management Review*, 5: 133–8.

Sims, H.P., Jr. and D.A. Gioia (eds) (1986) *Social Cognitions in Organizations*. San Francisco: Jossey-Bass.

Sims, J.P., Jr. and A.D. Szilagyi (1975) 'Leader Reward Behavior and Subordinate Satisfaction and Performance', *Organizational Behavior and Human Performance*, 14: 426–37.

Singer, M.S. (1985) 'Tranformational vs. Transactional Leadership: A Study of New Zealand Company Managers', *Psychological Reports*, 57: 143–6.

Singer, M.S. and A.E. Singer (1986) 'Relation Between Transformational vs. Transactional Leadership Performance and Subordinates' Personality: An Exploratory Study', *Perceptual and Motor Skills*, 62: 775–80.

Singh, R. (1983) 'Leadership Style and Reward Allocation: Does Least Preferred Coworker Scale Measure Task and Relation Orientation?', *Organizational Behavior and Human Performance*, 32: 178–97.

Sinha, J.B.P. (1981) *The Nurturant Task Manager: A Model of the Effective Executive*. Atlantic Highlands, NJ: Humanities Press.

Sinha, J.B.P. (1984) 'A Model of Effective Leadership Styles in India', *International Studies of Management and Organization*, 14: 86–98.

Slocum, J.W., Jr. and H.P. Sims, Jr. (1980) 'A Typology for Integrating Technology, Organization, and Job Design', *Human Relations*, 33: 193–212.

Smircich, L. (1985) 'Is the Concept of Culture a Paradigm for Understanding Organizations and Ourselves?', pp. 55–72 in P.J. Frost, L.F. Moore, M.R. Louis, C.C. Lundberg and J. Martin (eds), *Organizational Culture*. Beverly Hills, CA: Sage.

Smith, P.B. (1973) *Groups Within Organizations*. London: Harper & Row.

Smith, P.B. (1984) 'The Effectiveness of Japanese Styles of Management: A Review and Critique', *Journal of Occupational Psychology*, 57: 121–36.

Smith, P.B. and J. Misumi (1989) 'Japanese Management: A Sun Rising in the West?' in C.L. Cooper and I. Robertson (eds), *International Review of Industrial and Organizational Psychology, Volume 4*. Chichester: Wiley.

Smith, P.B., J. Misumi, M.H. Tayeb, M.F. Peterson and M.H. Bond (in press) 'On the Generality of Leader Style Measures across Cultures', *Journal of Occupational Psychology*.

Smith, P.B., D. Moscow, C.L. Cooper and M.L. Berger (1969) 'Relationships Between Managers and their Work Associates', *Administrative Science Quarterly*, 14: 338–45.

Smith, P.B., M.H. Tayeb, J.B.P. Sinha and B.Bennett (1987) 'Leader Style and Leader Behaviour: the Case of the 9,9 Manager', unpublished manuscript, University of Sussex.

Stahl, M.J. (1983) 'Achievement, Power and Managerial Motivation: Selecting Managerial Talent with the Job Choice Exercise', *Personnel Psychology*, 36: 775–89.

Steel, R.P., A.J. Mento, B.L. Dilla, N.K. Ovalle and R.F. Lloyd (1985) 'Factors

Influencing the Success and Failure of Two Quality Circle Programs', *Journal of Management*, 11: 99–119.

Steel, R.P. and G.S. Shane (1986) 'Evaluation Research on Quality Circles: Technical and Analytic Implications', *Human Relations*, 39: 449–86.

Steele, F.I. (1977) 'Is the Culture Hostile to Organizational Development? The UK Example', pp. 23–32 in P.H. Mirvis and D.N. Berg (eds), *Failures in Organizational Development and Change: Cases and Essays for Learning*. New York: Wiley.

Stewart, R. (1976) *Contrasts in Management: A Study of the Different Types of Management Jobs, Their Demands and Choices*. London: McGraw-Hill.

Stewart, R. (1982a) 'A Model for Understanding Managerial Jobs and Behavior', *Academy of Management Review*, 7: 7–13.

Stewart, R. (1982b) *Choices for the Manager*. London: McGraw-Hill.

Stewart, R. (1982c) 'The Relevance of some Studies of Managerial Work and Behavior to Leadership Research', pp. 11–30 in J.G. Hunt, U. Sekaran and C.A. Schriesheim (eds), *Leadership: Beyond Establishment Views*. Carbondale, IL: Southern Illinois University Press.

Stogdill, R.M. (1948) 'Personal Factors Associated with Leadership: A Survey of the Literature', *Journal of Psychology*, 25: 35–71.

Stogdill, R.M. (1974) *Handbook of Leadership*. New York: Free Press.

Stogdill, R.M. and A.E. Coons (eds) (1957) *Leader Behavior: Its Description and Measurement*. Columbus, OH: Bureau of Business Research, Ohio State University.

Strauss, A. (1978) *Negotiations: Varieties, Contexts, Processes and Social Order*. San Francisco: Jossey-Bass.

Strauss, G. (1962) 'Tactics of Lateral Relationship: the Purchasing Agent', *Administrative Science Quarterly*, 7: 161–86.

Strube, M.J. and J.E. Garcia (1981) 'A Meta-Analytic Investigation of Fiedler's Contingency Model of Leadership Effectiveness', *Psychological Bulletin*, 90: 307–21.

Stryker, S. and A. Statham (1985) 'Symbolic Interaction and Role Theory', pp. 311–78 in G. Lindzey and E. Aronson (eds), *Handbook of Social Psychology, Volume 1* (Third edition). New York: Random House.

Tajfel, H. (1981) *Human Groups and Social Categories*. Cambridge: Cambridge University Press.

Takahashi, N. and S. Takamayagi (1985) 'Decision Procedure Models and Empirical Research: the Japanese Experience', *Human Relations*, 38: 767–80.

Takamiya, S. and K. Thurley (eds) (1985) *Japan's Emerging Multinationals: An International Comparison of Policies and Practices*. Tokyo: University of Tokyo Press.

Taylor, F.W. (1947) *Scientific Management*. New York: Harper & Row (first published 1911).

Taylor, J. and D.G. Bowers (1972) *The Survey of Organizations: a Machine-Scored Standardised Questionnaire Instrument*. Ann Arbor, MI: Institute for Social Research.

Terman, L.M. (1904) 'A Preliminary Study of the Psychology and Pedagogy of Leadership', *Journal of Genetic Psychology*, 11: 413–51.

Thibaut, J.W. and H.H. Kelley (1959) *The Social Psychology of Groups*. New York: Wiley.

Thompson, V.A. (1961) *Modern Organization*. New York: Knopf.

Tjosvold, D. (1986) 'Dynamics and Outcomes of Goal Interdependence in Organizations', *Journal of Psychology*, 120: 101–12.

Trevor, M. (1983) *Japan's Reluctant Multinationals: Japanese Management at Home and Abroad*. London: Frances Pinter.

Trice, H.M. and J.M. Beyer (1984) 'Studying Organizational Cultures through Rites and Ceremonials', *Academy of Management Review*, 9: 653–69.

Tsui, A.S. (1984a) 'A Multiple-Constituency Framework of Managerial Reputational Effectiveness', pp. 28–44 in J.G. Hunt, D.M. Hosking, C.A. Schriesheim and R. Stewart (eds), *Leaders and Managers: International Perspectives on Managerial Behaviour and Leadership*. New York: Pergamon.

Tsui, A.S. (1984b) 'A Role Set Analysis of Managerial Reputation', *Organizational Behavior and Human Performance*, 34: 64–96.

Tung, R.L. (1982) 'Selection and Training Procedures of US, European and Japanese Multinationals', *California Management Review*, 25: 57–71.

Tung, R.L. (1987) 'Expatriate Assignments: Enhancing Success and Minimising Failure', *Academy of Management Executive*, 1: 117–26.

Van Maanen, J. and S.R. Barley (1985) 'Cultural Organization: Fragments of a Theory', pp. 31–54 in P.J. Frost, L.F. Moore, M.R. Louis, C.C. Lundberg and J. Martin (eds), *Organizational Culture*. Beverly Hills, CA: Sage.

Van Maanen, J. and E.H. Schein (1979) 'Toward a Theory of Organizational Socialization', pp. 209–64 in B.M. Staw (ed.), *Research in Organizational Behavior, Volume 1*. Greenwich, CT: JAI Press.

Vecchio, R.P. (1983) 'Assessing the Validity of Fiedler's Contingency Model of Leadership Effectiveness: A Closer Look at Strube and Garcia', *Psychological Bulletin*, 93: 404–8.

Vecchio, R.P. and B.C. Gobdel (1984) 'The Vertical Dyad Linkage Model of Leadership: Problems and Prospects', *Organizational Behavior and Human Performance*, 34: 5–20.

Vroom, V.H. (1964) *Work and Motivation*. New York: Wiley.

Vroom, V.H. (1984) 'Leadership and Decision-Making', pp. 87–109 in *Osaka University 50th Anniversary International Symposium on Democratization and Leadership in Industrial Organizations*. Osaka: Faculty of Human Sciences, Osaka University, Japan.

Vroom, V.H. and A.G. Jago (1978) 'On the Validity of the Vroom–Yetton Model', *Journal of Applied Psychology*, 63: 151–62.

Vroom, V.H. and P.W. Yetton (1973) *Leadership and Decision-Making*, Pittsburgh: University of Pittsburgh Press.

Wagner, J.A. and R.Z Gooding (1987) 'Shared Influence and Organizational Behavior: a Meta-analysis of Situational Variables Expected to Moderate Participation–Outcome Relationships', *Academy of Management Journal*, 30: 524–41.

Wahrman, R. and M.D. Pugh (1972) 'Competence and Conformity: Another Look at Hollander's Study', *Sociometry*, 35: 376–86.

Wakabayashi, M. and G. Graen (1984) 'The Japanese Career Progress Study: a 7 Year Follow-up', *Journal of Applied Psychology*, 69: 603–14.

Waldman, D.A., B.M. Bass and W.O. Einstein (1987) 'Leadership and Outcomes of Performance Appraisal Processes', *Journal of Occupational Psychology*, 60: 177–86.

Walter, G.A. (1985) 'Culture Collisions in Mergers and Acquisitions', pp. 301–14 in P.J. Frost, L.F. Moore, M.R. Louis, C.C. Lundberg and J. Martin (eds), *Organizational Culture*. Beverly Hills, CA: Sage.

Wanous, J.P. (1972) 'Occupational Preferences: Perceptions of Valence and Instrumentality, and Objective Data', *Journal of Applied Psychology*, 56: 152–5.

Weber, M. (1947) *The Theory of Economic and Social Organization* (tr. A.M. Henderson and T. Parsons). New York: Free Press (first published 1921).

Weick, K.E. (1976) 'Educational Organizations as Loosely-Coupled Systems', *Administrative Science Quarterly*, 21: 1–19.

Weiner, B., I. Frieze, A. Kukla, L. Reed, S. Rest and R.M. Rosenbaum (1971) 'Perceiving the Causes of Success and Failure', pp. 95–120 in E.E. Jones, D.E. Kanouse,

H.H. Kelley, R.E. Nisbett, S. Valins and B. Weiner (eds), *Attribution: Perceiving the Causes of Behaviour*. Morristown, NJ: General Learning Press.

Weiss, H.M. and S. Adler (1981) 'Cognitive Complexity and the Structure of Implicit Leadership Theories', *Journal of Applied Psychology*, 66: 69–78.

West, M.A. (1987) 'Role Innovation in the World of Work', *British Journal of Social Psychology*, 26: 305–16.

White, M. and M. Trevor (1983) *Under Japanese Management*. London, Heinemann.

Whitehead, A.N. (1929) *Process and Reality: an Essay in Cosmology*. Cambridge: Cambridge University Press.

Whitely, W. (1984) 'An Exploratory Study of Managers' Reactions to Properties of Verbal Communication', *Personnel Psychology*, 33: 77–89.

Whyte, W.F. and L.K. Williams (1963) 'Supervisory Leadership: An International Comparison', unpublished paper cited in A.S. Tannenbaum 'Organizational Psychology', pp. 280–334 in *Handbook of Cross-Cultural Psychology, Volume 5*. Boston, MA: Allyn and Bacon.

Williams, R. (1961) *The Long Revolution*. London: Chatto and Windus.

Wood, R.E. and T.R. Mitchell (1981) 'Manager Behavior in a Social Context: The Impact of Impression Management on Attributions and Disciplinary Actions', *Organizational Behavior and Human Performance*, 28: 356–78.

Wynne, B.E. and P.L. Hunsaker (1975) 'A Human Information-Processing Approach to the Process of Leadership', pp. 7–25 in J.G. Hunt and L.L. Larson (eds), *Leadership Frontiers*. Kent, OH: Kent State University.

Yang, K.S. (1986) 'Chinese Personality and its Change', pp. 106–70 in M.H. Bond (ed.), *The Psychology of the Chinese People*. Hong Kong: Oxford University Press.

Yukl, G.A. (1981) *Leadership in Organizations*. Englewood Cliffs, NJ: Prentice-Hall.

Yukl, G.A. and W. Nemeroff (1979) 'Identification and Measurement of Specific Categories of Leadership Behavior: A Progress Report', pp. 164–200 in J.G. Hunt and L.L. Larson (eds), *Crosscurrents in Leadership*. Carbondale, IL: Southern Illinois State University Press.

Yukl, G. and D. van Fleet (1982) 'Cross-situational, Multi-method Research on Military Leader Effectiveness', *Organizational Behavior and Human Performance*, 30: 87–108.

Index